The Utopia of Rules

Also by David Graeber

Toward an Anthropological Theory of Value
The False Coin of Our Own Dreams

Fragments of an Anarchist Anthropology

Lost People
Magic and the Legacy of Slavery in Madagascar

Possibilities
Essays on Hierarchy, Rebellion, and Desire

Direct Action
An Ethnography

Debt
The First 5,000 Years

Revolutions in Reverse
Essays on Politics, Violence, Art,
and Imagination

The Democracy Project
A History, A Crisis, A Movement

The Utopia of Rules

On Technology, Stupidity, and the
Secret Joys of Bureaucracy

David Graeber

MELVILLE HOUSE
BROOKLYN • LONDON

THE UTOPIA OF RULES

The following chapters originally appeared, in somewhat different form, in the following publications:

"Dead Zones of the Imagination: An Essay on Structural Stupidity" as "Dead Zones of the Imagination: On Violence, Bureaucracy, and Interpretive Labor. The 2006 Malinowski Memorial Lecture," in *HAU: The Journal of Ethnographic Theory*, vol. 2, no. 2, 2012.

"Of Flying Cars and the Declining Rate of Profit," in *The Baffler*, no. 19, 2012.

"On Batman and the Problem of Constituent Power" as "Super Position," in *The New Inquiry*, October 8, 2012.

Melville House Publishing
46 John Street and
Brooklyn, NY 11201

8 Blackstock Mews
Islington
London N4 2BT

mhpbooks.com / facebook.com/mhpbooks / @melvillehouse

Paperback ISBN: 978-1-61219-518-6

Design by Adly Elewa

Printed in the United States of America
12 14 16 18 19 17 15 13

A catalog record for this book is available from the Library of Congress.

Contents

The Utopia of Rules

Introduction

The Iron Law of Liberalism and the Era of Total Bureaucratization

Nowadays, nobody talks much about bureaucracy. But in the middle of the last century, particularly in the late sixties and early seventies, the word was everywhere. There were sociological tomes with grandiose titles like *A General Theory of Bureaucracy*,[1] *The Politics of Bureaucracy*,[2] or even *The Bureaucratization of the World*,[3] and popular paperback screeds with titles like *Parkinson's Law*,[4] *The Peter Principle*,[5] or *Bureaucrats: How to Annoy Them*.[6] There were Kafkaesque novels, and satirical films. Everyone seemed to feel that the foibles and absurdities of bureaucratic life and bureaucratic procedures were one of the defining features of modern existence, and as such, eminently worth discussing. But since the seventies, there has been a peculiar falling off.

Consider, for example, the following table, which diagrams how frequently the word "bureaucracy" appears in books written in English over the last century and a half. A subject of only moderate interest until the postwar period, it shoots into prominence starting in the fifties and then, after a pinnacle in 1973, begins a slow but inexorable decline.

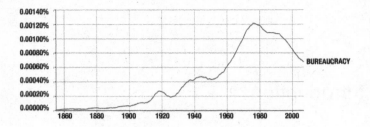

Why? Well, one obvious reason is that we've just become accustomed to it. Bureaucracy has become the water in which we swim. Now let's imagine another graph, one that simply documented the average number of hours per year a typical American—or a Briton, or an inhabitant of Thailand—spent filling out forms or otherwise fulfilling purely bureaucratic obligations. (Needless to say, the overwhelming majority of these obligations no longer involve actual, physical paper.) This graph would almost certainly show a line much like the one in the first graph—a slow climb until 1973. But here the two graphs would diverge—rather than falling back, the line would continue to climb; if anything, it would do so more precipitously, tracking how, in the late twentieth century, middle-class citizens spent ever more hours struggling with phone trees and web interfaces, while the less fortunate spent ever more hours of their day trying to jump through the increasingly elaborate hoops required to gain access to dwindling social services.

I imagine such a graph would look something like this:

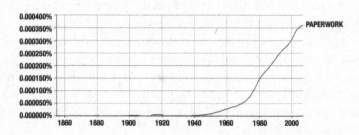

This is not a graph of hours spent on paperwork, just of how often the word "paperwork" has been used in English-language books. But absent time machines that could allow us to carry out a more direct investigation, this is about as close as we're likely to get.

By the way, most similar paperwork-related terms yield almost identical results:

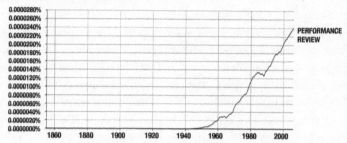

The essays assembled in this volume are all, in one way or another, about this disparity. We no longer like to think about bureaucracy, yet it informs every aspect of our existence. It's as if, as a planetary civilization, we have decided to clap our hands over our ears and start humming whenever the topic comes up. Insofar as we are even willing to discuss it, it's still in the terms popular in the sixties and early seventies. The social movements of the sixties were, on the whole, left-wing in inspiration, but they were also rebellions against bureaucracy, or, to put it more accurately, rebellions against the bureaucratic mindset, against the soul-destroying conformity of the postwar welfare states. In the face of the gray functionaries of both state-capitalist and state-socialist regimes, sixties rebels stood for individual expression and spontaneous conviviality, and against ("rules and regulations, who needs them?") every form of social control.

With the collapse of the old welfare states, all this has come to seem decidedly quaint. As the language of antibureaucratic individualism has been adopted, with increasing ferocity, by the Right, which insists on "market solutions" to every social problem, the mainstream Left has increasingly reduced itself to fighting a kind of pathetic rearguard action, trying to salvage remnants of the old welfare state: it has acquiesced with—often even spearheaded—attempts to make government efforts more "efficient" through the partial privatization of services and the incorporation of ever-more "market principles," "market incentives," and market-based "accountability processes" into the structure of the bureaucracy itself.

The result is a political catastrophe. There's really no other way to put it. What is presented as the "moderate" Left solution to any social problems—and radical left solutions are, almost everywhere now, ruled out *tout court*—has invariably come to be some nightmare fusion of the worst elements of bureaucracy and the worst elements of capitalism. It's as if someone had consciously tried to create the least appealing possible political position. It is a testimony to the genuine lingering power of leftist ideals that anyone would even consider voting for a party that promoted this sort of thing—because surely, if they do, it's not because they actually think these are good policies, but because these are the only policies anyone who identifies themselves as left-of-center is allowed to set forth.

Is there any wonder, then, that every time there is a social crisis, it is the Right, rather than the Left, which becomes the venue for the expression of popular anger?

The Right, at least, *has* a critique of bureaucracy. It's not a very good one. But at least it exists. The Left has none. As a result, when those who identify with the Left do have anything negative to say about bureaucracy, they are usually forced to adopt a watered-down version of the right-wing critique.[7]

This right-wing critique can be disposed of fairly quickly. It has its origins in nineteenth-century liberalism.[8] The story that emerged in middle-class circles in Europe in the wake of the

French revolution was that the civilized world was experiencing a gradual, uneven, but inevitable transformation away from the rule of warrior elites, with their authoritarian governments, their priestly dogmas, and their caste-like stratification, to one of liberty, equality, and enlightened commercial self-interest. The mercantile classes in the Middle Ages undermined the old feudal order like termites munching from below—termites, yes, but the good kind. The pomp and splendor of the absolutist states that were being overthrown were, according to the liberal version of history, the last gasps of the old order, which would end as states gave way to markets, religious faith to scientific understanding, and fixed orders and statuses of Marquis and Baronesses and the like to free contracts between individuals.

The emergence of modern bureaucracies was always something of a problem for this story because it didn't really fit. In principle, all these stuffy functionaries in their offices, with their elaborate chains of command, should have been mere feudal holdovers, soon to go the way of the armies and officer corps that everyone was expecting to gradually become unnecessary as well. One need only flip open a Russian novel from the late nineteenth century: all the scions of old aristocratic families—in fact, almost everyone in those books—had been transformed into either military officers or civil servants (no one of any notice seems to do anything else), and the military and civil hierarchies seemed to have nearly identical ranks, titles, and sensibilities. But there was an obvious problem. If bureaucrats were just holdovers, why was it that everywhere—not just in backwaters like Russia but in booming industrial societies like England and Germany—every year seemed to bring more and more of them?

There followed stage two of the argument, which was, in its essence, that bureaucracy represents an inherent flaw in the democratic project.[9] Its greatest exponent was Ludwig von Mises, an exiled Austrian aristocrat, whose 1944 book

Bureaucracy argued that by definition, systems of government administration could never organize information with anything like the efficiency of impersonal market pricing mechanisms. However, extending the vote to the losers of the economic game would inevitably lead to calls for government intervention, framed as high-minded schemes for trying to solve social problems through administrative means. Von Mises was willing to admit that many of those who embraced such solutions were entirely well-meaning; however, their efforts could only make matters worse. In fact, he felt they would ultimately end up destroying the political basis of democracy itself, since the administrators of social programs would inevitably form power-blocs far more influential than the politicians elected to run the government, and support ever-more radical reforms. Von Mises argued that as a result, the social welfare states then emerging in places like France or England, let alone Denmark or Sweden, would, within a generation or two, inevitably lead to fascism.

In this view, the rise of bureaucracy was the ultimate example of good intentions run amok. Ronald Reagan probably made the most effective popular deployment of this line of thought with his famous claim that, "the nine most terrifying words in the English language are, 'I'm from the government and I'm here to help.'"

The problem with all this is that it bears very little relation to what actually happened. First of all, historically, markets simply did not emerge as some autonomous domain of freedom independent of, and opposed to, state authorities. Exactly the opposite is the case. Historically, markets are generally either a side effect of government operations, especially military operations, or were directly created by government policy. This has been true at least since the invention of coinage, which was first created and promulgated as a means of provisioning soldiers; for most of Eurasian history, ordinary people used informal credit arrangements and physical money, gold, silver, bronze, and the kind of impersonal markets they made possible remained mainly an adjunct to the mobilization of legions, sacking of cities, extraction of tribute, and disposing of loot. Modern central banking systems were likewise first created to finance wars. So there's one initial problem with the conventional history. There's another even more dramatic one. While the idea that the market is somehow opposed to and independent of government has been used at least at least since the nineteenth century to justify laissez faire economic policies designed to lessen the role of government, they never actually have that effect. English liberalism, for instance, did not lead to a reduction of state bureaucracy, but the exact opposite: an endlessly ballooning array of legal clerks, registrars, inspectors, notaries, and police officials who made the liberal dream of a world of free contract between autonomous individuals possible. It turned out that maintaining a free market economy required a thousand times more paperwork than a Louis XIV-style absolutist monarchy.

This apparent paradox—that government policies intending to reduce government interference in the economy actually end up producing more regulations, more bureaucrats, and more police—can be observed so regularly that I think we are justified in treating it as a general sociological law. I propose to call it "the iron law of liberalism":

> **The Iron Law of Liberalism** states that any market reform, any government initiative intended to reduce red tape and promote market forces will have the ultimate effect of increasing the total number of regulations, the total amount of paperwork, and the total number of bureaucrats the government employs.

French sociologist Emile Durkheim was already observing this tendency at the turn of the twentieth century,[10] and eventually, it became impossible to ignore. By the middle of the century, even right-wing critics like von Mises were willing to admit—at least in their academic writing—that markets don't really regulate themselves, and that an army of administrators was indeed required to keep any market system going. (For von Mises, that army only became problematic when it was deployed to alter market outcomes that caused undue suffering for the poor.)[11] Still, right-wing populists soon realized that, whatever the realities, making a target of bureaucrats was almost always effective. Hence, in their public pronouncements, the condemnation of what U.S. governor George Wallace, in his 1968 campaign for President, first labeled "pointy-headed bureaucrats" living off hardworking citizens' taxes, was unrelenting.

Wallace is actually a crucial figure here. Nowadays, Americans mainly remember him as a failed reactionary, or even a snarling lunatic: the last die-hard Southern segregationist standing with an axe outside a public school door. But in terms of his broader legacy, he could just as well be represented as a kind of political genius. He was, after all, the first politician to create a national platform for a kind of right-wing populism that was soon to prove so infectious that by now, a generation later, it has come to be adopted by pretty much everyone, across the political spectrum. As a result, amongst working-class Americans, government is now generally seen as being made up of two sorts of people: "politicians," who are blustering crooks and liars but can at least occasionally be voted out of office, and "bureaucrats," who are condescending elitists almost impossible to uproot. There is assumed to be a kind of tacit alliance between what came to be seen as the parasitical poor (in America usually pictured in overtly racist terms) and the equally parasitical self-righteous officials whose existence depends on subsidizing the poor using other people's money. Again, even the mainstream Left—or what it is supposed to pass for a Left these days—has come to offer little more than a watered-down version of this right-wing language. Bill Clinton, for instance, had spent so much of his career bashing civil servants that after the Oklahoma City bombing, he actually felt moved to remind Americans that public servants were human beings unto themselves, and promised never to use the word "bureaucrat" again.[12]

In contemporary American populism—and increasingly, in the rest of the world as well—there can be only one alternative to "bureaucracy," and that is "the market." Sometimes this is held to mean that government should be run more like a business. Sometimes it is held to mean we should simply get the bureaucrats out of the way and let nature take its course, which means letting people attend to the business of their lives untrammelled by endless rules and regulations imposed on them from above, and so allowing the magic of the marketplace to provide its own solutions.

"Democracy" thus came to mean the market; "bureaucracy," in turn, government interference with the market; and this is pretty much what the word continues to mean to this day.

It wasn't always so. The rise of the modern corporation, in the late nineteenth century, was largely seen at the time as a matter of applying modern, bureaucratic techniques to the private sector—and these techniques were assumed to be required, when operating on a large scale, because they were more efficient than the networks of personal or informal connections that had dominated a world of small family firms. The pioneers of these new, private bureaucracies were the United States and Germany, and Max Weber, the German sociologist, observed that Americans in his day were particularly inclined to see public and private bureaucracies as essentially the same animal:

> The body of officials actively engaged in a "public" office, along with the respective apparatus of material

implements and the files, make up a "bureau." In private enterprise, "the bureau" is often called "the office" . . .

It is the peculiarity of the modern entrepreneur that he conducts himself as the "first official" of his corporation, in the very same way in which the ruler of a specifically modern bureaucratic state spoke of himself as "the first servant" of the state. The idea that the bureau activities of the state are intrinsically different in character from the management of private economic offices is a continental European notion and, by way of contrast, is totally foreign to the American way. [13]

In other words, around the turn of the century, rather than anyone complaining that government should be run more like a business, Americans simply assumed that governments and business—or big business, at any rate—were run the same way.

True, for much of the nineteenth century, the United States was largely an economy of small family firms and high finance—much like Britain's at the time. But America's advent as a power on the world stage at the end of the century corresponded to the rise of a distinctly American form: corporate—bureaucratic—capitalism. As Giovanni Arrighi pointed out, an analogous corporate model was emerging at the same time in Germany, and the two countries—the United States and Germany—ended up spending most of the first half of the next century battling over which would take over from the declining British empire and establish its own vision for a global economic and political order. We all know who won. Arrighi makes another interesting point here. Unlike the British Empire, which had taken its free market rhetoric seriously, eliminating its own protective tariffs with the famous Anti–Corn Law Bill of 1846, neither the German or American regimes had ever been especially interested in free trade. The Americans in particular were much more concerned with creating structures of international administration.

The very first thing the United States did, on officially taking over the reins from Great Britain after World War II, was to set up the world's first genuinely planetary bureaucratic institutions in the United Nations and the Bretton Woods institutions—the International Monetary Fund, World Bank, and GATT, later to become the WTO. The British Empire had never attempted anything like this. They either conquered other nations, or traded with them. The Americans attempted to administer everything and everyone.

British people, I've observed, are quite proud that they are not especially skilled at bureaucracy; Americans, in contrast, seem embarrassed by the fact that on the whole, they're really quite good at it.[14] It doesn't fit the American self-image. We're supposed to be self-reliant individualists. (This is precisely why the right-wing populist demonization of bureaucrats is so effective.) Yet the fact remains the United States is—and for a well over a century has been—a profoundly bureaucratic society. The reason it is so easy to overlook is because most American bureaucratic habits and sensibilities—from the clothing to the language to the design of forms and offices—emerged from the private sector. When novelists and sociologists described the "Organization Man," or "the Man in the Gray Flannel Suit," the soullessly conformist U.S. equivalent to the Soviet apparatchik, they were not talking about functionaries in the Department of Landmarks and Preservation or the Social Security Administration—they were describing corporate middle management. True, by that time, corporate bureaucrats were not actually being *called* bureaucrats. But they were still setting the standard for what administrative functionaries were supposed to be like.

The impression that the word "bureaucrat" should be treated as a synonym for "civil servant" can be traced back to the New Deal in the thirties, which was also the moment when bureaucratic structures and techniques first became dramatically visible in many ordinary people's lives. But in fact, from the very beginning, Roosevelt's New Dealers worked in close coordination with the battalions of lawyers, engineers, and corporate bureaucrats employed by firms like Ford, Coca Cola, or Proctor & Gamble, absorbing much of their style and sensibilities, and—as the United States shifted to war footing in the forties—so did the gargantuan bureaucracy of the U.S. military. And, of course, the United States has never really gone off war footing ever since. Still, through these means, the word "bureaucrat" came to attach itself almost exclusively to civil servants: even if what they do all day is sit at desks, fill out forms, and file reports, neither middle managers nor military officers are ever quite considered bureaucrats. (Neither for that matter are police, or employees of the NSA.)

In the United States, the lines between public and private have long been blurry. The American military, for example, is famous for its revolving door—high-ranking officers involved in procurement regularly end up on the boards of corporations that operate on military contracts. On a broader level, the need to preserve certain domestic industries for military purposes, and to develop others, has allowed the U.S. government to engage in practically Soviet-style industrial planning without ever having to admit it's doing so. After all, pretty much anything, from maintaining a certain number of steel plants, to doing the initial research to set up the Internet, can be justified on grounds of military preparedness. Yet again, since this kind of planning operates via an alliance between military bureaucrats and corporate bureaucrats, it's never perceived as something bureaucratic at all.

Still, with the rise of the financial sector, things have reached a qualitatively different level—one where it is becoming almost impossible to say what is public and what is private. This is not just due to the much-noted outsourcing of one-time government functions to private corporations. Above all, it's due to the way the private corporations themselves have come to operate.

Let me give an example. A few weeks ago, I spent several hours on the phone with Bank of America, trying to work out how to get access to my account information from overseas. This involved speaking to four different representatives, two referrals to nonexistent numbers, three long explanations of complicated and apparently arbitrary rules, and two failed attempts to change outdated address and phone number information lodged on various computer systems. In other words, it was the very definition of a bureaucratic runaround. (Neither was I able, when it was all over, to actually access my account.)

Now, there is not the slightest doubt in my mind that, were I to actually locate a bank manager and demand to know how such things could happen, he or she would immediately insist that the bank was not to blame—that it was all an effect of an arcane maze of government regulations. However, I am equally confident that, were it possible to investigate how these regulations came about, one would find that they were composed jointly by aides to legislators on some banking committee and lobbyists and attorneys employed by the banks themselves, in a process greased by generous contributions to the coffers of those same legislators' reelection campaigns. And the same would be true of anything from credit ratings, insurance premiums, mortgage applications, to, for that matter, the process of buying an airline ticket, applying for a scuba license, or trying to requisition an ergonomic chair for one's office in an ostensibly private university. The vast majority of the paperwork we do exists in just this sort of in-between zone—ostensibly private, but in fact entirely shaped by a government that provides the legal framework, underpins the rules with its courts and all of the elaborate mechanisms of enforcement that come with them, but—crucially—works closely with the private concerns to ensure that the results will guarantee a certain rate of private profit.

In cases like this the language we employ—derived as it is from the right-wing critique—is completely inadequate. It tells us nothing about what is actually going on.[15]

Consider the word "deregulation." In today's political discourse, "deregulation" is—like "reform"—almost invariably treated as a good thing. Deregulation means less bureaucratic meddling, and fewer rules and regulations stifling innovation and commerce. This usage puts those on the left-hand side of the political spectrum in an awkward position, since opposing deregulation—even, pointing out that it was an orgy of this very "deregulation" that led to the banking crisis of 2008—seems to imply a desire for more rules and regulations, and therefore, more gray men in suits standing in the way of freedom and innovation and generally telling people what to do.

But this debate is based on false premises. Let's go back to banks. There's no such thing as an "unregulated" bank. Nor could there be. Banks are institutions to which the government has granted the power to create money—or, to be slightly more technical about it, the right to issue IOUs that the government will recognize as legal tender, and, therefore, accept in payment of taxes and to discharge other debts within its own national territory. Obviously no government is about to grant anyone—least of all a profit-seeking firm—the power to create as much money as they like under any circumstances. That would be insane. The power to create money is one that, by definition, governments can only grant under carefully circumscribed (read: regulated) conditions. And indeed this is what we always find: government regulates everything from a bank's reserve requirements to its hours of operation; how much it can charge in interest, fees, and penalties; what sort of security precautions it can or must employ; how its records must be kept and reported; how and when it must inform its clients of their rights and responsibilities; and pretty much everything else.

So what are people actually referring to when they talk about "deregulation"? In ordinary usage, the word seems to mean "changing the regulatory structure in a way that I like." In practice this can refer to almost anything. In the case of airlines or telecommunications in the seventies and eighties, it meant changing the system of regulation from one that encouraged a few large firms to one that fostered carefully supervised competition between midsize firms. In the case of banking, "deregulation" has usually meant exactly the opposite: moving away from a situation of managed competition between mid-sized firms to one where a handful of financial conglomerates are allowed to completely dominate the market. This is what makes the term so handy. Simply by labeling a new regulatory measure "deregulation," you can frame it in the public mind as a way to reduce bureaucracy and set individual initiative free, even if the result is a fivefold increase in the actual number of forms to be filled in, reports to be filed, rules and regulations for lawyers to interpret, and officious people in offices whose entire job seems to be to provide convoluted explanations for why you're not allowed to do things.[16]

This process—the gradual fusion of public and private power into a single entity, rife with rules and regulations whose ultimate purpose is to extract wealth in the form of profits—does not yet have a name. That in itself is significant. These things can happen largely because we lack a way to talk about them. But one can see its effects in every aspect of our lives. It fills our days with paperwork. Application forms get longer and more elaborate. Ordinary documents like bills or tickets or memberships in sports or book clubs come to be buttressed by pages of legalistic fine print.

I'm going to make up a name. I'm going to call this the age of "total bureaucratization." (I was tempted to call this the age of "predatory bureaucratization" but it's really the all-encompassing nature of the beast I want to highlight here.) It had its first stirrings, one might say, just at the point where public discussion of bureaucracy began to fall off in the late seventies, and it began to get seriously under way in the eighties. But it truly took off in the nineties.

In an earlier book, I suggested that the fundamental historical break that ushered in our current economic regime occurred in 1971, the date that the U.S. dollar went off the gold standard. This is what paved the way first for the financialization of capitalism, but ultimately, for much more profound long-term changes that I suspect will ultimately spell the end of capitalism entirely. I still think that. But here we are speaking of much more short-term effects. What did financialization mean for the deeply bureaucratized society that was postwar America?[17]

I think what happened is best considered as a kind of shift in class allegiances on the part of the managerial staff of major corporations, from an uneasy, de facto alliance with their own workers, to one with investors. As John Kenneth Galbraith long ago pointed out, if you create an organization geared to produce perfumes, dairy products, or aircraft fuselages, those who make it up will, if left to their own devices, tend to concentrate their efforts on producing more and better perfumes, dairy products, or aircraft fuselages, rather than thinking primarily of what will make the most money for the shareholders. What's more, since for most of the twentieth century, a job in a large bureaucratic mega-firm meant a lifetime promise of employment, everyone involved in the process—managers and workers alike—tended to see themselves as sharing a certain common interest in this regard, over and against meddling owners and investors. This kind of solidarity across class lines even had a name: it was called "corporatism." One mustn't romanticize it. It was among other things the philosophical basis of fascism. Indeed, one could well argue that fascism simply took the idea that workers and managers had common interests, that organizations like corporations or communities formed organic wholes, and that financiers were an alien, parasitical force, and drove them to their ultimate, murderous extreme. Even in its more benign social democratic versions, in Europe or America, the attendant politics often came tinged with chauvinism[18]—but they also ensured that the investor class was always seen as to some extent outsiders, against whom white-collar and blue-collar workers could be considered, at least to some degree, to be united in a common front.

From the perspective of sixties radicals, who regularly watched antiwar demonstrations attacked by nationalist teamsters and construction workers, the reactionary implications of corporatism appeared self-evident. The corporate suits and the well-paid, Archie Bunker elements of the industrial proletariat were clearly on the same side. Unsurprising then that the left-wing critique of bureaucracy at the time focused on the ways that social democracy had more in common with fascism than its proponents cared to admit. Unsurprising, too, that this critique seems utterly irrelevant today.[19]

What began to happen in the seventies, and paved the way for what we see today, was a kind of strategic pivot of the upper echelons of U.S. corporate bureaucracy—away from the workers, and towards shareholders, and eventually, towards the financial structure as a whole. The mergers and acquisitions, corporate raiding, junk bonds, and asset stripping that began under Reagan and Thatcher and culminated in the rise of private equity firms were merely some of the more dramatic early mechanisms through which this shift of allegiance worked itself out. In fact, there was a double movement: corporate management became more financialized, but at the same time, the financial sector became corporatized, with investment banks, hedge funds, and the like largely replacing individual investors. As a result the investor class and the executive class became almost indistinguishable. (Think here of the term "financial management," which came to refer simultaneously to how the highest ranks of the corporate bureaucracy ran their firms, and how investors managed their portfolios.) Before long, heroic CEOs were being lionized in the media, their success largely measured by the number of employees they could fire. By the nineties, lifetime employment, even for white-collar workers, had become a thing of the past. When corporations wished to win loyalty, they increasingly did it by paying their employees in stock options.[20]

At the same time, the new credo was that everyone should look at the world through the eyes of an investor—that's why, in the eighties, newspapers began firing their labor reporters, but ordinary TV news reports came to be accompanied by crawls at the bottom of the screen displaying the latest stock quotes. The common cant was that through participation in personal retirement funds and investment funds of one sort or another, everyone would come to own a piece of capitalism. In reality, the magic circle was only really widened to include the higher paid professionals and the corporate bureaucrats themselves.

Still, that extension was extremely important. No political revolution can succeed without allies, and bringing along a certain portion of the middle class—and, even more crucially, convincing the bulk of the middle classes that they had some kind of stake in finance-driven capitalism—was critical. Ultimately, the more liberal members of this professional-managerial elite became the social base for what came to pass as "left-wing" political parties, as actual working-class organizations like trade unions were cast into the wilderness. (Hence, the U.S. Democratic Party, or New Labour in Great Britain, whose leaders engage in regular ritual acts of public abjuration of the very unions that have historically formed their strongest base of support). These were of course people who already tended to work in thoroughly bureaucratized environments, whether schools, hospitals, or corporate law firms. The actual working class, who bore a traditional loathing for such characters, either dropped out of politics entirely, or were increasingly reduced to casting protest votes for the radical Right.[21]

This was not just a political realignment. It was a cultural transformation. And it set the stage for the process whereby the bureaucratic techniques (performance reviews, focus groups, time allocation surveys . . .) developed in financial and corporate circles came to invade the rest of society—education, science, government—and eventually, to pervade almost every aspect of everyday life. One can best trace the process, perhaps, by following its language. There is a peculiar idiom that first emerged in such circles, full of bright, empty terms like vision, quality, stakeholder, leadership, excellence, innovation, strategic goals, or best practices. (Much of it traces back to "self-actualization" movements like Lifespring, Mind Dynamics, and EST, which were extremely popular in corporate boardrooms in the seventies, but it quickly became a language unto itself.) Now, imagine it would be possible to create a map of some major city, and then place one tiny blue dot on the location of every document that uses at least three of these words. Then imagine that we could watch it change over time. We would be able to observe this new corporate bureaucratic culture spread like blue stains in a petri dish, starting in the financial districts, on to boardrooms, then government offices and universities, then, finally, engulfing any location where any number of people gather to discuss the allocation of resources of any kind at all.

For all its celebration of markets and individual initiative, this alliance of government and finance often produces results that bear a striking resemblance to the worst excesses of bureaucratization in the former Soviet Union or former colonial backwaters of the Global South. There is a rich anthropological literature, for instance, on the cult of certificates, licenses, and diplomas in the former colonial world. Often the argument is that in countries like Bangladesh, Trinidad, or Cameroon, which hover between the stifling legacy of colonial domination and their own magical traditions, official credentials are seen as a kind of material fetish—magical objects conveying power in their own right, entirely apart from the real knowledge, experience, or training they're supposed to represent. But since the eighties, the real explosion of credentialism has been in what are supposedly the most "advanced" economies, like the United States, Great Britain, or Canada. As one anthropologist, Sarah Kendzior, puts it:

> "The United States has become the most rigidly credentialised society in the world," write James Engell and Anthony Dangerfield in their 2005 book *Saving Higher Education in the Age of Money*. "A BA is required for jobs that by no stretch of imagination need two years of full-time training, let alone four."
>
> The promotion of college as a requirement for a middle-class life . . . has resulted in the exclusion of the non-college educated from professions of public influence. In 1971, 58 percent of journalists had a college degree. Today, 92 percent do, and at many publications, a graduate degree in journalism is required—despite the fact that most renowned journalists have never studied journalism. [22]
>
> Journalism is one of many fields of public influence—including politics—in which credentials function as *de facto* permission to speak, rendering those who lack them less likely to be employed and less able to afford to stay in their field. Ability is discounted

without credentials, but the ability to purchase credentials rests, more often than not, on family wealth.[23]

One could repeat the story in field after field, from nurses to art teachers, physical therapists to foreign policy consultants. Almost every endeavor that used to be considered an art (best learned through doing) now requires formal professional training and a certificate of completion, and this seems to be happening, equally, in both the private and public sectors, since, as already noted, in matters bureaucratic, such distinctions are becoming effectively meaningless. While these measures are touted—as are all bureaucratic measures—as a way of creating fair, impersonal mechanisms in fields previously dominated by insider knowledge and social connections, the effect is often the opposite. As anyone who has been to graduate school knows, it's precisely the children of the professional-managerial classes, those whose family resources make them the least in need of financial support, who best know how to navigate the world of paperwork that enables them to get said support.[24] For everyone else, the main result of one's years of professional training is to ensure that one is saddled with such an enormous burden of student debt that a substantial chunk of any subsequent income one will get from pursuing that profession will henceforth be siphoned off, each month, by the financial sector. In some cases, these new training requirements can only be described as outright scams, as when lenders, and those prepared to set up the training programs, jointly lobby the government to insist that, say, all pharmacists be henceforth required to pass some additional qualifying examination, forcing thousands already practicing the profession into night school, which these pharmacists know many will only be able to afford with the help of high-interest student loans.[25] By doing this, lenders are in effect legislating themselves a cut of most pharmacists' subsequent incomes.[26]

The latter might seem an extreme case, but in its own way it's paradigmatic of the fusion of public and private power under the new financial regime. Increasingly, corporate profits in America are not derived from commerce or industry at all, but from finance—which means, ultimately, from other people's debts. These debts do not just happen by accident. To a large degree, they are engineered—and by precisely this kind of fusion of public and private power. The corporatization of education; the resulting ballooning of tuitions as students are expected to pay for giant football stadiums and similar pet projects of executive trustees, or to contribute to the burgeoning salaries of ever-multiplying university officials; the increasing demands for degrees as certificates of entry into any job that promises access to anything like a middle-class standard of living; resulting rising levels of indebtedness—all these form a single web. One result of all this debt is to render the government itself the main mechanism for the extraction of corporate profits. (Just think, here, of what happens if one tries to default on one's student loans: the entire legal apparatus leaps into action, threatening to seize assets, garnish wages, and apply thousands of dollars in additional penalties.) Another is to force the debtors themselves to bureaucratize ever-increasing dimensions of their own lives, which have to be managed as if they were themselves a tiny corporation measuring inputs and outputs and constantly struggling to balance its accounts.

It's also important to emphasize that while this system of extraction comes dressed up in a language of rules and regulations, in its actual mode of operation, it has almost nothing to do with the rule of law. Rather, the legal system has itself become the means for a system of increasingly arbitrary extractions. As the profits from banks and credit card companies derive more and more from "fees and penalties" levied on their customers—so much so that those living check to check can regularly expect to be charged eighty dollars for a five-dollar overdraft—financial firms have come to play by an entirely different set of rules. I once attended a conference on the crisis in the banking system where I was able to have a brief, informal chat with an economist for one of the Bretton Woods institutions (probably best I not say which). I asked him why everyone was still waiting for even one bank official to be brought to trial for any act of fraud leading up to the crash of 2008.

OFFICIAL: Well, you have to understand the approach taken by U.S. prosecutors to financial fraud is always to negotiate a settlement. They don't want to have to go to trial. The upshot is always that the financial institution has to pay a fine, sometimes in the hundreds of millions, but they don't actually admit to any criminal liability. Their lawyers simply say they are not going to contest the charge, but if they pay, they haven't technically been found guilty of anything.

ME: So you're saying if the government discovers that Goldman Sachs, for instance, or Bank of America, has committed fraud, they effectively just charge them a penalty fee.

OFFICIAL: That's right.

ME: So in that case . . . okay, I guess the real question is this: has there ever been a case where the amount the firm had to pay was *more* than the amount of money they made from the fraud itself?

OFFICIAL: Oh no, not to my knowledge. Usually it's substantially less.

ME: So what are we talking here, 50 percent?

OFFICIAL: I'd say more like 20 to 30 percent on average. But it varies considerably case by case.

ME: Which means . . . correct me if I'm wrong, but doesn't that effectively mean the government is saying, "you can commit all the fraud you like, but if we catch you, you're going to have to give us our cut"?

OFFICIAL: Well, obviously I can't put it that way myself as long as I have this job . . .

And of course, the power of those same banks to charge account-holders eighty bucks for an overdraft is enforced by the same court system content to merely collect a piece of the action when the bank itself commits fraud.

Now, on one level, this might just seem like another example of a familiar story: the rich always play by a different set of rules. If the children of bankers can regularly get off the hook for carrying quantities of cocaine that would almost certainly have earned them decades in a federal penitentiary if they happened to be poor or Black, why should things be any different when they grow up to become bankers themselves? But I think there is something deeper going on here, and it turns on the very nature of bureaucratic systems. Such institutions always create a culture of complicity. It's not just that some people get to break the rules—it's that loyalty to the organization is to some degree measured by one's willingness to pretend this isn't happening. And insofar as bureaucratic logic is extended to the society as a whole, all of us start playing along.

This point is worth expanding on. What I am saying is that we are not just looking at a double standard, but a particular kind of double standard typical of bureaucratic systems everywhere. All bureaucracies are to a certain degree utopian, in the sense that they propose an abstract ideal that real human beings can never live up to. Take the initial point about credentialism. Sociologists since Weber always note that it is one of the defining features of any bureaucracy that those who staff it are selected by formal, impersonal criteria—most often, some kind of written test. (That is, bureaucrats are not, say, elected like politicians, but neither should they get the job just because they are someone's cousin.) In theory they are meritocracies. In fact everyone knows the system is compromised in a thousand different ways. Many of the staff are in fact there just because they are someone's cousin, and everybody knows it. The first criterion of loyalty to the organization becomes complicity. Career advancement is not based on merit, and not even based necessarily on being someone's cousin; above all, it's based on a willingness to play along with the fiction that career advancement is *based* on merit, even though everyone knows this not to be true.[27] Or with the fiction that rules and regulations apply to everyone equally, when, in fact, they are often deployed as a means for entirely arbitrary personal power.

This is how bureaucracies have always tended to work. But for most of history, this fact has only been important for those who actually operated within administrative systems: say, aspiring Confucian scholars in Medieval China. Most everyone else didn't really have to think about organizations very often; typically, they only encountered them every few years when it came time to register their fields and cattle for the local tax authorities. But as I've pointed out, the last two centuries have seen an explosion of bureaucracy, and the last thirty or forty years in particular have seen bureaucratic principles extended to every aspect of our existence. As a result, this culture of complicity has come to spread as well. Many of us actually act as if we believe that the courts really are treating the financial establishment as it should be treated, that they are even dealing with them too harshly; and that ordinary citizens really do deserve to be penalized a hundred times more harshly for an overdraft.

As whole societies have come to represent themselves as giant credentialized meritocracies, rather than systems of arbitrary extraction, everyone duly scurries about trying to curry favor by pretending they actually believe this is to be true.

So: what would a left-wing critique of total, or predatory, bureaucratization look like?

I think the story of the Global Justice Movement provides a hint—because it was a movement that, rather to its own surprise, discovered this was what it was about. I remember this quite well because I was deeply involved in the movement at the time. Back in the 1990s, "globalization," as touted by journalists like Thomas Friedman (but really, by the entire journalistic establishment in the United States and most of it in other wealthy countries) was portrayed as an almost natural force. Technological advances—particularly the Internet—were knitting the world together as never before, increased communication was leading to increased trade, and national borders were rapidly becoming irrelevant as free trade treaties united the globe into a single world market. In political debates of the time in the mainstream media, all of this was discussed as such a self-evident reality that anyone who objected to the process could be treated as if they were objecting to basic laws of nature—they were flat-earthers, buffoons, the left-wing equivalents of Biblical fundamentalists who thought evolution was a hoax.

Thus when the Global Justice Movement started, the media spin was that it was a rearguard action of hoary, carbuncular leftists who wished to restore protectionism, national sovereignty, barriers to trade and communication, and, generally, to vainly stand against the Inevitable Tide of History. The problem with this was that it was obviously untrue. Most immediately, there was the fact that the protestors' average age, especially in the wealthier countries, seemed to be about nineteen. More seriously, there was the fact that the movement was a form of globalization in itself: a kaleidoscopic alliance of people from every corner of the world, including organizations ranging from Indian farmers' associations, to the Canadian postal workers' union, to indigenous groups in Panama, to anarchist collectives in Detroit. What's more, its exponents endlessly insisted that despite protestations to the contrary, what the media was calling "globalization" had almost nothing to do with the effacement of borders and the free movement of people, products, and ideas. It was really about trapping increasingly large parts of the world's population behind highly militarized national borders within which social protections could be systematically withdrawn, creating a pool of laborers so desperate that they would be willing to work for almost nothing. Against it, they proposed a genuinely borderless world.

Obviously, these ideas' exponents did not get to say any of this on TV or major newspapers—at least not in countries like America, whose media is strictly policed by its own internal corporate bureaucrats. Such arguments were, effectively, taboo. But we discovered that there was something we could do that worked almost as well. We could besiege the summits where the trade pacts were negotiated and the annual meetings of the institutions through which the terms of what was called globalization were actually concocted, encoded, and enforced. Until the movement came to North America with the siege of the World Trade Meeting in Seattle in November 1999—and subsequent blockades against the IMF/World Bank Meetings in Washington—most Americans simply had no idea that any of these organizations even existed. The actions operated like a magic charm that exposed everything that was supposed to be hidden: all we had to do was show up and try to block access to the venue, and instantly we revealed the existence of a vast global bureaucracy of interlocking organizations that nobody was supposed to really think about. And of course, at the same time, we would magically whisk into existence thousands of heavily armed riot police ready to reveal just what those bureaucrats were willing to unleash against anyone—no matter how nonviolent—who tried to stand in their way.

It was a surprisingly effective strategy. Within a matter of two or three years, we had sunk pretty much every proposed new global trade pact, and institutions like the IMF had been effectively expelled from Asia, Latin America, and, indeed, most of the world's surface.[28]

The imagery worked because it showed everything people had been told about globalization to be a lie. This was not some natural process of peaceful trade, made possible by new technologies. What was being talked about in terms of "free trade" and the "free market" really entailed the self-conscious completion of the world's first effective[29] planetary-scale administrative bureaucratic system. The foundations for the system had been laid in the 1940s, but it was only with the waning of the Cold War that they became truly effective. In the process, they came to be made up—like most other bureaucratic systems being created on a smaller scale at the same time—of such a thorough entanglement of public and private elements that it was often quite impossible to pull them apart—even conceptually. Let us think about it this way: At the top were the trade bureaucracies like the IMF, World Bank, WTO and the G8s, along with treaty organizations like NAFTA or the EU. These actually developed the economic—and even social—policies followed by supposedly democratic governments in the global south. Just below were the large global financial firms like Goldman Sachs, Lehman Brothers, American Insurance Group, or, for that matter, institutions like Standard & Poors. Below that came the transnational mega-corporations. (Much of what was being called "international trade" in fact consisted merely of the transfer of materials back and forth between different branches of the same corporation.) Finally, one has to include the NGOs, which in many parts of the world come to provide many of the social services previously provided by government, with the result that urban planning in a city in Nepal, or health policy in a town in Nigeria, might well have been developed in offices in Zurich or Chicago.

At the time, we didn't talk about things in quite these terms—that "free trade" and "the free market" actually meant the creation of global administrative structures mainly aimed at ensuring the extraction of profits for investors, that "globalization" really meant bureaucratization. We often came close. But we rarely quite out and said it.

In retrospect, I think this is exactly what we should have emphasized. Even the emphasis on inventing new forms of democratic processes that was at the core of the movement— the assemblies, the spokescouncils, and so on—was, more than anything else, a way to show that people could indeed get on with one another—and even make important decisions and carry out complex collective projects—without anyone ever having to fill out a form, appeal a judgment, or threaten to phone security or the police.

The Global Justice Movement was, in its own way, the first major leftist antibureaucratic movement of the era of total bureaucratization. As such, I think it offers important lessons for anyone trying to develop a similar critique. Let me end by outlining three of them:

1. Do not underestimate the importance of sheer physical violence.

The armies of highly militarized police that appeared to attack the summit protestors were not some sort of weird side effect of "globalization." Whenever someone starts talking about the "free market," it's a good idea to look around for the man with the gun. He's never far away. Free-market liberalism of the nineteenth century corresponded with the invention of the modern police and private detective agencies,[30] and gradually, with the notion that those police had at least ultimate jurisdiction over virtually every aspect of urban life, from the regulation of street peddlers to noise levels at private parties, or even to the resolution of bitter fights with crazy uncles or college roommates. We are now so used to the idea that we at least *could* call the police to resolve virtually any difficult circumstance that many of us find it difficult to even imagine what people would have done before this was possible.[31] Because, in fact, for the vast majority of people throughout history—even those who lived in in large cities—there were simply no authorities to call in such circumstances. Or, at least, no impersonal bureaucratic ones who were, like the modern police, empowered to impose arbitrary resolutions backed by the threat of force.

Here I think it is possible to add a kind of corollary to the Iron Law of Liberalism. History reveals that political policies that favor "the market" have always meant even more people in offices to administer things, but it also reveals that they also mean an increase of the range and density of social relations that are ultimately regulated by the threat of violence. This obviously flies in the face of everything we've been taught to believe about the market, but if you observe what actually happens, it's clearly true. In a sense, even calling this a "corollary" is deceptive, because we're really just talking about two different ways of talking about the same thing. The bureaucratization of daily life means the imposition of impersonal rules and regulations; impersonal rules and regulations, in turn, can only operate if they are backed up by the threat of force.[32] And indeed, in this most recent phase of total bureaucratization, we've seen security cameras, police scooters, issuers of temporary ID cards, and men and women in a variety of uniforms acting in either public or private capacities, trained in tactics of menacing, intimidating, and ultimately deploying physical violence, appear just about everywhere—even in places such as playgrounds, primary schools, college campuses, hospitals, libraries, parks, or beach resorts, where fifty years ago their presence would have been considered scandalous, or simply weird.

All this takes place as social theorists continue to insist that the direct appeal to force plays less and less of a factor in maintaining structures of social control.[33] The more reports one reads, in fact, of university students being tasered for unauthorized library use, or English professors being jailed and charged with felonies after being caught jaywalking on campus, the louder the defiant insistence that the kinds of subtle symbolic power analyzed by English professors are what's really important. It begins to sound more and more like a desperate refusal to accept that the workings of power could really be so crude and simplistic as what daily evidence proves them to be.

In my own native New York, I have observed the endless multiplication of bank branches. When I was growing up, most bank offices were large, freestanding buildings, usually designed to look like Greek or Roman temples. Over the last thirty years, storefront branches of the same three or four megabanks have opened, it seems, on every third block in the more prosperous parts of Manhattan. In the greater New York area there are now literally thousands of them, each one having replaced some earlier shop that once provided material goods and services of one sort or another. In a way these are the perfect symbols of our age: stores selling pure abstraction—immaculate boxes containing little but glass and steel dividers, computer screens, and armed security. They define the perfect point of conjuncture between guns and information, since that's really all that's there. And that conjuncture has come to provide the framework for almost every other aspect of our lives.

When we think about such matters at all, we generally act as if this is all simply an effect of technology: this is a world whisked into being by computers. It even looks like one. And indeed, all these new bank lobbies do bear a striking resemblance to the stripped-down virtual reality one often found in 1990s video games. It's as if we have finally achieved the ability to make such virtual realities materialize, and in so doing, to reduce our lives, too, to a kind of video game, as we negotiate the various mazeways of the new bureaucracies. Since, in such video games, nothing is actually produced, it just kind of springs into being, and we really do spend our lives earning points and dodging people carrying weapons.

But this sense that we are living in a world created by computers is itself an illusion. To conclude that this was all an inevitable effect of technological development, rather than of social and political forces, would be making a terrible mistake. Here too the lessons of "globalization," which was supposed to have been somehow created by the Internet, are critically important:

2. Do not overestimate the importance of technology as a causative factor.

Just as what came to be called "globalization" was really a creation of new political alignments, policy decisions, and new bureaucracies—which were only later followed by physical technologies like containerized shipping, or the Internet—so the pervasive bureaucratization of everyday life made possible by the computers is not, itself, the result of technological development. Rather it's the other way around. Technological change is simply not an independent variable. Technology will advance, and often in surprising and unexpected ways. But the overall direction it takes depends on social factors.

This is easy to forget because our immediate experience of everyday bureaucratization is entirely caught up in new information technologies: Facebook, smartphone banking, Amazon, PayPal, endless handheld devices that reduce the world around us to maps, forms, codes, and graphs. Still, the key alignments that made all this possible are precisely those that I have been describing in this essay, that first took place in the seventies and eighties, with the alliance of finance and corporate bureaucrats, the new corporate culture that emerged from it, and its ability to invade educational, scientific, and government circles in such a way that public and private bureaucracies finally merged together in a mass of paperwork designed to facilitate the direct extraction of wealth. This was not a product of new technologies. To the contrary, the appropriate technologies took decades to emerge. In the seventies, computers were still something of a joke. Banks and government offices were keen on putting them into service, but for most of those on the receiving end, they were the very definition of bureaucratic idiocy; whenever something went terribly, obviously wrong, the reaction was always to throw up one's eyes and blame "some computer." After forty years and the endless investment of research funding into information technologies, we have gotten to the point where the kinds of computers bankers employ, and provide, are our very definition of infallible, magical efficiency.

Consider the ATM machine. In the last thirty years, I can't remember a single occasion in which I have asked an ATM machine for money and gotten an incorrect amount. Nor have I been able to find anyone I know who can. This is so true that in the wake of the 2000 U.S. presidential elections, when the public was being regaled with statistics on the 2.8 percent degree of error expected from this type of voting machine, or the 1.5 percent expected from that, some had the temerity to point out that in a country that defines itself as the world's greatest democracy, where elections are our very sacrament, we seem to just accept that voting machines will regularly miscount the vote, while every day hundreds of millions of ATM transactions take place with an overall zero percent rate of error. What does this say about what really matters to Americans as a nation?

Financial technology then has gone from a running gag to something so reliable that it can form the assumed backbone of our social reality. You never have to think about whether the cash machine will dispense the correct amount of cash. If it's working at all, it will not make a mistake. This gives financial abstractions an air of utter certainty—a "ready-to-hand" quality, as Martin Heidegger put it—such an essential part of the practical infrastructure of our daily projects and affairs that we never have to think about as something in itself at all. Meanwhile physical infrastructure like roads, escalators, bridges, and underground railways crumbles around us, and the landscape surrounding major cities is peppered with the futuristic visions of past generations now lying smelly, dirty, or abandoned. None of this just happened. It is, precisely, a matter of national priorities: the result of policy decisions that allocate funding for everything from landmark preservation to certain kinds of scientific research. This is the world that all those endless documents about "vision," "quality," "leadership," and "innovation" have actually produced. Rather than causing our current situation, the direction that technological change has taken is itself largely a function of the power of finance.

3. Always remember it's all ultimately about value (or: whenever you hear someone say that what their greatest value is rationality, they are just saying that because they don't want to admit to what their greatest value really is).

The "self-actualization" philosophy from which most of this new bureaucratic language emerged insists that we live in a timeless present, that history means nothing, that we simply create the world around us through the power of the will. This is a kind of individualistic fascism. Around the time the philosophy became popular in the seventies, some conservative Christian theologians were actually thinking along very similar lines: seeing electronic money as a kind of extension for God's creative power, which is then transformed into material reality through the minds of inspired entrepreneurs. It's easy to see how this could lead to the creation of a world where financial abstractions feel like the very bedrock of reality, and so many of our lived environments look like they were 3-D-printed from somebody's computer screen. In fact, the sense of a digitally generated world I've been describing could be taken as a perfect illustration of another social law—at least, it seems to me that it should be recognized as a law—that, if one gives sufficient social power to a class of people holding even the most outlandish ideas, they will, consciously or not, eventually contrive to produce a world organized in such a way that living in it will, in a thousand subtle ways, reinforce the impression that those ideas are self-evidently true.

In the north Atlantic countries, all this is the culmination of a very long effort to transform popular ideas about the origins of value. Most Americans, for instance, used to subscribe to a rough-and-ready version of the labor theory of value. It made intuitive sense in a world where most people were farmers, mechanics, or shopkeepers: the good things in life were assumed to exist because people took the trouble to produce them; doing so was seen as involving both brain and muscle, usually, in roughly equal proportions. In the mid-nineteenth century even mainstream politicians would often use language that might seem to have been taken straight from Karl Marx. So Abraham Lincoln:

> Labor is prior to, and independent of, capital. Capital
> is only the fruit of labor, and could never have existed
> if labor had not first existed. Labor is the superior of
> capital, and deserves much the higher consideration.[34]

The rise of bureaucratic capitalism in the Gilded Age was accompanied by a self-conscious effort, on the part of the new tycoons of the day, to put this kind of language aside, and to promulgate what was considered at the time the bold new philosophy—steel magnate Andrew Carnegie spoke of it as "The Gospel of Wealth"—that value was instead derived from capital itself. Carnegie and his allies embarked on a well-funded campaign of promoting the new gospel, not just in Rotary Clubs and Chambers of Commerce across the nation, but also in schools, churches, and civic associations.[35] The basic argument was that the very efficiency of the new giant firms these men directed could produce such a material bounty it would allow Americans to realize themselves through what they consumed rather than what they produced. In this view, value was ultimately a product of the very bureaucratic organization of the new conglomerates.

One thing that the global justice movement taught us is that politics is, indeed, ultimately about value; but also, that those creating vast bureaucratic systems will almost never admit what their values really are. This was as true of the Carnegies as it is today. Normally, they will—like the robber barons of the turn of the last century—insist that they are acting in the name of efficiency, or "rationality." But in fact this language always turns out to be intentionally vague, even nonsensical. The term "rationality" is an excellent case in point here. A "rational" person is someone who is able to make basic logical connections and assess reality in a non-delusional fashion. In other words, someone who isn't crazy. Anyone who claims to base their politics on rationality—and this is true on the left as well as on the right—is claiming that anyone who disagrees with them might as well be insane, which is about as arrogant a position as one could possibly take. Or else, they're using "rationality" as a synonym for "technical efficiency," and thus focusing on *how* they are going about something because they do not wish to talk about *what* it is they are ultimately going about. Neoclassical economics is notorious for making this kind of move. When an economist attempts to prove that it is "irrational" to vote in national elections (because the effort expended outweighs the likely benefit to the individual voter), they use the term because they do not wish to say "irrational for actors for whom civic participation, political ideals, or the common good are not values in themselves, but who view public affairs only in terms of personal advantage." There is absolutely no reason why one could not rationally calculate the best way to further one's political ideals through voting. But according to the economists' assumptions, anyone who takes this course might as well be out of their minds.

In other words, talking about rational efficiency becomes a way of avoiding talking about what the efficiency is actually for; that is, the ultimately irrational aims that are assumed to be the ultimate ends of human behavior. Here is another place where markets and bureaucracies ultimately speak the same language. Both claim to be acting largely in the name of individual freedom, and individual self-realization through consumption. Even supporters of the old Prussian bureaucratic state in the nineteenth century, like Hegel or Goethe, insisted that its authoritarian measures could be justified by the fact they allowed citizens to be absolutely secure in their property, and therefore, free to do absolutely anything they pleased in their own homes—whether that meant pursuing the arts, religion, romance, or philosophical speculation, or simply a matter of deciding for themselves what sort of beer they chose to drink, music they chose to listen to, or clothes they chose to wear. Bureaucratic capitalism, when it appeared in the United States, similarly justified itself on consumerist grounds: one could justify demanding that workers abandon any control over the conditions under which they worked if one could thus guarantee them a wider and cheaper range of products for them to use at home.[36] There was always assumed to be a synergy between impersonal, rule-bound organization—whether in the public sphere, or the sphere of production—and absolute free self-expression in the club, café, kitchen, or family outing. (At first, of course, this freedom was limited to male heads of household; over time, it was at least in principle extended to everyone.)

The most profound legacy of the dominance of bureaucratic forms of organization over the last two hundred years is that it has made this intuitive division between rational, technical means and the ultimately irrational ends to which they are put seem like common sense. This is true on the national level, where civil servants pride themselves on being able to find the most efficient means to pursue whatever national destiny their country's rulers happen to dream up: whether that be rooted in the pursuit of cultural brilliance, imperial conquest, the pursuit of a genuinely egalitarian social order, or the literal application of Biblical law. It is equally true on the individual level, where we all take for granted that human beings go out into the marketplace merely to calculate the most efficient way to enrich themselves, but that once they have the money, there's no telling what they might decide to do with it: whether it be to buy a mansion, or a race car, engage in a personal investigation of UFO disappearances, or simply lavish the money on one's kids. It all seems so self-evident that it's hard for us to remember that in most human societies that have existed, historically, such a division would make no sense at all. In most times and places, the way one goes about doing something is assumed to be the ultimate expression of who one is.[37] But it also seems as if the moment one divides the world into two spheres in this way—into the domain of sheer technical competence and a separate domain of ultimate values—each sphere will inevitably begin trying to invade the other. Some will declare that rationality, or even efficiency, are themselves values, that they are even ultimate values, and that we should somehow create a "rational" society (whatever that means). Others will insist that life should become art; or else, religion. But all such movements are premised on the very division they profess to overcome.

In the big picture it hardly matters, then, whether one seeks to reorganize the world around bureaucratic efficiency or market rationality: all the fundamental assumptions remain the same. This helps explain why it's so easy to move back and forth between them, as with those ex-Soviet officials who so cheerfully switched hats from endorsing total state control of the economy, to total marketization—and in the process, true to the Iron Law, managed to increase the total number of bureaucrats employed in their country dramatically.[38] Or how the two can fuse into an almost seamless whole, as in the current era of total bureaucratization.

For anyone who has ever been a refugee, or for that matter had to fill out the forty-page application required to get one's daughter considered for admission by a London music school, the idea that bureaucracy has anything to do with rationality, let alone efficiency, might seem odd. But this is the way it looks from the top. In fact, from inside the system, the algorithms and mathematical formulae by which the world comes to be assessed become, ultimately, not just measures of value, but the source of value itself.[39] Much of what bureaucrats do, after all, is evaluate things. They are continually assessing, auditing, measuring, weighing the relative merits of different plans, proposals, applications, courses of action, or candidates for promotion. Market reforms only reinforce this tendency. This happens on every level. It is felt most cruelly by the poor, who are constantly monitored by an intrusive army of moralistic box-tickers assessing their child-rearing skills, inspecting their food cabinets to see if they are really cohabiting with their partners, determining whether they have been trying hard enough to find a job, or whether their medical conditions are really sufficiently severe to disqualify them from physical labor. All rich countries now employ legions of functionaries whose primary function is to make poor people feel bad about themselves. But the culture of evaluation is if anything even more pervasive in the hyper-credentialized world of the professional classes, where audit culture reigns, and nothing is real that cannot be quantified, tabulated, or entered into some interface or quarterly report. Not only is this world ultimately a product of financialization, it's really just a continuation of it. Since what is the world of securitized derivatives, collateralized debt obligations, and other such exotic financial instruments but the apotheosis of the principle that value is ultimately a product of paperwork, and the very apex of a mountain of assessment forms which begins with the irritating caseworker determining whether you are really poor enough to merit a fee waiver for your children's medicine and ends with men in suits engaged in high-speed trading of bets over how long it will take you to default on your mortgage.

A critique of bureaucracy fit for the times would have to show how all these threads—financialization, violence, technology, the fusion of public and private—knit together into a single, self-sustaining web. The process of financialization has meant that an ever-increasing proportion of corporate profits come in the form of rent extraction of one sort or another. Since this is ultimately little more than legalized extortion, it is accompanied by ever-increasing accumulation of rules and regulations, and ever-more sophisticated, and omnipresent, threats of physical force to enforce them. Indeed they become so omnipresent that we no longer realize we're being threatened, since we cannot imagine what it would be like not to be. At the same time, some of the profits from rent extraction are recycled to select portions of the professional classes, or to create new cadres of paper-pushing corporate bureaucrats. This helps a phenomenon I have written about elsewhere: the continual growth, in recent decades, of apparently meaningless, make-work, "bullshit jobs"—strategic vision coordinators, human resources consultants, legal analysts, and the like—despite the fact that even those who hold such positions are half the time secretly convinced they contribute nothing to the enterprise. In the end, this is just an extension of the basic logic of class realignment that began in the seventies and eighties as corporate bureaucracies become extensions of the financial system.

Every now and then you chance on a particular example that brings everything together. In September 2013, I visited a tea factory outside Marseille that was currently being occupied by its workers. There had been a standoff with local police for over a year. What had brought things to such a pass? A middle-aged factory worker, who took me on a tour of the plant, explained that while ostensibly the issue was a decision to move the plant to Poland to take advantage of cheaper labor, the ultimate issue had to do with the allocation of profits. The oldest and most experienced of the hundred-odd workers there had spent years tinkering with, and improving, the efficiency of the giant machines used to package teabags. Output had increased and with them profits. Yet what did the owners do with the extra money? Did they give the workers a raise to reward them for increased productivity? In the old Keynesian days of the fifties and sixties they almost certainly would have. No longer. Did they hire more workers and expand production? No again. All they did was hire middle managers.

For years, he explained, there had only been two executives in the factory: the boss, and a human resources officer. As profits rose, more and more men in suits appeared, until there were almost a dozen of them. The suits all had elaborate titles but there was almost nothing for them to do, so they spent a lot of time walking the catwalks staring at the workers, setting up metrics to measure and evaluate them, writing plans and reports. Eventually, they hit on the idea of moving the entire operation overseas—largely, he speculated, because devising the plan created a retrospective excuse for their existence, though, he added, it probably didn't hurt that while the workers themselves would mostly lose their jobs, the executives who made the plan would likely be relocated to a more attractive location. Before long, the workers had seized the building, and the perimeter was swarming with riot cops.

A left critique of bureaucracy, therefore, is sorely lacking. This book is not, precisely, an outline for such a critique. Neither is it in any sense an attempt to develop a general theory of bureaucracy, a history of bureaucracy, or even of the current age of total bureaucracy. It is a collection of essays, each of which points at some directions a left-wing critique of bureaucracy might take. The first focuses on violence; the second, on technology; the third, on rationality and value.

The chapters do not form a single argument. Perhaps they could be said to circle around one, but mainly, they are an attempt to begin a conversation—one long overdue.

We are all faced with a problem. Bureaucratic practices, habits, and sensibilities engulf us. Our lives have come to be organized around the filling out of forms. Yet the language we have to talk about these things is not just woefully inadequate—it might as well have been designed to make the problem worse. We need to find a way to talk about what it is we actually object to in this process, to speak honestly about the violence it entails, but at the same time, to understand what is appealing about it, what sustains it, which elements carry within them some potential for redemption in a truly free society, which are best considered the inevitable price to pay for living in any complex society, which can and should be entirely eliminated entirely. If this book plays even a modest role in sparking such a conversation, it will have made a genuine contribution to contemporary political life.

1

Dead Zones of the Imagination
An Essay on Structural Stupidity

Let me begin with a story about bureaucracy.

In 2006, my mother had a series of strokes. It soon became obvious that she would eventually be incapable of living at home without assistance. Since her insurance would not cover home care, a series of social workers advised us to put in for Medicaid. To qualify for Medicaid, however, one's total worth can only amount to six thousand dollars. We arranged to transfer her savings—this was, I suppose, technically a scam, though it's a peculiar sort of scam since the government employs thousands of social workers whose main work seems to involve telling citizens exactly how to perpetuate said scam—but shortly thereafter, she had another, very serious stroke, and found herself in a nursing home undergoing long-term rehabilitation. When she emerged from that, she was definitely going to need home care, but there was a problem:

her social security check was being deposited directly, and she was barely able to sign her name, so unless I acquired power of attorney over her account and was thus able to pay her monthly rent bills for her, the money would immediately build up and disqualify her, even after I filled out the enormous raft of Medicaid documents I needed to file to qualify her for pending status.

I went to her bank, picked up the requisite forms, and brought them to the nursing home. The documents needed to be notarized. The nurse on the floor informed me there was an in-house notary, but I needed to make an appointment; she picked up the phone and put me through to a disembodied voice, who then transferred me to the notary. The notary proceeded to inform me I first had to get authorization from the head of social work, and hung up. So I acquired his name and room number and duly took the elevator downstairs and appeared at his office—only to discover that the head of social work was, in fact, the disembodied voice that had referred me to the notary in the first place. The head of social work picked up the phone, said, "Marjorie, that was me, you're driving this man crazy with this nonsense and you're driving me crazy, too," and, after a small apologetic gesture, proceeded to secure me an appointment for early the next week.

The next week the notary duly appeared, accompanied me upstairs, made sure I'd filled out my side of the form (as had been repeatedly emphasized to me), and then, in my mother's presence, proceeded to fill out her own. I was a little puzzled that she didn't ask my mother to sign anything, only me, but I figured that she knew what she was doing. The next day I took the document to the bank, where the woman at the desk took one look, asked why my mother hadn't signed it, and showed it to her manager, who told me to take it back and do it right. It seemed that the notary indeed had no idea what she was doing. So I got new set of forms, duly filled out my side of each, and made a new appointment. On the appointed day the notary appeared, and after a few awkward remarks about how difficult these banks are (why does each bank insist on having its own, completely different power of attorney form?), she took me upstairs. I signed, my mother signed—with some difficulty, she was finding it hard at this point even to prop herself up—and the next day I returned to the bank. Another woman at a different desk examined the forms and asked why I had signed the line where it said to write my name and printed my name on the line where it said to sign.

"I did? Well, I just did exactly what the notary told me to do."

"But it clearly says 'signature' here."

"Oh, yes, it does, doesn't it? I guess she told me wrong. Again. Well . . . all the information is still there, isn't it? It's just those two bits that are reversed. So is that really a problem? The situation is kind of pressing, and I'd really rather not have to wait to make another appointment."

"Well, normally we don't even accept these forms without all the signatories being here in person."

"My mother had a stroke. She's bedridden. That's why I need power of attorney in the first place."

She said she'd check with the manager, and after ten minutes returned, the manager hanging just within earshot in the background, to announce the bank could not accept the forms in their present state—and in addition, even if they were filled out correctly, I would still need a letter from my mother's doctor certifying that she was mentally competent to sign such a document.

I pointed out that no one had mentioned any such letter previously.

"What?" the manager suddenly interjected. "Who gave you those forms and didn't tell you about the letter?"

Since the culprit was one of the more sympathetic bank

employees, I dodged the question,[40] noting instead that in the bankbook it was printed, quite clearly, "in trust for David Graeber." He of course replied that would only matter if she was dead.

As it happened, the whole problem soon became academic: my mother did indeed die a few weeks later.

At the time, I found this experience extremely disconcerting. Having spent much of my life leading a fairly bohemian student existence comparatively insulated from this sort of thing, I found myself asking my friends: is this what ordinary life, for most people, is really like? Running around feeling like an idiot all day? Being somehow put in a position where one actually does end up acting like an idiot? Most were inclined to suspect that this was indeed what life is mostly like. Obviously, the notary was unusually incompetent. Still, I had to spend over a month not long after dealing with the ramifying consequences of the act of whatever anonymous functionary in the New York Department of Motor Vehicles had inscribed my given name as "Daid," not to mention the Verizon clerk who spelled my surname "Grueber." Bureaucracies public and private appear—for whatever historical reasons—to be organized in such a way as to guarantee that a significant proportion of actors will not be able to perform their tasks as expected. It's in this sense that I've said one can fairly say that bureaucracies are utopian forms of organization. After all, is this not what we always say of utopians: that they have a naïve faith in the perfectibility of human nature and refuse to deal with humans as they actually are? Which is, are we not also told, what leads them to set impossible standards and then blame the individuals for not living up to them?[41] But in fact all bureaucracies do this, insofar as they set demands they insist are reasonable, and then, on discovering that they are not reasonable (since a significant number of people will always be unable to perform as expected), conclude that the problem is not with the demands themselves but with the individual inadequacy of each particular human being who fails to live up to them.

On a purely personal level, probably the most disturbing thing was how dealing with these forms somehow rendered me stupid, too. How could I not have noticed that I was printing my name on the line that said "signature"? It was written right there! I like to think that I am not, ordinarily, a particularly stupid person. In fact I've made something of a career out convincing others that I'm smart. Yet I was doing obviously foolish things; and not because I wasn't paying attention; in fact, I had been investing a great deal of mental and emotional energy in the whole affair. The problem, I realized, was not with the energy spent, but with the fact that most of this energy was being sunk into attempts to try to understand and influence whoever, at any moment, seemed to have some kind of bureaucratic power over me—when, in fact, all that was required was the accurate interpretation of one or two Latin words, and correct performance of certain purely mechanical functions. Spending so much of my time worrying about how not to seem like I was rubbing the notary's face in her incompetence, or imagining what might make me seem sympathetic to various bank officials, made me less inclined to notice when they told me to do something foolish. It was an obviously misplaced strategy, since insofar as anyone had the power to bend the rules they were usually not the people I was talking to; moreover, if I did encounter someone who did have such power, they would invariably inform me directly or indirectly that if I did complain in any way, even about a purely structural absurdity, the only possible result would be to get some junior functionary in trouble.

As an anthropologist, all this struck me as strangely familiar. We anthropologists have made something of a specialty out of dealing with the ritual surrounding birth, marriage, death, and similar rites of passage. We are particularly concerned with ritual gestures that are socially efficacious: where the mere act of saying or doing something makes it socially true. (Think of phrases like "I apologize," "I surrender, or "I pronounce you man and wife.") Humans being the social creatures that they are, birth and death are never mere biological events. It normally takes a great deal of work to turn a newborn baby into a person—someone with a name and social relationships (mother, father . . .) and a home, towards whom others have responsibilities, who can someday be expected to have responsibilities to them as well. Usually, much of this work is done through ritual. Such rituals, as anthropologists have noted, can vary wildly in form and content: they might involve baptisms, confirmations, fumigations, first haircuts, isolation, declarations, the making and waving and burning and burying of ritual paraphernalia, spells. Death is even more complicated because those same social relationships that one has acquired in life have to be gradually severed, rearranged. It often takes years, repeated burials (even reburials), burning, bleaching and rearranging of bones, feasts, and ceremonies before someone is entirely dead. In most existing societies at this point in history, those rituals may or may not be carried out, but it is precisely paperwork, rather than any other form of ritual, that is socially efficacious in this way, that actually effects the change. My mother, for example, wished to be cremated without ceremony; my main memory of the funeral home though was of the plump, good-natured clerk who walked me through a fourteen-page document he had to file in order to obtain a death certificate, written in ballpoint on carbon paper so it came out in triplicate. "How many hours a day do you spend filling out forms like that?" I asked. He sighed. "It's all I do," holding up a hand bandaged from some kind of incipient carpal tunnel syndrome. He had to. Without those forms, neither my mother, nor any of the other people cremated at his establishment, would be legally—hence socially—dead.

Why, then, I wondered, are there not vast ethnographic tomes about American or British rites of passage, with long chapters about forms and paperwork?

There is an obvious answer. Paperwork is boring. One can describe the ritual surrounding it. One can observe how people talk about or react to it. But when it comes to the paperwork itself, there just aren't that many interesting things one can say about it. How is the form laid out? What about the color scheme? Why did they choose to ask for certain bits of information and not others? Why place of birth and not, say, place where you went to grade school? What's so important about the signature? But even so, even the most imaginative commentator pretty quickly runs out of questions.

In fact, one could go further. Paperwork is *supposed* to be boring. And it's getting more so all the time. Medieval charters were often quite beautiful, full of calligraphy and heraldic embellishments. Even in the nineteenth century some of this remained: I have a copy of my grandfather's birth certificate, issued in Springfield, Illinois, in 1858, and it's quite colorful, with Gothic letters, scrolls and little cherubs (it's also written entirely in German). My father's, in contrast, issued in Lawrence, Kansas, in 1914, is monochrome and utterly unadorned, just lines and boxes, though they are filled out in a nice florid hand. My own, issued in New York in 1961, lacks even that: it's typed and stamped and utterly without character. But of course the computer interfaces used for so many forms nowadays are more boring still. It's as if the creators of these documents were gradually trying to strip them of anything even slightly profound, or remotely symbolic.

It's hardly surprising that all this might drive an anthropologist to despair. Anthropologists are drawn to areas of density. The interpretative tools we have at our disposal are best suited to wend our way through complex webs of meaning or signification—we seek to understand intricate ritual symbolism, social dramas, poetic forms, or kinship networks. What all these have in common is that they tend to be both infinitely rich, and, at the same time, open-ended. If one sought out to exhaust every meaning, motive, or association packed into a single Romanian harvest ritual, or Zande witchcraft accusation, or Mexican family saga, one could easily spend a lifetime—quite a number of lifetimes, in fact, if one were also out to trace the fan of relations with other elements in the larger social or symbolic fields such work invariably opens up. Paperwork in contrast is designed to be maximally simple and self-contained. Even when forms are complex, even bafflingly complex, it's by an endless accretion of very simple but apparently contradictory elements, like a maze composed entirely of the endless juxtaposition of two or three very simple geometrical motifs. And like a maze, paperwork doesn't really open on anything outside itself. As a result, there just isn't very much to interpret. Clifford Geertz became famous for offering a "thick description" of Balinese cockfights where he tried to demonstrate that, if one were able to unpack everything going on in a given match, one would be able to understand everything about Balinese society: they're conceptions of the human condition, of society, hierarchy, nature, all the fundamental passions and dilemmas of human existence. This simply would not be possible to do with a mortgage application, no matter how dense the document itself; and even if some defiant soul set out to write such an analysis—just to prove it could be done—it would be even harder to imagine anyone else actually reading it.

One might object: but haven't great novelists often written compelling literature about bureaucracy? Of course they have. But they have managed to do this by embracing the very circularity and emptiness—not to mention idiocy—of bureaucracy, and producing literary works that partake of something like the same mazelike, senseless form. This is why almost all great literature on the subject takes the form of horror-comedy. Franz Kafka's *The Trial* is of course the paradigm (as is *The Castle*), but one can cite any number of others: from Stanislaw Lem's *Memoirs Found in a Bathtub*, which is pretty much straight Kafka, to Ismail Kadare's *Palace of Dreams* and José Saramago's *All the Names*, to any number of works that might be said to be informed by the bureaucratic spirit, such as much of Italo Calvino or most anything by Borges. Joseph Heller's *Catch-22*, which takes on military bureaucracies, and *Something Happened*, about corporate bureaucracies, are considered latter-day masterworks in this genre, as is David Foster Wallace's unfinished *The Pale King*, an imaginative meditation on the nature of boredom set in a Midwestern office of the U.S. Internal Revenue Service. It's interesting that just about all these works of fiction not only emphasize the comic senselessness of bureaucratic life, but mix it with at least an undertone of violence. This is more obvious in some authors (Kafka and Heller, for example) than others, but it almost always seems to be lurking just underneath the surface. What's more, contemporary stories that are explicitly *about* violence have a tendency to also become stories about bureaucracy, since, after all, most acts of extreme violence either take place in bureaucratic environments (armies, prisons . . .) or else, they are almost immediately surrounded by bureaucratic procedures (crime).

Great writers, then, know how to deal with a vacuum. They embrace it. They stare into the abyss until the abyss stares back into them. Social theory, in contrast, abhors a vacuum—or, this is certainly true if its approach to bureaucracy is anything to go on. Stupidity and violence are precisely the elements it is least inclined to talk about.[42]

The lack of critical work is especially odd because on the surface, you would think academics are personally positioned to speak of the absurdities of bureaucratic life. Of course, this is in part because they *are* bureaucrats—increasingly so. "Administrative responsibilities," going to committee meetings, filling out forms, reading and writing letters of support, placating the whims of minor deans—all this takes up an ever-expanding portion of the average academic's time. But academics are also reluctant bureaucrats, in the sense that even when "admin," as it's called, ends up becoming most of what a professor actually does, it is always treated as something tacked on—not what they are really qualified for, certainly, and not the work that defines who they really are.[43] They are scholars—people who research, analyze, and interpret things—even if increasingly, they're really scholarly souls trapped in a bureaucrat's body. You might think that an academic's reaction would be to research, analyze, and interpret this very phenomenon: how does it happen that we all end up spending more and more of our time on paperwork? What is the meaning of paperwork anyway? What are the social dynamics behind it? Yet for some reason, this never happens.[44]

It has been my experience that when academics gather around the water cooler (or the academic equivalent of a water cooler, which is usually a coffee machine) they rarely talk about their "real" work but spend almost all their time complaining about administrative responsibilities. But in those ever-shrinking moments where they are allowed to think profound thoughts, this seems to be the last thing they'd wish to think about.

But there is something even deeper going on here, I suspect—something that bears on the very nature of what universities are and why they exist.

Consider, for example, the extraordinary prominence in U.S. social science in the postwar period of two continental theorists: German sociologist Max Weber in the fifties and sixties, and French historian and social philosopher Michel Foucault ever since. Each attained a kind of intellectual hegemony in the United States that they never managed to achieve in their own countries. What made them so appealing to American academics? No doubt their popularity had much to do with the ease with which each could be adopted as a kind of anti-Marx, their theories put forth (usually in crudely simplified form) as ways of arguing that power is not simply or primarily a matter of the control of production but rather a pervasive, multifaceted, and unavoidable feature of any social life.

But I also think that a large part of the appeal was their attitude toward bureaucracy. Indeed, it sometimes seems that these were the only two intelligent human beings in twentieth century history who honestly believed that the power of bureaucracy lies in its effectiveness. That is, that bureaucracy really works. Weber saw bureaucratic forms of organization as the very embodiment of Reason in human affairs, so obviously superior to any alternative form of organization that they threatened to engulf everything, locking humanity in a joyless "iron cage," bereft of spirit and charisma. Foucault was more subversive, but he was subversive in a way that only endowed bureaucratic power with more effectiveness, not less. In his work on asylums, clinics, prisons, and the rest, absolutely every aspect of human life—health, sexuality, work, morality, our very conceptions of truth—became nothing in and of themselves, but merely products of one or another form of professional or administrative discourse. Through concepts like governmentality and biopower, he argued that state bureaucracies end up shaping the parameters of human existence in ways far more intimate than anything Weber would have imagined. For Foucault, all forms of knowledge became forms of power, shaping our minds and bodies through largely administrative means.

It's hard to avoid the suspicion that Weber and Foucault's popularity owed much to the fact that the American university system during this period had itself increasingly become an institution dedicated to producing functionaries for an imperial administrative apparatus, operating on a global scale. In the immediate wake of World War II, when the United States was first establishing its global administrative apparatus, all this was often fairly explicit. Sociologists like Talcott Parsons and Edward Shils[45] were deeply embedded in the Cold War establishment at Harvard, and the stripped-down version of Weber they created was quickly stripped down even further and adopted by State Department functionaries and the World Bank as "development theory," and actively promoted as an alternative to Marxist historical materialism in the battleground states of the Global South. At that time, even anthropologists like Margaret Mead, Ruth Benedict, and Clifford Geertz had no compunctions against cooperating closely with the military-intelligence apparatus, or even the CIA.[46] All this changed with the war in Vietnam. During the course of campus mobilizations against the war, this kind of complicity was thrown under a spotlight, and Parsons—and with him, Weber—came to be seen as the very embodiment of everything radicals sought to reject.

With Weber dethroned, it was at first unclear who, if anyone, would replace him. For a while there was a lot of interest in German Marxism: Adorno, Benjamin, Marcuse, Lukacs, Fromm. But the focus eventually shifted to France, where the uprising of May 1968 had produced an efflorescence of extremely creative social theory—in France it was just called " '68 thought"— that was simultaneously radical in temperament, and hostile to almost every traditional manifestation of leftist politics, from union organizing to insurrection.[47] Different theorists shifted in and out of fashion, but over the course of the eighties, Foucault managed to establish himself in a way no one—even, really, Weber—has before or since. Or, at least, he did so within those disciplines that considered themselves in any way oppositional. Ultimately, it might be better to speak here of the emergence of a kind of division of academic labor within the American higher education system, with the optimistic side of Weber reinvented (in even more simplified form) for the actual train-ing of bureaucrats under the name of "rational choice theory," while his pessimistic side was relegated to the Foucauldians. Foucault's ascendancy in turn was precisely within those fields of academic endeavor that absorbed former campus radicals, or those who identified with them. These disciplines were almost completely divorced from any access to political power, or increasingly, any influence on social movements, as well—a distance that gave Foucault's emphasis on the "power/knowledge" nexus (the assertion that forms of knowledge are always also forms of social power—indeed, the most important forms of social power) a particular appeal.

No doubt any such pocket historical summary can only be a bit caricaturish and unfair. Still, I believe there is a profound truth here. It is not just that academics are drawn to areas of density, where our skills at interpretation are best deployed. We also have an increasing tendency to identify what's interesting with what's important, and to assume that places of density are also places of power. The power of bureaucracy shows just how often exactly the opposite is in fact the case.

But this essay is not just—or not even primarily—about bureaucracy. It is primarily about violence. What I would like to argue is that situations created by violence—particularly structural violence, by which I mean forms of pervasive social inequality that are ultimately backed up by the threat of physical harm—invariably tend to create the kinds of willful blindness we normally associate with bureaucratic procedures. To put it crudely: it is not so much that bureaucratic procedures are inherently stupid, or even that they tend to produce behavior that they themselves define as stupid—though they do do that—but rather, that they are invariably ways of managing social situations that are already stupid because they are founded on structural violence. This approach, I think, has the potential to tell us a great deal about both how bureaucracy has come to pervade every aspect of our lives, and why we don't notice it.

·

Now, I admit that this emphasis on violence might seem odd. We are not used to thinking of nursing homes or banks or even HMOs as violent institutions—except perhaps in the most abstract and metaphorical sense. But the violence I'm referring to here is not abstract. I am not speaking of conceptual violence. I am speaking of violence in the literal sense: the kind that involves, say, one person hitting another over the head with a wooden stick. All of these are institutions involved in the allocation of resources within a system of property rights regulated and guaranteed by governments in a system that ultimately rests on the threat of force. "Force" in turn is just a euphemistic way to refer to violence: that is, the ability to call up people dressed in uniforms, willing to threaten to hit others over the head with wooden sticks.

It is curious how rarely citizens in industrial democracies actually think about this fact, or how instinctively we try to discount its importance. This is what makes it possible, for example, for graduate students to be able to spend days in the stacks of university libraries poring over Foucault-inspired theoretical tracts about the declining importance of coercion as a factor in modern life without ever reflecting on that fact that, had they insisted on their right to enter the stacks without showing a properly stamped and validated ID, armed men would have been summoned to physically remove them, using whatever force might be required. It's almost as if the more we allow aspects of our everyday existence to fall under the purview of bureaucratic regulations, the more everyone concerned colludes to downplay the fact (perfectly obvious to those actually running the system) that all of it ultimately depends on the threat of physical harm.

Actually, the very use of the term "structural violence" is an excellent case in point. When I first began working on this essay, I simply took it for granted that the term referred to actual violence that operates in an indirect form. Imagine, if you will, some warlike tribe (let's call them the Alphas) that sweeps out of the desert and seizes a swath of land inhabited by peaceful farmers (let's call them the Omegas). But instead of exacting tribute, they appropriate all the fertile land, and arrange for their children to have privileged access to most forms of practical education, at the same time initiating a religious ideology that holds that they are intrinsically superior beings, finer and more beautiful and more intelligent, and that the Omegas, now largely reduced to working on their estates, have been cursed by the divine powers for some terrible sin, and have become stupid, ugly, and base. And perhaps the Omegas internalize their disgrace and come to act as if they believe they really are guilty of something. In a sense perhaps they do believe it. But on a deeper level it doesn't make a lot of sense to ask whether they do or not. The whole arrangement is the fruit of violence and can only be maintained by the continual threat of violence: the fact that the Omegas are quite aware that if anyone directly challenged property arrangements, or access to education, swords would be drawn and people's heads would almost certainly end up being lopped off. In a case like this, what we talk about in terms of "belief" are simply the psychological techniques people develop to accommodate themselves to this reality. We have no idea how they would act, or what they would think, if the Alphas' command of the means of violence were to somehow disappear.

This is what I had in mind when I first began using the phrase "structural violence"—structures that could only be created and maintained by the threat of violence, even if in their ordinary, day-to-day workings, no actual physical violence need take place. If one reflects on the matter, the same can be said of most phenomena that are ordinarily referred to as "structural violence" in the literature—racism, sexism, class privilege—even if their actual mode of operation is infinitely more complex.

Here I was probably inspired most by my readings in feminist literature, which often does speak of structural violence in this way.[48] It is widely noted, for instance, that rates of sexual assault increase dramatically at precisely the moments when women begin challenging "gender norms" of work, comportment, or dress. It's really quite the same as the conquerors suddenly taking out their swords again. But for the most part, academics do not use the term this way. The current usage really harkens back to sixties "Peace Studies," and it is used it to refer to "structures" that, it is claimed, have the same effects as violence, even though they may not involve physical acts of violence at all.[49] The list of structures is pretty much the same list (racism, sexism, poverty, and the rest), but the implication is there *could*, for example, exist a system of patriarchy that operated in the total absence of domestic violence or sexual assault, or a system of racism that was in no way backed up by government-enforced property rights—despite the fact that, to my knowledge, no example of either has ever been observed.[50] Once again, it's puzzling why anyone would make such an argument, unless they were for some reason determined to insist that the physical violence isn't the essence of the thing, that this isn't what really needs to be addressed. To pose the question of violence directly would, apparently, mean opening a series of doors that most academics seem to feel would really better be left shut.

Most of these doors lead directly to the problem of what we call "the state"—and the bureaucratic structures through which it actually exercises power. Is the state's claim to a monopoly of violence ultimately the problem, or is the state an essential part of any possible solution? Is the very practice of laying down rules and then threatening physical harm against anyone who does not follow them itself objectionable, or is it just that the authorities are not deploying such threats in the right way? To talk of racism, sexism, and the rest as a bunch of abstract structures floating about is the best way to dodge such questions entirely.

In many of the rural communities anthropologists are most familiar with, where modern administrative techniques are explicitly seen as alien impositions, things much more resemble my example of the Alphas and Omegas. We are usually dealing with conquered populations of one sort or another—hence, with people who are keenly aware that current arrangements are the fruit of violence. As a result, it would never occur to anyone to deny that the government is a fundamentally coercive institution—even if they might also be perfectly willing to concede that in certain respects, it could also be a benevolent one. In the part of rural Madagascar where I did my fieldwork, for example, everyone took it for granted that states operate primarily by inspiring fear. It was assumed to be just as true of the old Malagasy kingdoms as of the subsequent French colonial regime, or its contemporary Malagasy successor, which was seen as basically a slightly retooled version of the same thing. On the other hand, the fear it inspired was decidedly sporadic, since much of the time, the state, or its representatives, were not really around. Government played almost no role in regulating the minutiae of daily life: there were no building codes, no open container laws, no mandatory licensing and insurance of vehicles, no rules about who could buy or sell or smoke or build or eat or drink what where, where people could play music or tend their animals. Or anyway, if there were such laws, no one knew what they were because it never occurred to anyone, even the police, to enforce them—even in town, and definitely not in the surrounding countryside, where such matters were entirely regulated by custom, deliberation by communal assemblies, or magical taboo. In such contexts, it became all the more apparent that the main business of government bureaucracy was the registration of taxable property, and maintaining the infrastructure that allowed those who collected taxes to show up and take their things away.

This situation actually created some interesting dilemmas for my own research. I had done a good deal of work in the Malagasy national archives before heading out to the countryside. The nineteenth-century Merina kingdom had brought in foreign missionaries to help them train a civil service, and the records were all still there, along with those of the colonial regime. As a result, from about 1875 to 1950, I had quite a wealth of data for the community I was studying: census data, school records, and above all, precise figures about the size of each family and its holdings in land and cattle—and in the earlier period, slaves. But as soon as I arrived I discovered this was precisely what most people assumed an outsider arriving from the capital would be most likely to ask about, and therefore, which they were least inclined to tell them. In fact, people were willing to talk about almost anything else. As a result, I had almost completely different sorts of data for the two historical periods.

As I got to know people better, I slowly realized that it wasn't just that the government didn't regulate daily life—in most important respects, the government didn't do anything at all. State power has a tendency to ebb and flow in Malagasy history, and this was a definite ebb. There were government offices, of course, and people sat in them typing and registering things, but it was mainly just for show—they were barely paid, received no materials (they had to buy their own paper), everyone lied on their tax assessments, and no one really paid the taxes anyway. Police just patrolled the highway and would not go into the countryside at all. Yet everyone would talk about the government as if it actually existed, hoping outsiders wouldn't notice, which might possibly lead to someone in some office in the capital deciding they might have to do something about the situation. So on one level, bureaucratic power had almost no effect on people. On another, it colored everything.

Part of the reason was the initial impact of conquest nearly a hundred years before. At the time, most inhabitants of the Merina kingdom had been slaveholders, at the heart of a great kingdom. An important thing to remember about slavery is that it is never seen—by anyone really—as a moral relationship, but one of simple arbitrary power: the master can order the slave to do whatever he pleases, and there's really nothing the slave can do about it.[51] When the French overthrew the Merina kingdom and took over Madagascar in 1895, they simultaneously abolished slavery and imposed a government that similarly did not even pretend to be based on a social contract or the will of the governed, but was simply based on superior firepower. Unsurprisingly, most Malagasy concluded that they had all been effectively turned into slaves. This had profound relations on how people came to deal with one another. Before long, any relation of command—that is, any ongoing relationship between adults where one renders the other a mere extension of his or her will—was considered morally objectionable, essentially just variations on slavery, or the state. Proper Malagasy people didn't act this way. So even though the Malagasy government was far away, its shadow was everywhere. In the community I studied, such associations were most likely to come to the fore when people spoke of the great slave-holding families of the nineteenth century, whose children went on to become the core of the colonial-era administration, largely (it was always remarked) by dint of their devotion to education and skill with paperwork, and whose descendants still mostly worked in fancy offices in the capital, far from the worries and responsibilities of rural life. In other contexts, relations of command, particularly in bureaucratic contexts, were linguistically coded: they were firmly identified with French; Malagasy, in contrast, was seen as the language appropriate to deliberation, explanation, and consensus decision-making. Minor functionaries, when they wished to impose arbitrary dictates, would almost invariably switch to French.

I have particularly vivid memories of one occasion when an affable minor official who had had many conversations with me in Malagasy was flustered one day to discover me dropping by at exactly the moment everyone had apparently decided to go home early to watch a football game. (As I mentioned, they weren't really doing anything in these offices anyway.)

"The office is closed," he announced, in French, pulling himself up into an uncharacteristically formal pose. "If you have any business at the office you must return tomorrow at eight a.m."

This puzzled me. He knew English was my native language; he knew I spoke fluent Malagasy; he had no way to know I could even understand spoken French. I pretended confusion and replied, in Malagasy, "Excuse me? I'm sorry, I don't understand you."

His response was to pull himself up even taller and just say the same thing again, slightly slower and louder. I once again feigned incomprehension. "I don't get it," I said, "why are you speaking to me in a language I don't even know?" He did it again.

In fact, he proved utterly incapable of repeating the sentence in the vernacular, or, for that matter, of saying anything else at all in Malagasy. I suspected this was because if he had switched to everyday language, he would not feel he could be nearly so abrupt. Others later confirmed this was exactly what was happening: if he were speaking Malagasy, he would at the very least have had to explain why the office had closed at such an unusual time. In literary Malagasy, the French language can actually be referred to as *ny teny baiko*, "the language of command." It was characteristic of contexts where explanations, deliberation, and, ultimately, consent, were not required, since such contexts were shaped by the presumption of unequal access to sheer physical force. In this instance, the actual means to deploy such force was no longer present. The official could not in fact call the police, and nor would he want to—he just wanted me to go away, which, after teasing him for a moment with my language games, I did. But he couldn't even evoke the kind of attitude such power allows one to adopt without calling up the shadow of the colonial state.

In Madagascar, bureaucratic power was somewhat redeemed in most people's minds by its connection to education, which was held in near-universal esteem. To enter into the world of government, bureaus, and gendarme stations was also to enter into the world of novels, world history, technology, and potential travel overseas. It was not therefore irredeemably bad or intrinsically absurd.

But the Malagasy state was also not particularly violent. Comparative analysis suggests there is a direct relation however between the level of violence employed in a bureaucratic system, and the level of absurdity and ignorance it is seen to produce. Keith Breckenridge, for example, has documented at some length the regimes of "power without knowledge" typical of colonial South Africa,[52] where coercion and paperwork largely substituted for the need for understanding African subjects. The actual installation of apartheid that began in the 1950s, for example, was heralded by a new pass system that was designed to simplify earlier rules that obliged African workers to carry extensive documentation of labor contracts, substituting a single identity booklet, marked with their "names, locale, fingerprints, tax status, and their officially prescribed 'rights' to live and work in the towns and cities," and nothing else.[53] Government functionaries appreciated it for streamlining administration, police for relieving them of the responsibility of having to actually talk to African workers. African workers, for their parts, universally referred to the new document as the "dompas," or "stupid pass," for precisely that reason.

Andrew Mathews's brilliant ethnography of the Mexican forestry service in Oaxaca likewise demonstrates that it is precisely the near-total inequality of power between government officials and local farmers that allows foresters to remain in a kind of ideological bubble, maintaining simple black-and-white ideas about forest fires (for instance) that allow them to remain pretty much the only people in Oaxaca who don't understand what effects their regulations actually have.[54]

There are traces of the link between coercion and absurdity even in the way we talk about bureaucracy in English: note for example, how most of the colloquial terms that specifically refer to bureaucratic foolishness—SNAFU, Catch-22, and the like—derive from military slang. More generally, political scientists have long observed a "negative correlation," as David Apter put it,[55] between coercion and information: that is, while relatively democratic regimes tend to be awash in too much information, as everyone bombards political authorities with explanations and demands, the more authoritarian and repressive a regime, the less reason people have to tell it anything—which is why such regimes are forced to rely so heavily on spies, intelligence agencies, and secret police.

Violence's capacity to allow arbitrary decisions, and thus to avoid the kind of debate, clarification, and renegotiation typical of more egalitarian social relations, is obviously what allows its victims to see procedures created on the basis of violence as stupid or unreasonable. Most of us are capable of getting a superficial sense of what others are thinking or feeling just by observing their tone of voice, or body language—it's usually not hard to get a sense of people's immediate intentions and motives, but going beyond that superficial often takes a great deal of work. Much of the everyday business of social life, in fact, consists in trying to decipher others' motives and perceptions. Let us call this "interpretive labor." One might say, those relying on the fear of force are not obliged to engage in a lot of interpretative labor, and thus, generally speaking, they do not.

As an anthropologist, I know I am treading perilous ground here. When they do turn their attention to violence, anthropologists tend to emphasize exactly the opposite aspect: the ways that acts of violence are meaningful and communicative—even the ways that they can resembles poetry.[56] Anyone suggesting otherwise is likely to be instantly accused of a kind of philistinism: "are you honestly suggesting that violence is *not* symbolically powerful, that bullets and bombs are *not* meant to communicate something?" So for the record: no, I'm not suggesting that. But I am suggesting that this might not be the most important question. First of all, because it assumes that "violence" refers primarily to *acts* of violence—actual shovings, punchings, stabbings, or explosions—rather than to the *threat* of violence, and the kinds of social relations the pervasive threat of violence makes possible.[57] Second of all, because this seems to be one area where anthropologists, and academics more generally, are particularly prone to fall victim to the confusion of interpretive depth and social significance. That is, they automatically assume that what is most interesting about violence is also what's most important.

Let me take these points one at a time. Is it accurate to say that acts of violence are, generally speaking, also acts of communication? It certainly is. But this is true of pretty much any form of human action. It strikes me that what is really important about violence is that it is perhaps the only form of human action that holds out even the possibility of having social effects *without* being communicative. To be more precise: violence may well be the only way it is possible for one human being to do something which will have relatively predictable effects on the actions of a person about whom they understand nothing. In pretty much any other way in which you might try to influence another's actions, you must at least have some idea about who you think they are, who they think you are, what they might want out of the situation, their aversions and proclivities, and so forth. Hit them over the head hard enough, and all of this becomes irrelevant.

It is true that the effects one can have by disabling or killing someone are very limited. But they are real enough—and critically, it is possible to know in advance exactly what they are going to be. Any alternative form of action cannot, without some sort of appeal to shared meanings or understandings, have any predictable effects at all. What's more, while attempts to influence others by the threat of violence do require some level of shared understandings, these can be pretty minimal. Most human relations—particularly ongoing ones, whether between longstanding friends or longstanding enemies—are extremely complicated, dense with history and meaning. Maintaining them requires a constant and often subtle work of imagination, of endlessly trying to see the world from others' points of view. This is what I've already referred to as "interpretive labor." Threatening others with physical harm allows the possibility of cutting through all this. It makes possible relations of a far more simple and schematic kind ("cross this line and I will shoot you," "one more word out of any of you and you're going to jail"). This is of course why violence is so often the preferred weapon of the stupid. One might even call it the trump card of the stupid, since (and this is surely one of the tragedies of human existence) it is the one form of stupidity to which it is most difficult to come up with an intelligent response.

I do need to introduce one crucial qualification here. Everything, here, depends on the balance of forces. If two parties are engaged in a relatively equal contest of violence—say, generals commanding opposing armies—they have good reason to try to get inside each other's heads. It is only when one side has an overwhelming advantage in their capacity to cause physical harm that they no longer need to do so. But this has very profound effects, because it means that the most characteristic effect of violence, its ability to obviate the need for "interpretive labor," becomes most salient when the violence itself is least visible—in fact, where acts of spectacular physical violence are least likely to occur. These are of course precisely what I have just defined as situations of structural violence, systematic inequalities ultimately backed up by the threat of force. For this reason, situations of structural violence invariably produce extreme lopsided structures of imaginative identification.

These effects are often most visible when the structures of inequality take the most deeply internalized forms. Gender is again a classic case in point. For example, in American situation comedies of the 1950s, there was a constant staple: jokes about the impossibility of understanding women. The jokes (told, of course, by men) always represented women's logic as fundamentally alien and incomprehensible. "You have to love them," the message always seemed to run, "but who can really understand how these creatures think?" One never had the impression the women in question had any trouble understanding men. The reason is obvious. Women had no choice but to understand men. In America, the fifties were the heyday of a certain ideal of the one-income patriarchal family, and among the more affluent, the ideal was often achieved. Women with no access to their own income or resources obviously had no choice but to spend a great deal of time and energy understanding what their menfolk thought was going on.[58]

This kind of rhetoric about the mysteries of womankind appears to be a perennial feature of such patriarchal arrangements. It is usually paired with a sense that, though illogical and inexplicable, women still have access to mysterious, almost mystical wisdom ("women's intuition") unavailable to men. And of course something like this happens in any relation of extreme inequality: peasants, for example, are always represented as being both oafishly simple, but somehow, also, mystically wise. Generations of women novelists—Virginia Woolf comes most immediately to mind (*To the Lighthouse*)—have documented the other side of such arrangements: the constant efforts women end up having to expend in managing, maintaining, and adjusting the egos of oblivious and self-important men, involving the continual work of imaginative identification, or interpretive labor. This work carries over on every level. Women everywhere are always expected to continually imagine what one situation or another would look like from a male point of view. Men are almost never expected to do the same for women. So deeply internalized is this pattern of behavior that many men react to any suggestion that they might do otherwise as if it were itself an act of violence. A popular exercise among high school creative writing teachers in America, for example, is to ask students to imagine they have been transformed, for a day, into someone of the opposite sex, and describe what that day might be like. The results, apparently, are uncannily uniform. The girls all write long and detailed essays that clearly show they have spent a great deal of time thinking about the subject. Usually, a good proportion of the boys refuse to write the essay entirely. Those who do make it clear they have not the slightest conception what being a teenage girl might be like, and are outraged at the suggestion that they should have to think about it.[59]

Nothing I am saying here is particularly new to anyone familiar with Feminist Standpoint Theory or Critical Race Studies. Indeed, I was originally inspired to these broader reflections by a passage by bell hooks:

> Although there has never been any official body of black people in the United States who have gathered

as anthropologists and/or ethnographers to study whiteness, black folks have, from slavery on, shared in conversations with one another "special" knowledge of whiteness gleaned from close scrutiny of white people. Deemed special because it is not a way of knowing that has been recorded fully in written material, its purpose was to help black folks cope and survive in a white supremacist society. For years black domestic servants, working in white homes, acted as informants who brought knowledge back to segregated communities—details, facts, psychoanalytic readings of the white "Other."[60]

If there is a limitation in the feminist literature, I would say, it's that it can be if anything a tad too generous, tending to emphasize the insights of the oppressed over the blindness or foolishness of their oppressors.[61]

Could it be possible to develop a general theory of interpretive labor? We'd probably have to begin by recognizing that there are two critical elements here that, while linked, need to be formally distinguished. The first is the process of imaginative identification as a form of knowledge, the fact that within relations of domination, it is generally the subordinates who are effectively relegated the work of understanding how the social relations in question really work. Anyone who has ever worked in a restaurant kitchen, for example, knows that if something goes terribly wrong and an angry boss appears to size things up, he is unlikely to carry out a detailed investigation, or even to pay serious attention to the workers all scrambling to explain their version of what happened. He is much more likely to tell them all to shut up and arbitrarily impose a story that allows instant judgment: i.e., "you, Joe, you wouldn't have made a mistake like that; you, Mark, you're the new guy, you must have screwed up—if you do it again, you're fired." It's those who do not have the power to hire and fire who are left with the work of figuring out what actually did go wrong so as to make sure it doesn't happen again. The same thing usually happens with ongoing relations: everyone knows that servants tend to know a great deal about their employers' families, but the opposite almost never occurs.

The second element is the resultant pattern of sympathetic identification. Curiously, it was Adam Smith, in his *Theory of Moral Sentiments*, who first observed the phenomenon we now refer to as "compassion fatigue." Human beings, he proposed, are normally inclined not only to imaginatively identify with their fellows, but as a result, to spontaneously feel one another's joys and sorrows. The poor, however, are so consistently miserable that otherwise sympathetic observers are simply overwhelmed, and are forced, without realizing it, to blot out their existence entirely. The result is that while those on the bottom of a social ladder spend a great deal of time imagining the perspectives of, and genuinely caring about, those on the top, it almost never happens the other way around.

Whether one is dealing with masters and servants, men and women, employers and employees, rich and poor, structural inequality—what I've been calling structural violence—invariably creates highly lopsided structures of the imagination. Since I think Smith was right to observe that imagination tends to bring with it sympathy, the result is that victims of structural violence tend to care about its beneficiaries far more than those beneficiaries care about them. This might well be, after the violence itself, the single most powerful force preserving such relations.

At this point I can return to the question of bureaucracy.

In contemporary industrialized democracies, the legitimate administration of violence is turned over to what is euphemistically referred to as "criminal law enforcement"—particularly, to police officers. I say "euphemistically" because generations of police sociologists have pointed out that only a very small proportion of what police actually do has anything to do with enforcing criminal law—or with criminal matters of any kind. Most of it has to do with regulations, or, to put it slightly more technically, with the scientific application of physical force, or the threat of physical force, to aid in the resolution of administrative problems.[62] In other words they spend most of their time enforcing all those endless rules and regulations about who can buy or smoke or sell or build or eat or drink what where that don't exist in places like small-town or rural Madagascar.

So: Police are bureaucrats with weapons.

If you think about it, this is a really ingenious trick. Because when most of us think about police, we do not think of them as enforcing regulations. We think of them as fighting crime, and when we think of "crime," the kind of crime we have in our minds is violent crime.[63] Even though, in fact, what police mostly do is exactly the opposite: they bring the threat of force to bear on situations that would otherwise have nothing to do with it. I find this all the time in public discussions. When trying to come up with a hypothetical example of a situation in which police are likely to be involved, people will almost invariably think of some act of interpersonal violence: a mugging or assault. But even a moment's reflection should make it clear that, when most real acts of physical assault do occur, even in major cities like Marseille or Montevideo or Minneapolis—domestic violence, gang fights, drunken brawls—the police do not get involved. Police are only likely to be called in if someone dies, or is so seriously hurt they end up in the hospital. But this is because the moment an ambulance is involved, there is also paperwork; if someone is treated in the hospital, there has to be a cause of injury, the circumstances become relevant, police reports have to be filed. And if someone dies there are all sorts of forms, up to and including municipal statistics. So the only fights which police are sure to get involved in are those that generate some kind of paperwork. The vast majority of muggings or burglaries aren't reported either, unless there are insurance forms to be filled out, or lost documents that need to be replaced, and which can only be replaced if one files a proper police report. So most violent crime does not end up involving the police.

On the other hand, try driving down the street of any one of those cities in a car without license plates. We all know what's going to happen. Uniformed officers armed with sticks, guns, and/or tasers will appear on the scene almost immediately, and if you simply refuse to comply with their instructions, violent force will, most definitely, be applied.

Why are we so confused about what police really do? The obvious reason is that in the popular culture of the last fifty years or so, police have become almost obsessive objects of imaginative identification in popular culture. It has come to the point that it's not at all unusual for a citizen in a contemporary industrialized democracy to spend several hours a day reading books, watching movies, or viewing TV shows that invite them to look at the world from a police point of view, and to vicariously participate in their exploits. And these imaginary police do, indeed, spend almost all of their time fighting violent crime, or dealing with its consequences.

If nothing else, all this throws an odd wrinkle into Weber's famous worries about the iron cage: the danger that modern society will become so well organized by faceless technocrats that charismatic heroes, enchantment, and romance will completely disappear.[64] Actually, as it turns out, bureaucratic society does indeed have a tendency to produce its own, unique forms of charismatic hero. These have, since the late nineteenth century, arrived in the form of an endless assortment of mythic detectives, police officers, and spies—all, significantly, figures whose job is to operate precisely where bureaucratic structures for ordering information encounter the actual application of physical violence. Bureaucracy, after all, has been around for thousands of years, and bureaucratic societies, from Sumer and Egypt, to Imperial China, have produced great literature. But modern North Atlantic societies are the very first to have created genres of literature where the heroes themselves are bureaucrats, or operate entirely within bureaucratic environments.[65]

It strikes me that contemplating the role of the police in our society actually allows us some interesting insights into social theory. Now, I must admit that over the course of this essay I have not been especially kind to academics and most of their theoretical habits and predilections. I wouldn't be surprised if some were inclined to read what I've written as an argument that social theory is largely pointless—the self-important fantasies of a cloistered elite who refuse to accept the simple realities of power. But this is not what I'm arguing at all. This essay is itself an exercise in social theory, and if I didn't think such exercises had the potential to throw important light on areas that would otherwise remain obscure, I would not have written it. The question is what kind, and to what purpose.

Here a comparison of bureaucratic knowledge and theoretical knowledge is revealing. Bureaucratic knowledge is all about schematization. In practice, bureaucratic procedure invariably means ignoring all the subtleties of real social existence and reducing everything to preconceived mechanical or statistical formulae. Whether it's a matter of forms, rules, statistics, or questionnaires, it is always a matter of simplification. Typically, it's not very different from the boss who walks into the kitchen to make arbitrary snap decisions as to what went wrong: in either case it is a matter of applying very simple pre-existing templates to complex and often ambiguous situations. The result often leaves those forced to deal with bureaucratic administration with the impression that they are dealing with people who have for some arbitrary reason decided to put on a set of glasses that only allows them to see only 2 percent of what's in front of them. But surely, something very similar happens in social theory as well. Anthropologists like to describe what they do as "thick description," but in fact an ethnographic description, even a very good one, captures at best 2 percent of what's happening in any particular Nuer feud or Balinese cockfight. A theoretical work that draws on ethnographic descriptions will typically focus on only a tiny part of *that*, plucking perhaps one or two strands out of an endlessly complex fabric of human circumstance, and using them as the basis on which to make generalizations: say, about the dynamics of social conflict, the nature of performance, or the principle of hierarchy.

I am not trying to say there's anything wrong in this kind of theoretical reduction. To the contrary, I am convinced some such process is necessary if one wishes to say something dramatically new about the world.

Consider the role of structural analysis, of the sort that in the sixties and seventies was made famous by anthropologists like Claude Lévi-Strauss, or classicists like Paul Vernant. Academic fashion being what it is, structural analysis is currently considered definitively passé, and most anthropology students find Claude Lévi-Strauss's entire corpus vaguely ridiculous. This strikes me as unfortunate. Certainly insofar as Structuralism claimed to be a single, grandiose theory of the nature of thought, language, and society, providing the key to unlocking all the mysteries of human culture, it was indeed ridiculous and has been justifiably abandoned. But structural analysis wasn't a theory, it was a technique, and to toss that too out the window, as has largely been done, robs us of one our most ingenious tools. Because the great merit of structural analysis is that it provides a well-nigh foolproof technique for doing what any good theory should do: simplifying and schematizing complex material in such a way as to be able to say something unexpected. This is incidentally how I came up with the point about Weber and heroes of bureaucracy a few paragraphs above. It all came from an experiment demonstrating structural analysis to students at a seminar at Yale.

The basic principle of structural analysis, I was explaining, is that the terms of a symbolic system do not stand in isolation—they are not to be thought of in terms of what they "stand for," but are defined by their relations to each other. One has to first define the field, and then look for elements in that field that are systematic inversions of each other. Take vampires. First you place them: vampires are stock figures in American horror movies. American horror movies constitute a kind of cosmology, a universe unto themselves. Then you ask: what, within this cosmos, is the opposite of a vampire? The answer is obvious. The opposite of a vampire is a werewolf. On one level they are the same: they are both monsters that can bite you and by biting you, turn you, too, into one of their own kind. In most others ways each is an exact inversion of the other. Vampires are rich. They are typically aristocrats. Werewolves are always poor. Vampires are fixed in space: they have castles or crypts that they have to retreat to during the daytime; werewolves are usually homeless derelicts, travelers, or otherwise on the run. Vampires control other creatures (bats, wolves, humans that they hypnotize or render thralls.) Werewolves can't control themselves. Yet—and this is really the clincher in this case—each can be destroyed only by its own negation: vampires, by a stake, a simple sharpened stick that peasants use to construct fences; werewolves, by a silver bullet, something literally made from money.

By observing these axes of inversion, we can get a sense of what such symbols are really about: that vampires, for instance, are not necessarily so much about death, or fear, but about power; about the simultaneous feelings of attraction and repulsion that relations of domination tend to create.

Obviously this is an extremely simple example. What I've described is just the initial move, there's a whole series of more sophisticated ones that normally follow: inversions within inversions, mediating terms, levels of hierarchical encompassment . . . There's no need to go into any of that here. My point is just that even by making this initial move, one will almost invariably discover something one would not have thought of otherwise. It's a way of radically simplifying reality that leads to insights one would almost certainly never have achieved if one had simply attempted to take on the world in its full complexity.

I often used that example when explaining structural analysis to students. Students always liked it. One time, I suggested we try collectively try our hands at another analysis, of a similar pop culture figure, and someone suggested James Bond.

This made sense to me: James Bond is clearly a mythical figure of some kind. But who was his mythic opposite? The answer soon became obvious. James Bond was the structural inversion of Sherlock Holmes. Both are London-based crime-fighters, and both permanent adolescents after their own fashion, even mild sociopaths, but otherwise, they are opposites in almost every way:

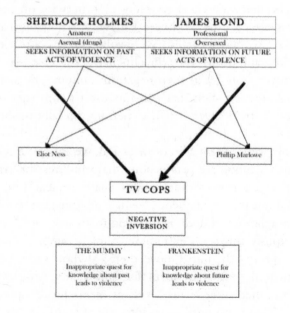

Where Holmes is asexual but fond of cocaine and opium, Bond is oversexed, but uninterested in drugs except for liquor. Holmes is an amateur. Bond is the quintessential professional—he seems to have no life outside his work. Yet Holmes is an amateur who is almost preternaturally disciplined and competent, far more than the professionals at Scotland Yard, while Bond is a professional who is always allowing himself to become distracted, blowing his cover, getting captured, or disobeying direct orders from his boss.[66]

All this, though, really just sets up the key inversion, which is in terms of what they actually *do*: Sherlock Holmes seeks information about past acts of violence inside his country, while James Bond seeks information about future acts of violence outside it.

It was in mapping out the field that I came to realize that everything here was organized, precisely, around the relation between information and violence—and that Sherlock Holmes and James Bond are, between them, the quintessential charismatic heroes of bureaucracy. The classic TV cop, or hero of any of the literally hundreds of "maverick-cop-who-breaks-all-the-rules" movies that Hollywood has trundled out since the 1960s, is clearly a kind of synthesis of these two figures: crime-fighters who exist within, but are constantly bursting out, of the bureaucratic order, which is nonetheless their entire meaning and existence.[67]

One might object that all this is a simplification of a much richer, more complex and nuanced, tradition of popular culture. Of course it is. That's the whole point. Structural analysis of this sort makes a virtue of simplification. For my own part, I see Lévi-Strauss as a kind of heroic figure too, a man with the sheer intellectual courage to pursue a few simple principles as far as they would go, no matter how apparently absurd or just plain wrong the results could sometimes be (the story of Oedipus is really about eyes and feet; all social organizations are simply systems for the exchange of women)—or, if you prefer, how much violence he thus did to reality. Because it's a productive violence. And nobody actually gets hurt.

As long as one remains within the domain of theory, then, I would argue that simplification is not necessarily a form of stupidity—it can be a form of intelligence. Even of brilliance. The problems arise at the moment that violence is no longer metaphorical. Here let me turn from imaginary cops to real ones. Jim Cooper, a former LAPD officer turned sociologist,[68] has observed that the overwhelming majority of those who end up getting beaten or otherwise brutalized by police turn out to be innocent of any crime. "Cops don't beat up burglars," he writes. The reason, he explained, is simple: the one thing most guaranteed to provoke a violent reaction from police is a challenge to their right to, as he puts it, "define the situation." That is, to say "no, this isn't a possible crime situation, this is a citizen-who-pays-your-salary-walking-his-dog situation, so shove off," let alone the invariably disastrous, "wait, why are you handcuffing that guy? He didn't do anything!" It's "talking back" above all that inspires beat-downs, and that means challenging whatever administrative rubric (an orderly or a disorderly crowd? A properly or improperly registered vehicle?) has been applied by the officer's discretionary judgment. The police truncheon is precisely the point where the state's bureaucratic imperative for imposing simple administrative schema and its monopoly on coercive force come together. It only makes sense then that bureaucratic violence should consist first and foremost of attacks on those who insist on alternative schemas or interpretations. At the same time, if one accepts Jean Piaget's famous definition of mature intelligence as the ability to coordinate between multiple perspectives (or possible perspectives) one can see, here, precisely how bureaucratic power, at the moment it turns to violence, becomes literally a form of infantile stupidity.

This analysis, too, is no doubt a simplification, but it's a productive one. Let me try to demonstrate this by applying some of these insights to understanding the type of politics that can emerge within a fundamentally bureaucratic society.

One of the central arguments of this essay so far is that structural violence creates lopsided structures of the imagination. Those on the bottom of the heap have to spend a great deal of imaginative energy trying to understand the social dynamics that surround them—including having to imagine the perspectives of those on top—while the latter can wander about largely oblivious to much of what is going on around them. That is, the powerless not only end up doing most of the actual, physical labor required to keep society running, they also do most of the interpretive labor as well.

This much seems to be the case wherever one encounters systematic inequality. It was just as true in ancient India or medieval China as it is anywhere today. And it will, presumably, remain true so long as structural inequalities endure. However, our own bureaucratic civilization introduces a further element. Bureaucracies, I've suggested, are not themselves forms of stupidity so much as they are ways of organizing stupidity—of managing relationships that are already characterized by extremely unequal structures of imagination, which exist because of the existence of structural violence. This is why even if a bureaucracy is created for entirely benevolent reasons, it will still produce absurdities. And this, in turn, is why I began the essay the way I did. I have no reason to believe anyone involved in my mother's power of attorney drama (even the bank manager) was anything other than well-intentioned. Yet an absurd and apparently endless run-around nonetheless ensued.

Why does this happen? Because even the most benevolent bureaucracies are really just taking the highly schematized, minimal, blinkered perspectives typical of the powerful, turning them into ways of limiting that power or ameliorating its most pernicious effects. Surely, bureaucratic interventions along these lines have done an enormous amount of good in the world. The European social welfare state, with its free education and universal health care, can justly be considered—as Pierre Bourdieu once remarked—one of the greatest achievements of human civilization. But at the same time, in taking forms of willful blindness typical of the powerful and giving them the prestige of science—for instance, by adopting a whole series of assumptions about the meaning of work, family, neighborhood, knowledge, health, happiness, or success that had almost nothing to do with the way poor or working-class people actually lived their lives, let alone what they found meaningful in them—it set itself up for a fall. And fall it did. It was precisely the uneasiness this blindness created even in the minds of its greatest beneficiaries that allowed the Right to mobilize popular support for the policies that have gutted and devastated even the most successful of these programs since the eighties.

And how was this uneasiness expressed? Largely, by the feeling that bureaucratic authority, by its very nature, represented a kind of war against the human imagination. This becomes particularly clear if we look at the youth rebellions from China to Mexico to New York that culminated in the insurrection of May 1968 in Paris. All were rebellions first and foremost against bureaucratic authority; all saw bureaucratic authority as fundamentally stifling of the human spirit, of creativity, conviviality, imagination. The famous slogan "All power to the imagination," painted on the walls of the Sorbonne, has haunted us ever since—endlessly repeated on posters, buttons, flyers, manifestos, films, and song lyrics, largely because it seems to embody something fundamental, not just to the spirit of sixties rebellion, but to the very essence of what we have come to call "the Left."

This is important. Actually it could not be more important. Because I think what happened in '68 reveals a contradiction at the very core of Leftist thought, from its very inception—a contradiction that only fully revealed itself at precisely the high-water mark of its historical success. In the introduction to this volume, I suggested that the contemporary Left suffers from the lack of a coherent critique of bureaucracy. But if you really go back to the beginnings—to the idea that emerged around the time of the French Revolution that the political spectrum can be divided into a right- and left-wing in the first place—it becomes clear that the Left, in its essence, *is* a critique of bureaucracy, even if it's one that has, again and again, been forced to accommodate itself in practice to the very bureaucratic structures and mindset it originally arose to oppose.[69]

In this sense, the Left's current inability to formulate a critique of bureaucracy that actually speaks to its erstwhile constituents is synonymous with the decline of the Left itself. Without such a critique, radical thought loses its vital center—it collapses into a fragmented scatter of protests and demands.

It seems that every time the Left decides to take a safe, "realistic" course, it just digs itself deeper. To understand how this happened, let alone what we might be able to do about it, I think it will be necessary to reexamine some very basic assumptions: first and foremost, about what it means to say one is being "realistic" to begin with.

Be realistic: demand the impossible.
(another '68 slogan)

So far, I have been discussing how structural violence creates lopsided structures of the imagination and how bureaucracy becomes a way of managing such situations—and the forms of structural blindness and stupidity they inevitably entail. Even at their best, bureaucratic procedures are ways to turn stupidity, as it were, against itself.

Why do movements challenging such structures so often end up creating bureaucracies instead? Normally, they do so as a kind of compromise. One must be realistic and not demand too much. Welfare state reforms seem more realistic than demanding a broad distribution of property; a "transitional" stage of state socialism seems more realistic than jumping immediately to giving power to democratically organized workers' councils, and so forth. But this raises another question. When we speak of being "realistic," exactly what reality is it we are referring to?

Here, I think an anecdote about an activist group I was once involved with might prove instructive.

From early 2000 to late 2002, I was working with the New York Direct Action Network—the principal group responsible for organizing mass actions as part of the global justice movement in New York City at that time. I call it a "group," but technically DAN was not a group at all but a decentralized network, operating on principles of direct democracy according to an elaborate, but quite effective, form of consensus process. It played a central role in ongoing efforts to create new organizational forms. DAN existed in a purely political space. It had no concrete resources—not even a significant treasury—to administer.

Then one day someone gave DAN a car.

The DAN car caused a minor, but ongoing, crisis. We soon discovered that legally, it is impossible for a decentralized network to own a car. Cars can be owned by individuals, or they can be owned by corporations (which are fictive individuals), or by governments. But they cannot be owned by networks. Unless we were willing to incorporate ourselves as a nonprofit corporation (which would have required a complete reorganization and an abandonment of most of our egalitarian principles) the only expedient was to find a volunteer willing to claim to be the legal owner. But then that person was held responsible for all outstanding fines and insurance fees, and had to provide written permission to allow anyone else to drive the car out of state. And, of course, only he could retrieve the car if it were impounded. One courageous activist did agree to undertake the responsibility, but as a result, weekly meetings were overwhelmed by reportbacks about his latest legal problems. Before long the DAN car had become such an endless source of tribulation that we decided to organize a fundraiser, throwing a big party where we provided a sledgehammer to anyone willing to pay five dollars to take a whack at the thing.

It struck me there was something profound to this story. Why is it that projects like DAN's—projects aimed at democratizing society—are so often perceived as idle dreams that melt away as soon as they encounter hard material reality? In our case, at least, it had nothing to do with inefficiency: police chiefs across the country had called us the best organized force they'd ever had to deal with. It seems to me that the reality effect (if one may call it that) comes rather from the fact that radical projects tend to founder—or at least become endlessly difficult—the moment they enter into the world of large, heavy objects: buildings, cars, tractors, boats, industrial machinery. This in turn is not because these objects are somehow intrinsically difficult to administer democratically—history is full of communities that successfully engage in the democratic administration of common resources—it's because, like the DAN car, they are surrounded by endless government regulation, and are effectively impossible to hide from the government's armed representatives. In America, I have seen endless examples of this dilemma. A squat is legalized after a long struggle; suddenly, building inspectors arrive to announce it will take ten thousand dollars' worth of repairs to bring it up to code. Organizers are therefore forced to spend the next several years organizing bake sales and soliciting contributions. This means setting up bank accounts, which means, in turn, adhering to legal regulations that specify how any group receiving funds, or dealing with the government, must be organized (again, *not* as an egalitarian collective). All these regulations are enforced by violence. True, in ordinary life, police rarely come in swinging billy clubs to enforce building code regulations, but, as anarchists often are often uniquely positioned to find out, if one simply pretends the state and its regulations don't exist, this will, eventually, happen. The rarity with which the nightsticks actually appear just helps to make the violence harder to see. This in turn makes the effects of all these regulations—regulations that almost always assume that normal relations between individuals are mediated by the market, and that normal groups are organized internally by relations of hierarchy and command—seem to emanate not from the government's monopoly of the use of force, but from the largeness, solidity, and heaviness of the objects themselves.

When one is asked to be "realistic," then, the reality one is normally being asked to recognize is not one of natural, material facts, nor some supposed ugly truth about human nature. Being "realistic" usually means taking seriously the effects of the systematic threat of violence. This possibility even threads our language. Why, for example, is a building referred to as "real property," or "real estate"? The "real" in this usage is not derived from Latin *res*, or "thing": it's from the Spanish *real*, meaning, "royal," "belonging to the king." All land within a sovereign territory ultimately belongs to the sovereign—legally this is still the case. This is why the state has the right to impose its regulations. But sovereignty ultimately comes down to a monopoly on what is euphemistically referred to as "force"—that is, violence. Just as the Italian philosopher Giorgio Agamben argued that from the perspective of sovereign power, something is alive because you can kill it, so property is "real" because the state can seize or destroy it.

In the same way, when one takes a "realist" position in International Relations, one assumes that states will use whatever capacities they have at their disposal, including force of arms, to pursue their national interests. What "reality" is one recognizing? Certainly not material reality. The idea that nations are human-like entities with purposes and interests is purely metaphysical. The King of France had purposes and interests. "France" does not. What makes it seem "realistic" to suggest it does is simply that those in control of nation-states have the power to raise armies, launch invasions, and bomb cities, and can otherwise threaten the use of organized violence in the name of what they describe as their "national interests"—and that it would be foolish to ignore that possibility. National interests are real because they can kill you.

The critical term here is "force," as in "the state's monopoly on the use of coercive force." Whenever we hear this word invoked, we find ourselves in the presence of a political ontology in which the power to destroy, to cause others pain or to threaten to break, damage, or mangle others' bodies (or just lock them in a tiny room for the rest of their lives) is treated as the social equivalent of the very energy that drives the cosmos. Contemplate, if you will, the metaphors and displacements that make it possible to construct the following two sentences:

> Scientists investigate the nature of physical laws so as to understand the forces that govern the universe.

> Police are experts in the scientific application of physical force in order to enforce the laws that govern society.

This is to my mind the essence of right-wing thought: a political ontology that through such subtle means allows violence to define the very parameters of social existence and common sense.[70]

This is why I say that the Left has always been, in its essential inspiration, antibureaucratic. Because it has always been founded on a different set of assumptions about what is ultimately real—that is, about the very grounds of political being. Obviously Leftists don't deny the reality of violence. Many Leftist theorists think about it quite a lot. But they don't tend to give it the same foundational status. Instead, I would argue that Leftist thought is founded on what I will call a "political ontology of the imagination" (though it could also, perhaps just as well, have been called an ontology of creativity or making or invention.) Nowadays, most of us tend to identify this tendency with the legacy of Marx, with his emphasis on social revolution and forces of material production. Marx was ultimately only a man of his time, and his terms emerged from much wider arguments about value, labor, and creativity current in radical circles of his day, whether in the workers' movement, or for that matter in various strains of Romanticism and bohemian life emerging around him in Paris and London at the time. Marx himself, for all his contempt for the utopian Socialists of his day, never ceased to insist that what makes human beings different from animals is that architects, unlike bees, first raise their structures in the imagination. It was the unique property of humans, for Marx, that they first envision things, and only then bring them into being. It was this process he referred to as "production."

Around the same time, utopian Socialists like St. Simon were arguing that artists needed to become the *avant-garde* or "vanguard," as he put it, of a new social order, providing the grand visions that industry now had the power to bring into being. What at the time might have seemed the fantasy of an eccentric pamphleteer soon became the charter for a sporadic, uncertain, but apparently permanent alliance that endures to this day. If artistic avant-gardes and social revolutionaries have felt a peculiar affinity for one another ever since, borrowing each other's languages and ideas, it appears to have been insofar as both have remained committed to the idea that the ultimate, hidden truth of the world is that it is something that we make, and could just as easily make differently. In this sense, a phrase like "all power to the imagination" expresses the very quintessence of the Left.

From a left perspective, then, the hidden reality of human life is the fact that the world doesn't just happen. It isn't a natural fact, even though we tend to treat it as if it is—it exists because we all collectively produce it. We imagine things we'd like and then we bring them into being. But the moment you think about it in these terms, it's obvious that something has gone terribly wrong. Since who, if they could simply imagine any world that they liked and then bring it into being, would create a world like this one?[71] Perhaps the leftist sensibility was expressed in its purest form in the words of Marxist philosopher John Holloway, who once wanted to title a book, "Stop Making Capitalism."[72] Capitalism, he noted, is not something imposed on us by some outside force. It only exists because every day we wake up and continue to produce it. If we woke up one morning and all collectively decided to produce something else, then we wouldn't have capitalism anymore. This is the ultimate revolutionary question: what are the conditions that would have to exist to enable us to do this—to just wake up and imagine and produce something else?

To this emphasis on forces of creativity and production, the Right tends to reply that revolutionaries systematically neglect the social and historical importance of the "means of destruction": states, armies, executioners, barbarian invasions, criminals, unruly mobs, and so on. Pretending such things are not there, or can simply be wished away, they argue, has the result of ensuring that left-wing regimes will in fact create far more death and destruction than those that have the wisdom to take a more "realistic" approach.

Obviously, this is something of a simplification, and one could make endless qualifications. The bourgeoisie of Marx's time, for instance, had an extremely productivist philosophy— one reason Marx could see it as a revolutionary force. Elements of the Right dabbled with the artistic ideal, and twentieth-century Marxist regimes often embraced essentially right-wing theories of power and paid little more than lip service to the determinant nature of production. On the other hand, in their obsession with jailing poets and playwrights whose work they considered threatening, they evinced a profound faith in the power of art and creativity to change the world—those running capitalist regimes rarely bothered, convinced that if they kept a firm hand on the means of productions (and, of course, the army and police), the rest would take care of itself.

One of the reasons it is difficult to see all this is because the word "imagination" can mean so many different things. In most modern definitions imagination is counterposed to reality; "imaginary" things are first and foremost things that aren't really there. This can cause a great deal of confusion when we speak of imagination in the abstract, because it makes it seem like imagination has much more do with Spenser's *Faerie Queene* than with a group of waitresses trying to figure out how to placate the couple at Table 7 before the boss shows up.

Still, this way of thinking about imagination is relatively new, and continues to coexist with much older ones. In the common Ancient and Medieval conception, for example, what we now call "the imagination" was not seen as opposed to reality per se, but as a kind of middle ground, a zone of passage connecting material reality and the rational soul. This was especially true for those who saw Reason as essentially an aspect of God, who felt that thought therefore partook in a divinity which in no way partook of—indeed, was absolutely alien to—material reality. (This became the dominant position in the Christian Middle Ages.) How, then, was it possible for the rational mind to receive sense impressions from nature?

The solution was to propose an intermediary substance, made out of the same material as the stars, the "pneuma," a kind of circulatory system through which perceptions of the material world could pass, becoming emotionally charged in the process and mixing with all sorts of phantasms, before the rational mind could grasp their significance. Intentions and desires moved in the opposite direction, circulating through the imagination before they could be realized in the world. It's only after Descartes, really, that the word "imaginary" came to mean, specifically, anything that is not real: imaginary creatures, imaginary places (Narnia, planets in faraway galaxies, the Kingdom of Prester John), imaginary friends. By this definition, a "political ontology of the imagination" could only be a contradiction in terms. The imagination cannot be the basis of reality. It is by definition that which we can think, but which has no reality.

I'll refer to this latter as "the transcendent notion of the imagination" since it seems to take as its model novels or other works of fiction that create imaginary worlds that presumably remain the same no matter how many times one reads them. Imaginary creatures—elves or unicorns or TV cops—are not affected by the real world. They cannot be, since they don't exist. In contrast, the kind of imagination I have been developing in this essay is much closer to the old, immanent, conception. Critically, it is in no sense static and free-floating, but entirely caught up in projects of action that aim to have real effects on the material world, and as such, always changing and adapting. This is equally true whether one is crafting a knife or a piece of jewelry, or trying to make sure one doesn't hurt a friend's feelings.

It was precisely in the mid- to late-eighteenth century, which saw the origins of industrial capitalism, modern bureaucratic society, and the political division between right and left, where the new transcendent concept of imagination really came to prominence. For Romantics, in particular, the Imagination came to take the place once held by the soul—rather than mediating between the rational soul and the material world, it *was* the soul, and the soul was that which was beyond any mere rationality. It's easy to see how the advent of an impersonal, bureaucratic order of offices, factories, and rational administration would also give rise to this sort of idea. But insofar as the imagination became a residual category, everything that the new order was not, it also was not purely transcendent; in fact, it necessarily became a kind of crazy hodgepodge of what I've been calling transcendent and immanent principles. On the one hand, the imagination was seen as the source of art, and all creativity. On the other, it was the basis of human sympathy, and hence morality.[73]

Two hundred and fifty years later, we might do well to begin to sort these matters out.

Because honestly, there's a lot at stake here. To get a sense of just how much, let's return for a moment to that '68 slogan: "All power to the imagination." Which imagination are we referring to? If one takes this to refer to the transcendent imagination—to an attempt to impose some sort of prefab utopian vision—the effects can be disastrous. Historically, it has often meant creating some vast bureaucratic machine designed to impose such utopian visions by violence. World-class atrocities are likely to result. On the other hand, in a revolutionary situation, one might by the same token argue that *not* giving full power to the other, immanent, sort of imagination—the practical common sense imagination of ordinary cooks, nurses, mechanics and gardeners—is likely to end up having exactly the same effects.

This confusion, this jumbling of different conceptions of imagination, runs throughout the history of leftist thought.

One can already see the tension in Marx. There is a strange paradox in his approach to revolution. As I've noted, Marx insists that what makes us human is that rather than relying on unconscious instinct like spiders and bees, we first raise structures in our imagination, and then try to bring those visions into being. When a spider weaves her web, she operates on instinct. The architect first draws up a plan, and only then starts building the foundations of his edifice. This is true, Marx insists, in all forms of material production, whether we are building bridges or making boots. Yet when Marx speaks of social creativity, his key example—the only kind of social creativity he ever talks about actually—is always revolution, and when he does that, he suddenly changes gears completely. In fact he reverses himself. The revolutionary should never proceed like the architect; he should never begin by drawing up a plan for an ideal society, then think about how to bring it into being. That would be utopianism. And for utopianism, Marx had nothing but withering contempt. Instead, revolution is the actual immanent practice of the proletariat, which will ultimately bear fruit in ways that we cannot possibly imagine from our current vantage point.

Why the discrepancy? The most generous explanation, I would suggest, is that Marx did understand, at least on some intuitive level, that the imagination worked differently in the domain of material production than it did in social relations; but also, that he lacked an adequate theory as to why. Perhaps, writing in the mid-nineteenth century, long before the rise of feminism, he simply lacked the intellectual tools.[74] Given the considerations already outlined in this essay, I think we can confirm that this is indeed the case. To put it in Marx's own terms: in both domains one can speak of alienation. But in each, alienation works in profoundly different ways.

To recall the argument so far: structural inequalities always create what I've called "lopsided structures of imagination," that is, divisions between one class of people who end up doing most of the imaginative labor, and others who do not. However, the sphere of factory production that Marx concerned himself with is rather unusual in this respect. It is one of the few contexts where it is the dominant class who end up doing more imaginative labor, not less.

Creativity and desire—what we often reduce, in political economy terms, to "production" and "consumption"—are essentially vehicles of the imagination. Structures of inequality and domination—structural violence, if you will—tend to skew the imagination. Structural violence might create situations where laborers are relegated to mind-numbing, boring, mechanical jobs, and only a small elite is allowed to indulge in imaginative labor, leading to the feeling, on the part of the workers, that they are alienated from their own labor, that their very deeds belong to someone else. It might also create social situations where kings, politicians, celebrities, or CEOs prance about oblivious to almost everything around them while their wives, servants, staff, and handlers spend all their time engaged in the imaginative work of maintaining them in their fantasies. Most situations of inequality I suspect combine elements of both.

The subjective experience of living inside such lopsided structures of imagination—the warping and shattering of imagination that results—is what we are referring to when we talk about "alienation."

The tradition of Political Economy, within which Marx was writing, tends to see work in modern societies as divided between two spheres: wage labor, for which the paradigm is always factories, and domestic labor—housework, childcare—relegated mainly to women. The first is seen primarily as a matter of creating and maintaining physical objects. The second is probably best seen as a matter of creating and maintaining people and social relations. The distinction is obviously a bit of a caricature: there has never been a society, not even Engels's Manchester or Victor Hugo's Paris, where most men were factory workers and most women worked exclusively as housewives. Still, this frames how we think about such issues today. It also points to the root of Marx's problem. In the sphere of industry, it is generally those on top that relegate to themselves the more imaginative tasks (i.e., they design the products and organize production), whereas when inequalities emerge in the sphere of social production, it is those on the bottom who end up expected to do the major imaginative work—notably, the bulk of what I've called the "labor of interpretation" that keeps life running.[75]

So far I have proposed that bureaucratic procedures, which have an uncanny ability to make even the smartest people act like idiots, are not so much forms of stupidity in themselves, as they are ways of managing situations already stupid because of the effects of structural violence. As a result, such procedures come to partake of the very blindness and foolishness they seek to manage. At their best, they become ways of turning stupidity against itself, much in the same way that revolutionary violence could be said to be. But stupidity in the name of fairness and decency is still stupidity, and violence in the name of human liberation is still violence. It's no coincidence the two so often seem to arrive together.

For much of the last century, the great revolutionary question has thus been: how does one affect fundamental change in society without setting in train a process that will end with the creation of some new, violent bureaucracy? Is utopianism the problem—the very idea of imagining a better world and then trying to bring it into being? Or is it something in the very nature of social theory? Should we thus abandon social theory? Or is the notion of revolution itself fundamentally flawed?

Since the sixties, one common solution has been to start by lowering one's sights. In the years leading up to May '68, the Situationists famously argued that it was possible to do this through creative acts of subversion that undermined the logic of what they called "the Spectacle," which rendered us passive consumers. Through these acts, we could, at least momentarily, recapture our imaginative powers. At the same time, they also felt that all such acts were small-scale dress rehearsals for the great insurrectionary moment to which they would necessarily lead—"the" revolution, properly speaking. This is what's largely gone today. If the events of May '68 showed anything, it was that if one does not aim to seize state power, there can be no fundamental, onetime break. As a result, among most contemporary revolutionaries, that millenarian element has almost completely fallen away. No one thinks the skies are about to open any time soon. There is a consolation, though: that as a result, insofar as one actually can come to experiencing genuine revolutionary freedom, one can begin to experience it immediately. Consider the following statement from the Crimethinc collective, probably the most inspiring young anarchist propagandists operating in the Situationist tradition today:

> We must make our freedom by cutting holes in the fabric of this reality, by forging new realities which will, in turn, fashion us. Putting yourself in new situations constantly is the only way to ensure that you make your decisions unencumbered by the inertia of habit, custom, law, or prejudice—and it is up to you to create these situations

> Freedom only exists in the moment of revolu-
> tion. And those moments are not as rare as you think.
> Change, revolutionary change, is going on constantly
> and everywhere—and everyone plays a part in it, con-
> sciously or not.

What is this but an elegant statement of the logic of direct action: the defiant insistence on acting as if one is already free?[76] The obvious question is how this approach can contribute to an overall strategy—one that should lead, perhaps not to a single moment of revolutionary redemption, but to a cumulative movement towards a world without states and capitalism. On this point, no one is completely sure. Most assume the process could only be one of endless improvisation. Insurrectionary moments there will surely be. Likely as not, quite a few of them. But they will most likely be one element in a far more complex and multifaceted revolutionary process whose outlines could hardly, at this point, be fully anticipated.

In retrospect, what seems strikingly naïve is the old assumption that a single uprising or successful civil war could, as it were, neutralize the entire apparatus of structural violence, at least within a particular national territory—that within that territory, right-wing realities could be simply swept away, to leave the field open for an untrammeled outpouring of revolutionary creativity. But the truly puzzling thing is that, at certain moments of human history, that appeared to be exactly what was happening. It seems to me that if we are to have any chance of grasping the new, emerging conception of revolution, we need to begin by thinking again about the quality of these insurrectionary moments.

One of the most remarkable things about such insurrectionary upheavals is how they can seem to burst out of nowhere—and then, often, dissolve away just as quickly. How is it that the same "public" that two months before say, the Paris Commune, or the Spanish Civil War, had voted in a fairly moderate social democratic regime will suddenly find itself willing to risk their lives for the same ultra-radicals who received a fraction of the actual vote? Or, to return to May '68, how is it that the same public that seemed to support or at least feel strongly sympathetic toward the student/worker uprising could almost immediately afterwards return to the polls and elect a right-wing government? The most common historical explanations—that the revolutionaries didn't really represent the public or its interests, but that elements of the public perhaps became caught up in some sort of irrational effervescence—seem obviously inadequate. First of all, they assume that "the public" is an entity with opinions, interests, and allegiances that can be treated as relatively consistent over time. In fact what we call "the public" is created, produced through specific institutions that allow specific forms of action—taking polls, watching television, voting, signing petitions or writing letters to elected officials or attending public hearings—and not others. These frames of action imply certain ways of talking, thinking, arguing, deliberating. The same "public" that may widely indulge in the use of recreational chemicals may also consistently vote to make such indulgences illegal; the same collection of citizens is likely to come to completely different decisions on questions affecting their communities if organized into a parliamentary system, a system of computerized plebiscites, or a nested series of public assemblies. In fact the entire anarchist project of reinventing direct democracy is premised on assuming this is the case.

To illustrate what I mean, consider that in English-speaking nations, the same collection of people referred to in one context as "the public" can in another be referred to as "the workforce." They become a "workforce," of course, when they are engaged in different sorts of activity. The "public" does not work—a sentence like "most of the American public works in the service industry" would never appear in a magazine or paper, and if a journalist were to attempt to write such a sentence, her editor would certainly change it to something else. It is especially odd since the public *does* apparently have to go to work: this is why, as leftist critics often complain, the media will always talk about how, say, a transport strike is likely to inconvenience the public, in their capacity of commuters, but it will never occur to them that those striking are themselves part of the public—or that if they succeed in raising wage levels, this will be a public benefit. And certainly the "public" does not go out into the streets. Its role is as audience to public spectacles, and consumers of public services. When buying or using goods and services privately supplied, the same collection of individuals become something else ("consumers"), just as in other contexts of action they are relabeled a "nation," "electorate," or "population."

All these entities are the product of bureaucracies and institutional practices that, in turn, define certain horizons of possibility. Hence when voting in parliamentary elections one might feel obliged to make a "realistic" choice; in an insurrectionary situation, on the other hand, suddenly anything seems possible.

What "the public," "the workforce," "the electorate," "consumers," and "the population" all have in common is that they are brought into being by institutionalized frames of action that are inherently bureaucratic, and therefore, profoundly alienating. Voting booths, television screens, office cubicles, hospitals, the ritual that surrounds them—one might say these are the very machinery of alienation. They are the instruments through which the human imagination is smashed and shattered. Insurrectionary moments are moments when this bureaucratic apparatus is neutralized. Doing so always seems to have the effect of throwing horizons of possibility wide open, which is only to be expected if one of the main things that that apparatus normally does is to enforce extremely limited horizons. (This is probably why, as Rebecca Solnit has so beautifully observed,[77] people often experience something very similar during natural disasters.) All of this would explain why revolutionary moments always seem to be followed by an outpouring of social, artistic, and intellectual creativity. Normally unequal structures of imaginative identification are disrupted; everyone is experimenting with trying to see the world from unfamiliar points of view; everyone feels not only the right, but usually the immediate practical need to re-create and reimagine everything around them.

The question, of course, is how to ensure that those who go through this experience are not immediately reorganized under some new rubric—the people, the proletariat, the multitude, the nation, the ummah, whatever it may be—that then gives way to the construction of a new set of rules, regulations, and bureaucratic institutions around it, which will inevitably come to be enforced by new categories of police. I actually think that here, some progress has been made. A lot of the credit goes to feminism. Since at least the seventies, there has been a self-conscious effort among those seeking radical change to shift the emphasis away from millenarian dreams and onto much more immediate questions about how those "holes cut in the fabric of reality" might actually be organized in a non-bureaucratic fashion, so that at least some of that imaginative power can be sustained over the long term. This was already true of the great Festivals of Resistance organized around trade summits by the Global Justice movement from 1998 to 2003, where the intricate details of the process of democratic planning for the actions was, if anything, more important than the actions themselves, but it became even more true in 2011 with the camps of the Arab Spring, the great assemblies of Greece and Spain, and finally, the Occupy movement in the United States. These were simultaneously direct actions, practical demonstrations of how real democracy could be thrown in the face of power, and experiments in what a genuinely non-bureaucratized social order, based on the power of practical imagination, might look like.

Such is the lesson, I think, for politics. If one resists the reality effect created by pervasive structural violence—the way that bureaucratic regulations seem to disappear into the very mass and solidity of the large heavy objects around us, the buildings, vehicles, large concrete structures, making a world regulated by such principles seem natural and inevitable, and anything else a dreamy fantasy—it *is* possible to give power to the imagination. But it also requires an enormous amount of work.

Power makes you lazy. Insofar as our earlier theoretical discussion of structural violence revealed anything, it was this: that while those in situations of power and privilege often feel it as a terrible burden of responsibility, in most ways, most of the time, power is all about what you *don't* have to worry about, *don't* have to know about, and *don't* have to do. Bureaucracies can democratize this sort of power, at least to an extent, but they can't get rid of it. It becomes forms of institutionalized laziness. Revolutionary change may involve the exhilaration of throwing off imaginative shackles, of suddenly realizing that impossible things are not impossible at all, but it also means most people will have to get over some of this deeply habituated laziness and start engaging in interpretive (imaginative) labor for a very long time to make those realities stick.

I have spent much of the last two decades thinking about how social theory might contribute to this process. As I've emphasized, social theory itself could be seen as kind of radical simplification, a form of calculated ignorance, a way of putting on a set of blinkers designed to reveal patterns one could never otherwise be able to see.

What I've been trying to do, then, is to put on one set of blinkers that allows us to see another. That's why I began the essay as I did, with the paperwork surrounding my mother's illness and death. I wanted to bring social theory to bear on those places that seem most hostile to it. There are dead zones that riddle our lives, areas so devoid of any possibility of interpretive depth that they repel every attempt to give them value or meaning. These are spaces, as I discovered, where interpretive labor no longer works. It's hardly surprising that we don't like to talk about them. They repel the imagination. But I also believe we have a responsibility to confront them, because if we don't, we risk becoming complicit in the very violence that creates them.

Let me explain what I mean by this. The tendency in existing social theory is to romanticize violence: to treat violent acts above all as ways to send dramatic messages, to play with symbols of absolute power, purification, and terror. Now, I'm not saying this is exactly untrue. Most acts of violence are also, in this sort of very literal sense, acts of terrorism. But I would also insist that focusing on these most dramatic aspects of violence makes it easy to ignore the fact that one of the salient features of violence, and of situations it creates, is that it is very boring. In American prisons, which are extraordinary violent places, the most vicious form of punishment is simply to lock a person in an empty room for years with absolutely nothing to do. This emptying of any possibility of communication or meaning is the real essence of what violence really is and does. Yes, sending someone into solitary is a way of sending a message to them, and to other prisoners. But the act consists largely of stifling out the possibility of sending any further messages of any kind.

It is one thing to say that, when a master whips a slave, he is engaging in a form of meaningful, communicative action, conveying the need for unquestioning obedience, and at the same time trying to create a terrifying mythic image of absolute and arbitrary power. All of this is true. It is quite another to insist that that is all that is happening, or all that we need to talk about. After all, if we do not go on to explore what "unquestioning" actually means—the master's ability to remain completely unaware of the slave's understanding of any situation, the slave's inability to say anything even when she becomes aware of some dire practical flaw in the master's reasoning, the forms of blindness or stupidity that result, the fact these oblige the slave to devote even more energy trying to understand and anticipate the master's confused perceptions—are we not, in however small a way, doing the same work as the whip? It's not really about making its victims talk. Ultimately, it's about participating in the process that shuts them up.

There is another reason I began with that story about my mother and the notary. As my apparently inexplicable confusion over the signatures makes clear, such dead zones can, temporarily at least, render *anybody* stupid. Just as, the first time I constructed this argument, I was actually unaware that most of these ideas had already been developed within feminist standpoint theory. That theory itself had been so marginalized I was only vaguely aware of it. These territories present us with a kind of bureaucratic maze of blindness, ignorance, and absurdity, and it is perfectly understandable that decent people seek to avoid them—in fact, that the most effective strategy of political liberation yet discovered lies precisely in avoiding them—but at the same time, it is only at our peril that we simply pretend that they're not there.

2

Of Flying Cars and the Declining Rate of Profit

"Contemporary reality is the beta-version of a science fiction dream."   —Richard Barbrook

There is a secret shame hovering over all us in the twenty-first century. No one seems to want to acknowledge it.

For those in what should be the high point of their lives, in their forties and fifties, it is particularly acute, but in a broader sense it affects everyone. The feeling is rooted in a profound sense of disappointment about the nature of the world we live in, a sense of a broken promise—of a solemn promise we felt we were given as children about what our adult world was supposed to be like. I am referring here not to the standard false promises that children are always given (about how the world is fair, authorities are well-meaning, or those who work hard shall be rewarded), but about a very specific generational promise—given above all to those who were children in the fifties, sixties, seventies, or even eighties—one that was never quite articulated as a promise but rather as a set of assumptions about what our adult world would be like. And since it was never quite promised, now that it has spectacularly failed to come true, we're left confused; indignant, but at the same time, embarrassed at our own indignation, ashamed we were ever so silly to believe our elders to begin with.

I am referring, of course, to the conspicuous absence, in 2015, of flying cars.

Well, all right, not just flying cars. I don't really care about flying cars—especially because I don't even drive. What I have in mind are all the technological wonders that any child growing up in the mid-to-late twentieth century simply assumed would exist by 2015. We all know the list: Force fields. Teleportation. Antigravity fields. Tricorders. Tractor beams. Immortality drugs. Suspended animation. Androids. Colonies on Mars. What happened to them? Every now and then it's widely trumpeted that one is about to materialize—clones, for instance, or cryogenics, or anti-aging medications, or invisibility cloaks—but when these don't prove to be false promises, which they usually are, they emerge hopelessly flawed. Point any of this out, and the usual response is a ritual invocation of the wonders of computers—why would you want an antigravity sled when you can have second life?—as if this is some sort of unanticipated compensation. But, even here, we're not nearly where people in the fifties imagined we'd have been by now. We still don't have computers you can have an interesting conversation with, or robots that can walk the dog or fold your laundry.

Speaking as someone who was eight years old at the time of the Apollo moon landing, I have very clear memories of calculating that I would be thirty-nine years of age in the magic year 2000, and wondering what the world around me would be like. Did I honestly expect I would be living in a world of such wonders? Of course. Everyone did. And so do I feel cheated now? Absolutely. Certainly, I didn't think I'd see *all* the things we read about in science fiction realized in my lifetime (even assuming my lifetime was not extended by centuries by some newly discovered longevity drug). If you asked me at the time, I'd have guessed about half. But it never occurred to me that I wouldn't see *any* of them.

I have long been puzzled and fascinated by the near silence surrounding this issue in public discourse. One does occasionally see griping about flying cars on the Internet, but it's muted, or very marginal. For the most part, the topic is treated almost as taboo. At the turn of the millennium, for instance, I was expecting an outpouring of reflections by forty-somethings in the popular media on what we had expected the world of 2000 to be like, and why we had all gotten it so wrong. I couldn't find a single one. Instead, just about all the authoritative voices—both Left and Right—began their reflections from the assumption that a world of technological wonders had, in fact, arrived.

To a very large extent, the silence is due to fear of being ridiculed as foolishly naïve. Certainly if one does raise the issue, one is likely to hear responses like "Oh, you mean all that Jetson stuff?" As if to say, but that was just for children! Surely, as grown-ups, we're supposed to understand that the Jetsons future was about as realistic as the Flintstones past. But of course it wasn't just the Jetsons. All serious science shows designed for children in the fifties, sixties, seventies, and even the eighties—the *Scientific American*s, the educational TV programs, the planetarium shows in national museums—all the authoritative voices who told us what the universe was like and why the sky was blue, who explained the periodic table of elements, also assured us that the future was indeed going to involve colonies on other planets, robots, matter transformation devices, and a world much closer to *Star Trek* than to our own.

The fact that all these voices turned out to be wrong doesn't just create a deep feeling of largely inexpressible betrayal; it also points to some conceptual problems about how we should even talk about history, now that things haven't unfolded as we thought they would. There are contexts where we really can't just wave our hands and make the discrepancy between expectations and reality go away. One obvious one is science fiction. Back in the twentieth century, creators of science fiction movies used to come up with concrete dates in which to place their futuristic fantasies. Often these were no more than a generation in the future. Thus in 1968, Stanley Kubrick felt that a moviegoing audience would find it perfectly natural to assume that only thirty-three years later, in 2001, we would have commercial moon flights, city-like space stations, and computers with humanlike personalities maintaining astronauts in suspended animation while traveling to Jupiter.[78] In fact about the only new technology from *2001* that actually did appear were video telephones, but those were already technically possible in 1968—at the time, they were simply unmarketable because no one really wanted to have one.[79] Similar problems crop up whenever a particular writer, or program, tries to create a grand mythos. According to the universe created by Larry Niven, which I got to know as a teenager, humans in this decade (2010s) are living under a one-world U.N. government and creating their first colony on the moon, while dealing with the social consequences of medical advances that have created a class of immortal rich people. In the *Star Trek* mythos developed around the same time, in contrast, humans would now be recovering from fighting off the rule of genetically engineered supermen in the Eugenics Wars of the 1990s—a war which ended when we shot them all in suspension pods into outer space. *Star Trek* writers in the 1990s were thus forced to start playing around with alternate time lines and realities just as a way of keeping the whole premise from falling apart.

By 1989, when the creators of *Back to the Future II* dutifully placed flying cars and antigravity hoverboards in the hands of ordinary teenagers in the year 2015, it wasn't clear if it was meant as a serious prediction, a bow to older traditions of imagined futures, or as a slightly bitter joke. At any rate, it marked one of the last instances of this sort of thing. Later science fiction futures were largely dystopian, moving from bleak technofascism into some kind of stone-age barbarism, as in *Cloud Atlas*, or else, studiously ambiguous: the writers remaining coy about the dates, which renders "the future" a zone of pure fantasy, no different really than Middle Earth or Cimmeria. They might even, as with *Star Wars*, place the future in the past, "a long time ago in a galaxy far, far away." This Future is, most often, not really a future at all, but more like an alternative dimension, a dream-time, some kind of technological Elsewhere, existing in days to come in the same sense that elves and dragon-slayers existed in the past; just another screen for the projection of moral dramas and mythic fantasies. Science fiction has now become just another set of costumes in which one can dress up a Western, a war movie, a horror flick, a spy thriller, or just a fairy tale.

I think it would be wrong, however, to say that our culture has completely sidestepped the issue of technological disappointment. Embarrassment over this issue has ensured that we've been reluctant to engage with it explicitly. Instead, like so many other cultural traumas, pain has been displaced; we can only talk about it when we think we're talking about something else.

In retrospect, it seems to me that entire fin de siècle cultural sensibility that came to be referred to as "postmodernism" might best be seen as just such a prolonged meditation on technological changes that never happened. The thought first struck me when watching one of the new *Star Wars* movies. The movie was awful. But I couldn't help but be impressed by the quality of the special effects. Recalling all those clumsy effects typical of fifties sci-fi films, the tin spaceships being pulled along by almost-invisible strings, I kept thinking about how impressed a 1950s audience would have been if they'd known what we could do by now—only to immediately realize, "actually, no.

They wouldn't be impressed at all, would they? They thought that we'd actually be *doing* this kind of thing by now. Not just figuring out more sophisticated ways to simulate it."

That last word, "simulate," is key. What technological progress we have seen since the seventies has largely been in information technologies—that is, technologies of simulation. They are technologies of what Jean Baudrillard and Umberto Eco used to call the "hyper-real"—the ability to make imitations more realistic than the original. The entire postmodern sensibility, the feeling that we had somehow broken into an unprecedented new historical period where we understood that there was nothing new; that grand historical narratives of progress and liberation were meaningless; that everything now was simulation, ironic repetition, fragmentation and pastiche: all this only makes sense in a technological environment where the only major breakthroughs were ones making it easier to create, transfer, and rearrange virtual projections of things that either already existed, or, we now came to realize, never really would. Surely, if we were really taking our vacations in geodesic domes on Mars, or toting about pocket-sized nuclear fusion plants or telekinetic mind-reading devices, no one would ever have been talking like this. The "postmodern" moment was simply a desperate way to take what could only otherwise be felt as a bitter disappointment, and dress it up as something epochal, exciting and new.

It's worthy of note that in the earliest formulations of post-modernism, which largely came out of the Marxist tradition, a lot of this technological subtext was not even subtext; it was quite explicit. Here's a passage from Frederick Jameson's original *Postmodernism, or the Cultural Logic of Late Capitalism*, in 1984:

> It is appropriate to recall the excitement of machinery in the moment of capital preceding our own, the exhilaration of futurism, most notably, and of Marinetti's

celebration of the machine gun and the motorcar. These are still visible emblems, sculptural nodes of energy which give tangibility and figuration to the motive energies of that earlier moment of modernization . . . the ways in which revolutionary or communist artists of the 1930s also sought to reappropriate this excitement of machine energy for a Promethean reconstruction of human society as a whole . . .

It is immediately obvious that the technology of our own moment no longer possesses this same capacity for representation: not the turbine, nor even Sheeler's grain elevators or smokestacks, not the baroque elaboration of pipes and conveyor belts, nor even the streamlined profile of the railroad train—all vehicles of speed still concentrated at rest—but rather the computer, whose outer shell has no emblematic or visual power, or even the casings of the various media themselves, as with that home appliance called television which articulates nothing but rather implodes, carrying its flattened image surface within itself.[80]

Where once the sheer physical power of technologies themselves gave us a sense of history sweeping forward, we are now reduced to a play of screens and images.

Jameson originally proposed the term "postmodernism" to refer to the cultural logic appropriate to a new phase of capitalism, one that Ernest Mandel had, as early as 1972, dubbed a "third technological revolution." Humanity, Mandel argued, stood on the brink of a transformation as profound as the agricultural or industrial revolutions had been: one in which computers, robots, new energy sources, and new information technologies would, effectively, replace old-fashioned industrial labor—the "end of work" as it soon came to be called—reducing us all to designers and computer technicians coming up with the crazy visions that cybernetic factories would actually produce.[81] End of work arguments became increasingly popular in the late seventies and early eighties, as radical thinkers pondered what would happen to traditional working-class struggle once there was no longer a working class. (The answer: it would turn into identity politics.)

Jameson thought of himself as exploring the forms of consciousness and historical sensibilities likely to emerge from this emerging new age. Of course, as we all know, these technological breakthroughs did not, actually, happen. What happened instead is that the spread of information technologies and new ways of organizing transport—the containerization of shipping, for example—allowed those same industrial jobs to be outsourced to East Asia, Latin America, and other countries where the availability of cheap labor generally allowed manufacturers to employ much less technologically sophisticated production-line techniques than they would have been obliged to employ at home. True, from the perspective of those living in Europe and North America, or even Japan, the results did seem superficially to be much as predicted. Smokestack industries did increasingly disappear; jobs came to be divided between a lower stratum of service workers and an upper stratum sitting in antiseptic bubbles playing with computers. But below it all lay an uneasy awareness that this whole new post-work civilization was, basically, a fraud. Our carefully engineered high-tech sneakers were not really being produced by intelligent cyborgs or self-replicating molecular nanotechnology; they were being made on the equivalent of old-fashioned Singer sewing machines, by the daughters of Mexican and Indonesian farmers who had, as the result of WTO or NAFTA-sponsored trade deals, been ousted from their ancestral lands. It was this guilty awareness, it seems to me, that ultimately lay behind the postmodern sensibility, its celebration of the endless play of images and surfaces, and its insistence that ultimately, all those modernist narratives that were supposed to give those images depth and reality had been proved to be a lie.

So: Why did the projected explosion of technological growth everyone was expecting—the moon bases, the robot factories—fail to materialize? Logically, there are only two possibilities. Either our expectations about the pace of technological change were unrealistic, in which case, we need to ask ourselves why so many otherwise intelligent people felt they were not. Or our expectations were not inherently unrealistic, in which case, we need to ask what happened to throw the path of technological development off course.

When cultural analysts nowadays do consider the question—which they rarely do—they invariably choose the first option. One common approach is to trace the problem back to illusions created by the Cold War space race. Why, many have asked, did both the United States and the Soviet Union become so obsessed with the idea of manned space travel in the fifties, sixties, and seventies? It was never an efficient way to engage in scientific research. Was it not the fact that both the Americans and Russians had been, in the century before, societies of pioneers, the one expanding across the Western frontier, the other, across Siberia? Was it not the same shared commitment to the myth of a limitless, expansive future, of human colonization of vast empty spaces, that helped convince the leaders of both superpowers they had entered into a new "space age" in which they were ultimately battling over control over the future itself? And did not that battle ultimate produce, on both sides, completely unrealistic conceptions of what that future would actually be like?[82]

Obviously there is truth in this. There were powerful myths at play. But most great human projects are rooted in some kind of mythic vision—this, in itself, proves nothing, one way or the other, about the feasibility of the project itself. In this essay, I want to explore the second possibility. It seems to me there are good reasons to believe that at least some of those visions were not inherently unrealistic—and that at least some of these science fiction fantasies (at this point we can't know which ones) could indeed have been brought into being. The most obvious reason is because in the past, they regularly had been. After all, if someone growing up at the turn of the century reading Jules Verne or H. G. Wells tried to imagine what the world would be like in, say, 1960, they imagined a world of flying machines, rocket ships, submarines, new forms of energy, and wireless communication . . . and that was pretty much exactly what they got. If it wasn't unrealistic in 1900 to dream of men traveling to the moon, why was it unrealistic in the sixties to dream of jet-packs and robot laundry-maids? If from 1750 to 1950 new power sources emerged regularly (steam, electric, petroleum, nuclear . . .) was it that unreasonable to imagine we'd have seen at least one new one since?

There is reason to believe that even by the fifties and sixties, the real pace of technological innovation was beginning to slow from the heady pace of the first half of the century. There was something of a last spate of inventions in the fifties when microwave ovens (1954), the pill (1957), and lasers (1958) all appeared in rapid succession. But since then, most apparent technological advances have largely taken the form of either clever new ways of combining existing technologies (as in the space race), or new ways to put existing technologies to consumer use (the most famous example here is television, invented in 1926, but only mass-produced in the late forties and early fifties, in a self-conscious effort to create new consumer demand to ensure the American economy didn't slip back into depression). Yet the space race helped convey the notion that this was an age of remarkable advances, and the predominant popular impression during the sixties was that the pace of technological change was speeding up in terrifying, uncontrollable ways. Alvin Toffler's 1970 breakaway bestseller *Future Shock* can be seen as a kind of high-water mark of this line of thought. In retrospect, it's a fascinating and revealing book.[83]

Toffler argued that almost all of the social problems of the 1960s could be traced back to the increasing pace of technological change. As an endless outpouring of new scientific breakthroughs continually transformed the very grounds of our daily existence, he wrote, Americans were left rudderless, without any clear idea of what normal life was supposed to be like. Perhaps it was most obvious in the case of the family, where, he claimed, not just the pill, but also the prospect of in vitro fertilization, test tube babies, and sperm and egg donation were about to make the very idea of motherhood obsolete. Toffler saw similar things happening in every domain of social life— nothing could be taken for granted. And humans were not psychologically prepared for the pace of change. He coined a term for the phenomenon: "accelerative thrust." This quickening of the pace of technological advance had begun, perhaps, with the industrial revolution, but by roughly 1850, he argued, the effect had become unmistakable. Not only was everything around us changing, most of it—the sheer mass of human knowledge, the size of the population, industrial growth, the amount of energy being consumed—was changing at an exponential rate. Toffler insisted that the only solution was to begin to create some kind of democratic control over the process—institutions that could assess emerging technologies and the effects they were likely to have, ban those technologies likely to be too socially disruptive, and guide development in directions that would foster social harmony.

The fascinating thing is that while many of the historical trends Toffler describes are accurate, the book itself appeared at almost precisely the moment when most of them came to an end. For instance, it was right around 1970 when the increase in the number of scientific papers published in the world—a figure that had been doubling every fifteen years since roughly 1685—began leveling off. The same is true of the number of books and patents. In other areas, growth did not just slow down—it stopped entirely. Toffler's choice of the word "acceleration" turns out to have been particularly unfortunate. For most of human history, the top speed at which human beings could travel had lingered around twenty-five miles per hour. By 1900 it had increased to perhaps 100 mph, and for the next seventy years it did indeed seem to be increasing exponentially. By the time Toffler was writing, in 1970, the record for the fastest speed at which any human had traveled stood at 24,791 mph, achieved by the crew of Apollo 10 while reentering the earth's atmosphere in 1969, just a year before. At such an exponential rate, it must have seemed reasonable to assume that within a matter of decades, humanity would be exploring other solar systems. Yet no further increase has occurred since 1970. The record for the fastest a human has ever traveled remains with the crew of Apollo 10. True, the maximum speed of commercial air flight did peak one year later, at 14,000 mph, with the launching of the Concorde in 1971. But airline speed has not only failed to increase since—it has actually decreased since the Concorde's abandonment in 2003.[84]

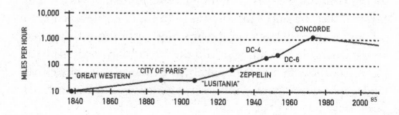

The fact that Toffler turned out to be wrong about almost everything had no deleterious effects on his own career. Charismatic prophets rarely suffer much when their prophecies fail to materialize. Toffler just kept retooling his analysis and coming up with new spectacular pronouncements every decade or so, always to great public recognition and applause. In 1980 he produced a book called *The Third Wave*,[86] its argument lifted directly from Ernest Mandel's "third technological revolution"—except that while Mandel argued these changes would spell the eventual end of capitalism, Toffler simply assumed that capitalism would be around forever. By 1990, he had become the personal intellectual guru of Republican congressman Newt Gingrich, who claimed that his own 1994 "Contract with America" was inspired, in part, by the understanding that the United States needed to move from an antiquated, materialist, industrial mindset to a new, free-market, information-age, Third Wave civilization.

There are all sorts of ironies here. Probably one of the greatest real-world achievements of *Future Shock* had been to inspire the government to create an Office of Technology Assessment (OTA) in 1972, more or less in line with Toffler's call for some sort of democratic oversight over potentially disruptive technologies. One of Gingrich's first acts on winning control of Congress in 1995 was to defund the OTA as an example of useless government waste. Again, none of this seemed to faze Toffler at all. By that time, he had long since given up trying to influence policy by appealing to the general public, or even really trying to influence political debate; he was, instead, making a living largely by giving seminars to CEOs and the denizens of corporate think tanks. His insights had, effectively, been privatized.

Gingrich liked to call himself a "conservative futurologist." This might seem oxymoronic; but actually, if you look back at Toffler's work in retrospect, the guru's politics line up precisely with his student's, and it's rather surprising anyone ever took him for anything else. The argument of *Future Shock* is the very definition of conservatism. Progress was always presented as a problem that needed to be solved. True, his solution was ostensibly to create forms of democratic control, but in effect, "democratic" obviously meant "bureaucratic," the creation of panels of experts to determine which inventions would be approved, and which put on the shelf. In this way, Toffler might best be seen as a latter day, intellectually lightweight version of the early nineteenth-century social theorist Auguste Comte. Comte, too, felt that he was standing on the brink of a new age—in his case, the industrial age—driven by the inexorable progress of technology, and that the social cataclysms of his times were really caused by the social system not having managed to adjust. The older, feudal order, had developed not only Catholic theology, a way of thinking about man's place in the cosmos perfectly suited to the social system of the time, but an institutional structure, the Church, that conveyed and enforced such ideas in a way that could give everyone a sense of meaning and belonging. The current, industrial age had developed its own system of ideas—science—but scientists had not succeeded in creating anything like the Catholic Church. Comte concluded that we needed to develop a new science, which he dubbed "sociology," and that sociologists should play the role of priests in a new Religion of Society that would inspire the masses with a love of order, community, work-discipline, and patriarchal family values. Toffler was less ambitious: his futurologists were not supposed to actually play the role of priests. But he shared the same feeling that technology was leading humans to the brink of a great historical break, the same fear of social breakdown, and, for that matter, the same obsession with the need to preserve the sacred role of motherhood—Comte wanted to put the image of a pregnant woman on the flag of his religious movement.

Gingrich did have another guru who was overtly religious: George Gilder, a libertarian theologian, and author, among other things, of a newsletter called the "Gilder Technology Report."

Gilder was also obsessed with the relation of technology and social change, but in an odd way, he was far more optimistic. Embracing an even more radical version of Mandel's Third Wave argument, he insisted that what we were seeing since the 1970s with the rise of computers was a veritable "overthrow of matter." The old, materialist, industrial society, where value came from physical labor, was giving way to an information age where value emerged directly from the minds of entrepreneurs, just as the world had originally appeared ex nihilo from the mind of God, just as money, in a proper supply-side economy, emerged ex nihilo from the Federal Reserve and into the hands of creative, value-creating, capitalists. Supply-side economic policies, he concluded, would ensure that investment would continue to steer away from old government boondoggles like the space program, and towards more productive information and medical technologies.

Gilder, who had begun his career declaring that he aspired to be "America's premier antifeminist," also insisted that such salutary developments could only be maintained by strict enforcement of traditional family values. He did not propose a new religion of society. He didn't feel he had to, since the same work could be done by the Christian evangelical movement that was already forging its strange alliance with the libertarian right.[87]

One would be unwise, perhaps, to dwell too much on such eccentric characters, however influential. For one thing, they came very late in the day. If there was a conscious, or semi-conscious, move away from investment in research that might have led to better rockets and robots, and towards research that would lead to such things as laser printers and CAT scans, it had already begun before the appearance of Toffler's *Future Shock* (1971), let alone Gilder's *Wealth and Poverty* (1981).[88] What their success does show is that the issues these men raised—the concern that existing patterns of technological development would lead to social upheaval, the need to guide technological development in directions that did not challenge existing structures of authority—found a receptive ear in the very highest corridors of power. There is every reason to believe that statesmen and captains of industry were indeed thinking about such questions, and had been for some time.[89]

So what happened? Over the course of the rest of this essay, which is divided into three parts, I am going to consider a number of factors that I think contributed to ensuring the technological futures we all anticipated never happened. These fall into two broad groups. One is broadly political, having to do with conscious shifts in the allocation of research funding; the other bureaucratic, a change in the nature of the systems administering scientific and technological research.

Thesis

There appears to have been a profound shift, beginning in the 1970s, from investment in technologies associated with the possibility of alternative futures to investment technologies that furthered labor discipline and social control

> "The bourgeoisie cannot exist without constantly revolutionizing the instruments of production, and thereby the relations of production, and with them the whole relations of society . . . All fixed, fast-frozen relations, with their train of ancient and venerable prejudices and opinions, are swept away, all new-formed ones become antiquated before they can ossify. All that is solid melts into air, all that is holy is profaned, and man is at last compelled to face with sober senses his real conditions of life, and his relations with his kind."
> —Marx and Engels, *Manifesto of the Communist Party* (1847)

"I said that fun was very important, too, that it was a direct
rebuttal of the kind of ethics and morals that were being
put forth in the country to keep people working in a rat
race which didn't make any sense because in a few years
the machines would do all the work anyway, that there
was a whole system of values that people were taught
to postpone their pleasure, to put all their money in the
bank, to buy life insurance, a whole bunch of things that
didn't make any sense to our generation at all."
—Abbie Hoffman, from the trial of the Chicago Seven (1970)

Since its inception in the eighteenth century, the system that
has come to be known as "industrial capitalism" has fostered
an extremely rapid rate of scientific advance and technological
innovation—one unparalleled in previous human history. Its
advocates have always held this out as the ultimate justification
for the exploitation, misery, and destruction of communities
the system also produced. Even its most famous detractors, Karl
Marx and Friedrich Engels, were willing to celebrate capitalism—if for nothing else—for its magnificent unleashing of the
"productive forces." Marx and Engels also believed that that
very tendency, or, to be more precise, capitalism's very need to
continually revolutionize the means of industrial production,
would eventually be its undoing.

Is it possible that they were right? And is it also possible that
in the sixties, capitalists, as a class, began to figure this out?

Marx's specific argument was that, for certain technical
reasons, value, and therefore profits, can only be extracted from
human labor. Competition forces factory owners to mechanize
production, so as to reduce labor costs, but while this is to the
short-term advantage of the individual firm, the overall effect
of such mechanization is actually to drive the overall rate of
profit of all firms down. For almost two centuries now, economists have debated whether all this is really true. But if it is true,

the otherwise mysterious decision by industrialists not to pour research funds into the invention of the robot factories that everyone was anticipating in the sixties, and instead to begin to relocate their factories to more labor-intensive, low-tech facilities in China or the Global South, makes perfect sense.[90]

I've already observed that there's reason to believe the pace of technological innovation in productive processes—the factories themselves—had already begun to slow down considerably in the fifties and sixties. Obviously it didn't look that way at the time. What made it appear otherwise were largely the side-effects of U.S. rivalry with the Soviet Union. This seems to have been true in two ways. One was a conscious policy: the Cold War saw frenetic efforts by U.S. industrial planners[91] to find ways to apply existing technologies to consumer purposes, to create an optimistic sense of burgeoning prosperity and guaranteed progress that, it was hoped, would undercut the appeal of radical working-class politics. The famous 1959 "kitchen debate" between Richard Nixon and Nikita Khrushchev made the politics quite explicit: "your communist 'worker's state' may have beat us into outer space," Nixon effectively argued, "but it's capitalism that creates technology like washing machines that actually improve the lives of the toiling masses." The other was the space race. In either case, the initiative really came from the Soviet Union itself. All this is difficult for Americans to remember, because with the end of the Cold War, the popular image of the USSR switched so quickly from terrifying rival to pathetic basket case—the exemplar of a society that "just didn't work." Back in the fifties, many U.S. planners were laboring under the suspicion that the Soviet system quite possibly worked much better than their own. Certainly, they keenly recalled the fact that in the 1930s, while the United States was mired in depression, the Soviet Union was maintaining almost unprecedented economic growth rates of 10 to 12 percent a year—an achievement quickly followed by the production of the vast tank armies that defeated Hitler, and of course, the launching of Sputnik in 1957, followed by the first manned spacecraft, the Vostok, in 1961. When Khrushchev assured Nixon that Soviet living standards would surpass those of the Americans in seven years, many Americans feared he might actually be right.

It's often said that the Apollo moon landing was the greatest historical achievement of Soviet communism. Surely, the United States would never have contemplated such a feat had it not been for the cosmic ambitions of the Soviet Politburo. Even putting things this way is a bit startling. "Cosmic ambitions?" We are used to thinking of the Politburo as a group of unimaginative grey bureaucrats, but while the Soviet Union was certainly run by bureaucrats, they were, from the beginning, bureaucrats who dared to dream astounding dreams. (The dream of world revolution was just the first.) Of course, most of their grandiose projects—changing the course of mighty rivers, that sort of thing—either turned out to be ecologically and socially disastrous, or, like Stalin's projected one-hundred-story Palace of the Soviets, which was to be topped by a twenty-story statue of Lenin, never got off the ground. And after the initial successes of the Soviet space program, most projects remained on the drawing board. But the Soviet leadership never ceased coming up with new ones. Even in the eighties, when the United States was attempting its own last—itself abortive— grandiose scheme, Star Wars, the Soviets were still planning and scheming ways to transform the world through creative uses of technology. Few outside of Russia now remember most of these projects, but vast resources were devoted to them. It's also worth noting that unlike the Star Wars project, which was a purely military project designed to sink the Soviet Union, most were peaceful: as for instance, the attempt to solve the world hunger problem by harvesting lakes and oceans with an edible bacteria called spirulina, or to solve world energy problems by a truly breathtaking plan to launch hundreds of gigantic solar power platforms into orbit and beaming the resulting electricity back to earth.[92]

Even the golden age of science fiction, which had its heyday in the fifties and sixties, and which first developed that standard repertoire of future inventions—force fields, tractor beams, warp drives—that any contemporary eight-year-old is familiar with (just as surely as they will know that garlic, crosses, stakes, and sunlight are what's most likely to be of help in slaying vampires) occurred in the United States and the USSR simultaneously.[93] Or consider *Star Trek*, that quintessence of American mythology. Is not the Federation of Planets—with its high-minded idealism, strict military discipline, and apparent lack of both class differences and any real evidence of multiparty democracy—really just an Americanized vision of a kinder, gentler Soviet Union, and above all, one that actually "worked"?[94]

What I find remarkable about *Star Trek*, in particular, is that there is not only no real evidence of democracy, but that almost no one seems to notice its absence. Granted, the *Star Trek* universe has been endlessly elaborated, with multiple series, movies, books and comics, even encyclopedias, not to mention decades' worth of every sort of fan fiction, so the question of the political constitution of the Federation did eventually have to come up. And when it did there was no real way anyone could say it was *not* a democracy. So one or two late references to the Federation as having an elected President and legislature were duly thrown in. But this is meaningless. Signs of real democratic life are entirely absent in the show—no character ever makes even a passing reference to elections, political parties, divisive issues, opinion polls, slogans, plebiscites, protests, or campaigns. Does Federation "democracy" even operate on a party system? If so, what are the parties? What sort of philosophy or core constituency does each represent? In 726 episodes we're not given the slightest clue.[95]

One might object: the characters themselves are part of

Fleet. They're in the military. True; but in real democratic societies, or even constitutional republics like the United States, soldiers and sailors regularly express political opinions about all sorts of things. You never see anyone in Star Fleet saying, "I never should have voted for those idiots pushing the expan-sionist policy, now look what a mess they've gotten into in Sector 5" or "when I was a student I was active in the campaign to ban terraforming of class-C planets but now I'm not sure we were right." When political problems do arise, and they regularly do, those sent in to deal with them are invariably bureaucrats, diplomats, and officials. *Star Trek* characters complain about bureaucrats all the time. They never complain about politicians. Because political problems are always addressed solely through administrative means.[96]

But this is of course exactly what one would expect under some form of state socialism. We tend to forget that such regimes, also, invariably claimed to be democracies. On paper, the USSR under Stalin boasted an exemplary constitution, with far more democratic controls than European parliamentary systems of the time. It was just that, much as in the Federation, none of this had any bearing on how life actually worked.

The Federation, then, is Leninism brought to its full and absolute cosmic success—a society where secret police, reeducation camps, and show trials are not necessary because a happy conjuncture of material abundance and ideological conformity ensures the system can now run entirely by itself.

While no one seems to know or much care about the Federation's political composition, its economic system has, from the eighties onward, been subject to endless curiosity and debate. *Star Trek* characters live under a regime of explicit communism. Social classes have been eliminated. So too have divisions based on race, gender, or ethnic origin.[97] The very existence of money, in earlier periods, is considered a weird and somewhat amusing historical curiosity. Menial labor has been automated into nonexistence. Floors clean themselves. Food, clothing, tools and weapons can be whisked into existence at will with a mere expenditure of energy, and even energy does not seem to be rationed in any significant way. All this did raise some hackles, and it would be interesting to write a political history of the debate over the economics of the future it sparked in the late eighties and early nineties. I well remember watching filmmaker Michael Moore, in a debate with editors of *The Nation*, pointing out that *Star Trek* showed that ordinary working-class Americans were far more amenable to overt anticapitalist politics than the beacons of the mainstream "progressive" left. It was around that time, too, that conservatives and libertarians on the Internet also began to take notice, filling newsgroups and other electronic forums with condemnations of the show as leftist propaganda.[98] But suddenly, we learned that money had not entirely disappeared. There was latinum. Those who traded in it, however, were an odious race who seemed to be almost exactly modeled on Medieval Christian stereotypes of Jews, except with oversized ears instead of oversized noses. (Amusingly, they were given a name, Ferengi, that is actually the Arabic and Hindi term for "annoying white person.")[99] On the other hand, the suggestion that the Federation was promoting communism was undercut by the introduction of the Borg, a hostile civilization so utterly communistic that individuality had been effaced completely, sucking any sentient life form it assimilated into one terrifying beehive mind.

By the time of the moon landing of 1969, U.S. planners no longer took their competition seriously. The Soviets had lost the space race, and as a result, the actual direction of American research and development could shift away from anything that might lead to the creation of Mars bases and robot factories, let alone become the technological basis for a communist utopia.

The standard line, of course, is that this shift of priorities was simply the natural result of the triumph of the market. The Apollo program was the quintessential Big Government project—Soviet-inspired in the sense that it required a vast national effort, coordinated by an equally vast government bureaucracy. As soon as the Soviet threat was safely out of the picture, this story goes, capitalism was free to revert to lines of technological development more in accord with its normal, decentralized, free-market imperatives—such as privately funded research into marketable products like touch-pad phones, adventurous little start-ups, and the like. This is, certainly, the line that men like Toffler and Gilder began taking in the late seventies and early eighties. But it's obviously wrong.

First of all, the amount of really innovative research being done in the private sector has actually declined since the heyday of Bell Labs and similar corporate research divisions in the fifties and sixties. Partly this is because of a change of tax regimes. The phone company was willing to invest so much of its profits in research because those profits were highly taxed—given the choice between sinking the money into higher wages for its workers (which bought loyalty) and research (which made sense to a company that was still locked in the old mind-set that said corporations were ultimately about making things, rather than making money), and having that same money simply appropriated by the government, the choice was obvious. After the changes in the seventies and eighties described in the introduction, all this changed. Corporate taxes were slashed. Executives, whose compensation now increasingly took the form of stock options, began not just paying the profits to investors in dividends, but using money that would otherwise be directed towards raises, hiring, or research budgets on stock buybacks, raising the values of the executives' portfolios but doing nothing to further productivity. In other words, tax cuts and financial reforms had almost precisely the opposite effect as their proponents claimed they would.

At the same time, the U.S. government never did abandon gigantic state-controlled schemes of technological development. It just shifted their emphasis sharply away from civilian projects like the space program and in the direction of military research—not just Star Wars, which was Reagan's version of a vast Soviet-scale project, but an endless variety of weapons projects, research in communications and surveillance technologies, and similar, "security-related" concerns. To some degree this had always been true: the billions poured into missile research alone had always dwarfed the relatively insignificant sums allocated to the space program. Yet by the 1970s, even much basic research came to be conducted following essentially military priorities. The most immediate reason we don't have robot factories is that, for the last several decades, some 95 percent of robotics research funding has been channeled through the Pentagon, which is of course far more interested in the kind of discoveries that might lead to the development of unmanned drones than fully automated bauxite mines or robot gardeners.

These military projects did have their own civilian spin-offs: the Internet is one. But they had the effect of guiding development in very specific directions.

One might suggest an even darker possibility. A case could be made that even the shift into R&D on information technologies and medicine was not so much a reorientation towards market-driven consumer imperatives, but part of an all-out effort to follow the technological humbling of the Soviet Union with total victory in the global class war: not only the imposition of absolute U.S. military dominance overseas, but the utter rout of social movements back home. The technologies that emerged were in almost every case the kind that proved most conducive to surveillance, work discipline, and social control. Computers have opened up certain spaces of freedom, as we're constantly reminded, but instead of leading to the workless utopia Abbie Hoffman or Guy Debord imagined, they have been employed in such a way as to produce the opposite effect. Information technology has allowed a financialization of capital that has driven workers ever more desperately into debt, while, at the same time, allowed employers to create new "flexible" work regimes that have destroyed traditional job security and led to a massive increase in overall working hours for almost all segments of the population. Along with the export of traditional factory jobs, this has put the union movement to rout and thus destroyed any real possibility of effective working-class politics.[100] Meanwhile, despite unprecedented investment in research on medicine and life sciences, we still await cures for cancer or even of the common cold; instead, the most dramatic medical breakthroughs we have seen have taken the form of drugs like Prozac, Zoloft, or Ritalin—tailor-made, one might say, to ensure that these new professional demands don't drive us completely, dysfunctionally, crazy.

When historians write the epitaph for neoliberalism, they will have to conclude that it was the form of capitalism that systematically prioritized political imperatives over economic ones. That is: given a choice between a course of action that will make capitalism *seem* like the only possible economic system, and one that will make capitalism actually *be* a more viable long-term economic system, neoliberalism has meant always choosing the former. Does destroying job security while increasing working hours really create a more productive (let alone innovative, loyal) workforce? There is every reason to believe that exactly the opposite is the case. In purely economic terms the result of neoliberal reform of labor markets is almost certainly negative—an impression that overall lower economic growth rates in just about all parts of the world in the eighties and nineties would tend to reinforce. However it has been spectacularly effective in depoliticizing labor. The same could be said of the burgeoning growth in armies, police, and private security services. They're utterly unproductive—nothing but a resource sink. It's quite possible, in fact, that the very weight of the apparatus created to ensure the ideological victory of capitalism will itself ultimately sink it. But it's also easy to see how, if the ultimate imperative of those running the world is choking off the possibility of any sense of an inevitable, redemptive future that will be fundamentally different than the world today must be a crucial part of the neoliberal project.

Antithesis

Yet even those areas of science and technology that did receive massive funding have not seen the breakthroughs originally anticipated

At this point, the pieces would seem to be falling neatly into place. By the 1960s, conservative political forces had become skittish about the socially disruptive effects of technological progress, which they blamed for the social upheavals of the era, and employers were beginning to worry about the economic impact of mechanization. The fading of the Soviet threat allowed for a massive reallocation of resources in directions seen as less challenging to social and economic arrangements—and ultimately, to ones that could support a campaign to sharply reverse the gains progressive social movements had made since the forties, thus achieving a decisive victory in what U.S. elites did indeed see as a global class war. The change of priorities was touted as a withdrawal of big-government projects and a return to the market, but it actually involved a shift in the orientation of government-directed research, away from programs like NASA—or, say, alternative energy sources—and toward even more intense focus on military, information, and medical technologies.

I think all this is true as far as it goes; but it can't explain everything. Above all, it cannot explain why even in those areas that have become the focus of well-funded research projects, we have not seen anything like the kind of advances anticipated fifty years ago. To take only the most obvious example: if 95 percent of robotics research has been funded by the military, why is there still no sign of Klaatu-style killer robots shooting death rays from their eyes? Because we *know* they've been working on that.

Obviously, there have been advances in military technology. It's widely acknowledged that one of the main reasons we all survived the Cold War is that while nuclear bombs worked more or less as advertised, the delivery systems didn't; Intercontinental Ballistic Missiles weren't really capable of hitting cities, let alone specific targets inside them, which meant there was little point in launching a nuclear first strike unless you were consciously intending to destroy the world. Contemporary cruise missiles, in contrast, are fairly accurate. Still, all those much-vaunted precision weapons never seem capable of taking out specific individuals (Saddam, Osama, Gaddafi), even if hundreds are dropped. Drones are just model airplanes, driven by remote control. And ray guns of any sort have not materialized, surely not for lack of trying—we have to assume the Pentagon has poured billions into coming up with one, but the closest they've come so far are lasers (a fifties technology) that might, if aimed correctly, make an enemy gunner looking directly at the beam go blind. This is not just unsporting, but rather pathetic. Phasers that can be set to stun do not appear to even be on the drawing boards; in fact, when it comes to infantry combat, the preferred weapon in 2011, almost everywhere, remains the AK-47, a Soviet design, named after the year it was first introduced: 1947.[101]

The same, as I've already noted, can be said of widely anticipated breakthroughs in medicine, and even (dare I say?) computers. The Internet is surely a remarkable thing. Still, if a fifties sci-fi fan were to appear in the present and ask what the most dramatic technological achievement of the intervening sixty years had been, it's hard to imagine the reaction would have been anything but bitter disappointment. He would almost certainly have pointed out that all we are really talking about here is a super-fast and globally accessible combination of library, post office, and mail order catalog. "Fifty years and this is the best our scientists managed to come up with? We were expecting computers that could actually think!"

All this is true, despite the fact that overall levels of research funding have increased dramatically since the 1970s. Of course, the proportion of that funding that comes from the corporate sector has increased even more dramatically, to the point where private enterprise is now funding twice as much research as the government. But the total increase is so large that the overall amount of government research funding, in real dollar terms, is still much higher than it was before. Again, while "basic," "curiosity-driven," or "blue skies" research—the kind that is not driven by the prospect of any immediate practical application, and which is therefore most likely to lead to unexpected break-throughs—is an ever-smaller proportion of the total, so much money is being thrown around nowadays that overall levels of basic research funding has actually gone up. Yet most honest assessments have agreed that the results have been surprisingly paltry. Certainly we no longer see anything like the continual stream of conceptual revolutions—genetic inheritance, relativity, psychoanalysis, quantum mechanics—that humanity had grown used to, and even to expect, a hundred years before.

Why?

One common explanation is that when funders do conduct basic research, they tend to put all their eggs in one gigantic basket: "Big Science," as it has come to be called. The Human Genome Project is often held out as an example. Initiated by the U.S. government, the project ended up spending almost three billion dollars and employing thousands of scientists and staff in five different countries, generating enormous expectations, only to discover that human gene sequences are nearly identical to those of chimpanzees, distinctly *less* complicated than the gene sequences of, say, rice, and that there would appear to be very little to be learned from them that's of immediate practical application. Even more—and I think this is really key—the hype and political investment surrounding such projects demonstrate the degree to which even basic research now seems to be driven by political, administrative, and marketing imperatives (the Human Genome Project for instance had its own corporate-style logo) that make it increasingly unlikely that anything particularly revolutionary will result.

Here, I think our collective fascination with the mythic origins of Silicon Valley and the Internet have blinded us to what's really going on. It has allowed us imagine that research and development is now driven, primarily, by small teams of plucky entrepreneurs, or the sort of decentralized cooperation that creates open-source software. It isn't. These are just the sort of research teams most likely to produce results. If anything, research has been moving in the opposite direction. It is still driven by giant, bureaucratic projects; what has changed is the bureaucratic culture. The increasing interpenetration of government, university, and private firms has led all parties to adopt language, sensibilities, and organizational forms that originated in the corporate world. While this might have helped somewhat in speeding up the creation of immediately marketable products—as this is what corporate bureaucracies are designed to do—in terms of fostering original research, the results have been catastrophic.

Here I can speak from experience. My own knowledge comes largely from universities, both in the United States and the UK. In both countries, the last thirty years have seen a veritable explosion of the proportion of working hours spent on administrative paperwork, at the expense of pretty much everything else. In my own university, for instance, we have not only more administrative staff than faculty, but the faculty, too, are expected to spend at least as much time on administrative responsibilities as on teaching and research combined.[102] This is more or less par for the course for universities worldwide. The explosion of paperwork, in turn, is a direct result of the introduction of corporate management techniques, which are always justified as ways of increasing efficiency, by introducing competition at every level. What these management techniques invariably end up meaning in practice is that everyone winds up spending most of their time trying to sell each other things: grant proposals; book proposals; assessments of our students' job and grant applications; assessments of our colleagues; prospectuses for new interdisciplinary majors, institutes, conference workshops, and universities themselves, which have now become brands to be marketed to prospective students or contributors. Marketing and PR thus come to engulf every aspect of university life.

The result is a sea of documents about the fostering of "imagination" and "creativity," set in an environment that might as well have been designed to strangle any actual manifestations of imagination and creativity in the cradle. I am not a scientist. I work in social theory. But I have seen the results in my own field of endeavor. No major new works of social theory have emerged in the United States in the last thirty years. We have, instead, been largely reduced to the equivalent of Medieval scholastics, scribbling endless annotations on French theory from the 1970s, despite the guilty awareness that if contemporary incarnations of Gilles Deleuze, Michel Foucault, or even Pierre Bourdieu were to appear in the U.S. academy, they would be unlikely to even make it through grad school, and if they somehow did make it, they would almost certainly be denied tenure.[103]

There was a time when academia was society's refuge for the eccentric, brilliant, and impractical. No longer. It is now the domain of professional self-marketers. As for the eccentric, brilliant, and impractical: it would seem society now has no place for them at all.

If all this is true in the social sciences, where research is still carried out largely by individuals, with minimal overhead, one can only imagine how much worse it is for physicists. And indeed, as one physicist has recently warned students pondering a career in the sciences, even when one does emerge from the usual decade-long period languishing as someone else's flunky, one can expect one's best ideas to be stymied at every point.

> You [will] spend your time writing proposals rather than doing research. Worse, because your proposals are judged by your competitors you cannot follow your curiosity, but must spend your effort and talents on anticipating and deflecting criticism rather than on solving the important scientific problems . . . It is proverbial that original ideas are the kiss of death for a proposal; because they have not yet been proved to work.[104]

That pretty much answers the question of why we don't have teleportation devices or antigravity shoes. Common sense dictates that if you want to maximize scientific creativity, you find some bright people, give them the resources they need to pursue whatever idea comes into their heads, and then leave them alone for a while. Most will probably turn up nothing, but one or two may well discover something completely unexpected. If you want to minimize the possibility of unexpected breakthroughs, tell those same people they will receive no resources at all unless they spend the bulk of their time competing against each other to convince you they already know what they are going to discover.[105]

That's pretty much the system we have now.[106]

In the natural sciences, to the tyranny of managerialism we can also add the creeping privatization of research results. As the British economist David Harvie has recently reminded us, "open source" research is not new. Scholarly research has always been open-source in the sense that scholars share materials and results. There is competition, certainly, but it is, as he nicely puts it, "convivial":

> Convivial competition is where I (or my team) wish to be the first to prove a particular conjecture, to explain a particular phenomenon, to discover a particular species, star or particle, in the same way that if I race my bike against my friend I wish to win. But convivial competition does not exclude cooperation, in that rival researchers (or research teams) will share preliminary results, experience of techniques and so on ... Of course, the shared knowledge, accessible through books, articles, computer software and directly, through dialogue with other scientists, forms an intellectual commons.[107]

Obviously this is no longer true of scientists working in the corporate sector, where findings are jealously guarded, but the spread of the corporate ethos within the academy and research institutes themselves has increasingly caused even publicly funded scholars to treat their findings as personal property. Less is published. Academic publishers ensure that findings that *are* published are more difficult to access, further enclosing the intellectual commons. As a result, convivial, open-source competition slides further into something much more like classic market competition.

There are all sorts of forms of privatization, up to and including the simple buying-up and suppression of inconvenient discoveries by large corporations for fear of their economic effects.[108] All this is much noted. More subtle is the way the managerial ethos itself militates against the implementation of anything remotely adventurous or quirky, especially, if there is no prospect of immediate results. Oddly, the Internet can be part of the problem here:

> Most people who work in corporations or academia have witnessed something like the following: A number of engineers are sitting together in a room, bouncing ideas off each other. Out of the discussion emerges a new concept that seems promising. Then some laptop-wielding person in the corner, having performed a quick Google search, announces that this "new" idea is, in fact, an old one; it—or at least vaguely similar—has already been tried. Either it failed, or it succeeded. If it failed, then no manager who wants to keep his or her job will approve spending money trying to revive it. If it succeeded, then it's patented and entry to the market is presumed to be unattainable, since the first people who thought of it will have "first-mover advantage" and will have created "barriers to entry." The number of seemingly promising ideas that have been crushed in this way must number in the millions.[109]

I could go on, but I assume the reader is getting the idea. A timid, bureaucratic spirit has come to suffuse every aspect of intellectual life. More often than not, it comes cloaked in a language of creativity, initiative, and entrepreneurialism. But the language is meaningless. The sort of thinkers most likely to come up with new conceptual breakthroughs are the least likely to receive funding, and if, somehow, breakthroughs nonetheless occur, they will almost certainly never find anyone willing to follow up on the most daring implications.

•

Let me return in more detail to some of the historical context briefly outlined in the introduction.

Giovanni Arrighi, the Italian political economist, has observed that after the South Sea Bubble, British capitalism largely abandoned the corporate form. The combination of high finance and small family firms that had emerged after the industrial revolution continued to hold throughout the next century—Marx's London, a period of maximum scientific and technological innovation; or Manchester; or Birmingham were not dominated by large conglomerates but mainly by capitalists who owned a single factory. (This is one reason Marx could assume capitalism was characterized by constant cutthroat competition.) Britain at that time was also notorious for being just as generous to its oddballs and eccentrics as contemporary America is intolerant. One common expedient was to allow them to become rural vicars, who, predictably, became one of the main sources for amateur scientific discoveries.[110]

As I mentioned, contemporary, bureaucratic, corporate capitalism first arose in the United States and Germany. The two bloody wars these rivals fought culminated, appropriately enough, in vast government-sponsored scientific programs to see who would be the first to discover the atom bomb. Indeed, even the structure of U.S. universities has always been based on the Prussian model. True, during these early years, both the United States and Germany did manage to find a way to cultivate their creative eccentrics—in fact, a surprising number of the most notorious ones that ended up in America (Albert Einstein was the paradigm) actually were German. During the war, when matters were desperate, vast government projects like the Manhattan Project were still capable of accommodating a whole host of bizarre characters (Oppenheimer, Feynman, Fuchs . . .). But as American power grew more and more secure, the country's bureaucracy became less and less tolerant of its outliers. And technological creativity declined.

The current age of stagnation seems to have begun after 1945, precisely at the moment the United States finally and definitively replaced the UK as organizer of the world economy.[111] True, in the early days of the U.S. Space Program—another period of panic—there was still room for genuine oddballs like Jack Parsons, the founder of NASA's Jet Propulsion Laboratory. Parsons was not only a brilliant engineer—he was also a Thelemite magician in the Aleister Crowley tradition, known for regularly orchestrating ceremonial orgies in his California home. Parsons believed that rocket science was ultimately just one manifestation of deeper, magical principles. But he was eventually fired.[112] U.S. victory in the Cold War guaranteed a corporatization of existing university and scientific bureaucracies sufficiently thorough to ensure that no one like him would ever get anywhere near a position of authority to start with.

Americans do not like to think of themselves as a nation of bureaucrats—quite the opposite, really—but, the moment we stop imagining bureaucracy as a phenomenon limited to government offices, it becomes obvious that this is precisely what we have become. The final victory over the Soviet Union did not really lead to the domination of "the market." More than anything, it simply cemented the dominance of fundamentally conservative managerial elites—corporate bureaucrats who use the pretext of short-term, competitive, bottom-line thinking to squelch anything likely to have revolutionary implications of any kind.

Synthesis

On the Movement from Poetic to Bureaucratic Technologies

> "All the labor-saving machinery that has hitherto been in-
> vented has not lessened the toil of a single human being."
> —John Stuart Mill

It is the premise of this book that we live in a deeply bureaucratic society. If we do not notice it, it is largely because bureaucratic practices and requirements have become so all-pervasive
that we can barely see them—or worse, cannot imagine doing
things any other way.

Computers have played a crucial role in all of this. Just as
the invention of new forms of industrial automation in the
eighteenth and nineteenth centuries had the paradoxical effect
of turning more and more of the world's population into full-
time industrial workers, so has all the software designed to
save us from administrative responsibilities in recent decades
ultimately turned us all into part or full-time administrators.
Just as university professors seem to feel it is inevitable that they
will spend more and more of their time managing grants, so
do parents simply accept that they will have to spend weeks of
every year filling out forty-page online forms to get their children into acceptable schools, and store clerks realize that they
will be spending increasing slices of their waking lives punch-
ing passwords into their phones to access, and manage, their
various bank and credit accounts, and pretty much everyone
understands that they have to learn how to perform jobs once
relegated to travel agents, brokers, and accountants.

Someone once figured out that the average American will
spend a cumulative six months of her life waiting for the light
to change. I don't know if similar figures are available for how
long she is likely to spend filling out forms, but it must be at
least that much. If nothing else, I think it's safe to say that no

population in the history of the world has spent nearly so much time engaged in paperwork.

Yet all of this is supposed to have happened after the overthrow of horrific, old-fashioned, bureaucratic socialism, and the triumph of freedom and the market. Certainly this is one of the great paradoxes of contemporary life, much though—like the broken promises of technology—we seem to have developed a profound reluctance to address the problem.

Clearly, these problems are linked—I would say, in many ways, they are ultimately the same problem. Nor is it merely a matter of bureaucratic, or more specifically managerial, sensibilities having choked off all forms of technical vision and creativity. After all, as we're constantly reminded, the Internet has unleashed all sorts of creative vision and collaborative ingenuity. What it has really brought about is a kind of bizarre inversion of ends and means, where creativity is marshaled to the service of administration rather than the other way around.

I would put it this way: in this final, stultifying stage of capitalism, we are moving from poetic technologies to bureaucratic technologies.

By poetic technologies, I refer to the use of rational, technical, bureaucratic means to bring wild, impossible fantasies to life. Poetic technologies in this sense are as old as civilization. They could even be said to predate complex machinery. Lewis Mumford used to argue that the first complex machines were actually made of people. Egyptian pharaohs were only able to build the pyramids because of their mastery of administrative procedures, which then allowed them to develop production line techniques, dividing up complex tasks into dozens of simple operations and assigning each to one team of workmen—even though they lacked mechanical technology more complex than the lever and inclined plane. Bureaucratic oversight turned armies of peasant farmers into the cogs of a vast machine. Even much later, after actual cogs had been invented, the design of complex machinery was always to some degree an elaboration of principles originally developed to organize people.[113]

Yet still, again and again, we see those machines—whether their moving parts are arms and torsos or pistons, wheels, and springs—being put to work to realize otherwise impossible fantasies: cathedrals, moon shots, transcontinental railways, and on and on. Certainly, poetic technologies almost invariably have something terrible about them; the poetry is likely to evoke dark satanic mills as much as it does grace or liberation. But the rational, bureaucratic techniques are always in service to some fantastic end.

From this perspective, all those mad Soviet plans—even if never realized—marked the high-water mark of such poetic technologies. What we have now is the reverse. It's not that vision, creativity, and mad fantasies are no longer encouraged. It's that our fantasies remain free-floating; there's no longer even the pretense that they could ever take form or flesh. Meanwhile, in the few areas in which free, imaginative creativity actually is fostered, such as in open-source Internet software development, it is ultimately marshaled in order to create even more, and even more effective, platforms for the filling out of forms. This is what I mean by "bureaucratic technologies": administrative imperatives have become not the means, but the end of technological development. Meanwhile, the greatest and most powerful nation that has ever existed on this earth has spent the last decades telling its citizens that we simply can no longer contemplate grandiose enterprises, even if—as the current environmental crisis suggests—the fate of the earth depends on it.

So what, then, are the political implications?

First of all, it seems to me that we need to radically rethink some of our most basic assumptions about the nature of capitalism. One is that capitalism is somehow identical to the market, and that both are therefore inimical to bureaucracy, which is a creature of the state. The second is that capitalism is in its nature technologically progressive. It would seem that Marx and Engels, in their giddy enthusiasm for the industrial revolutions of their day, were simply wrong about this. Or to be more precise: they were right to insist that the mechanization of industrial production would eventually destroy capitalism; they were wrong to predict that market competition would compel factory owners to go on with mechanization anyway. If it didn't happen, it can only be because market competition is not, in fact, as essential to the nature of capitalism as they had assumed. If nothing else, the current form of capitalism, where much of the competition seems to take the form of internal marketing within the bureaucratic structures of large semi-monopolistic enterprises, would presumably have come as a complete surprise to them.[114]

Defenders of capitalism generally make three broad historical claims: first, that it has fostered rapid scientific and technological development; second, that however much it may throw enormous wealth to a small minority, it does so in such a way that increases overall prosperity for everyone; third, that in doing so, it creates a more secure and democratic world. It is quite clear that in the twenty-first century, capitalism is not doing any of these things. In fact, even its proponents are increasingly retreating from any claim that it is a particularly good system, falling back instead on the claim that it is the only possible system—or at least, the only possible system for a complex, technologically sophisticated society such as our own.

As an anthropologist, I find myself dealing with this latter argument all the time.

SKEPTIC: You can dream your utopian dreams all you like, I'm talking about a political or economic system that could actually work. And experience has shown us that what we have is really the only option here.

ME: Our particular current form of limited representative government—or corporate capitalism—is the only possible political or economic system? Experience shows us no such thing. If you look at human history, you can find hundreds, even thousands of different political and economic systems. Many of them look absolutely nothing like what we have now.

SKEPTIC: Sure, but you're talking about simpler, small-scale societies, or ones with a much simpler technological base. I'm talking about modern, complex, technologically advanced societies. So your counter-examples are irrelevant.

ME: Wait, so you're saying that technological progress has actually limited our social possibilities? I thought it was supposed to be the other way around!

But even if you concede the point, and agree that for whatever reason, while a wide variety of economic systems might once have been equally viable, modern industrial technology has created a world in which this is no longer the case—could anyone seriously argue that current economic arrangements are also the only ones that will ever be viable under any possible *future* technological regime as well? Such a statement is self-evidently absurd. If nothing else, how could we possibly know?

Granted, there are people who take that position—on both ends of the political spectrum. As an anthropologist and anarchist, I have to deal fairly regularly with "anticivilizational" types who insist not only that current industrial technology can only lead to capitalist-style oppression, but that this must necessarily be true of any future technology as well: and therefore, that human liberation can only be achieved by a return to the Stone Age. Most of us are not such technological determinists. But ultimately, claims for the present-day inevitability of capitalism have to be based on some kind of technological determinism. And for that very reason, if the ultimate aim of neoliberal capitalism is to create a world where no one believes any other economic system could really work, then it needs to suppress not just any idea of an inevitable redemptive future, but really any radically different technological future at all. There's a kind of contradiction here. It cannot mean convincing us that technological change has come to an end—since that would mean capitalism is not really progressive. It means convincing us that technological progress is indeed continuing, that we do live in a world of wonders, but to ensure those wonders largely take the form of modest improvements (the latest iPhone!), rumors of inventions about to happen ("I hear they actually are going to have flying cars pretty soon"),[115] even more complex ways of juggling information and imagery, and even more complex platforms for the filling out of forms.

I do not mean to suggest that neoliberal capitalism—or any other system—could ever be permanently successful in this regard. First, there's the problem of trying to convince the world you are leading the way in terms of technological progress when you are actually holding it back. With its decaying infrastructure and paralysis in the face of global warming, the United States is doing a particularly bad job of this at the moment. (This is not to mention its symbolically devastating abandonment of the manned space program, just as China revs up its own.) Second, there's the fact that pace of change simply can't be held back forever. At best it can be slowed down. Breakthroughs will happen; inconvenient discoveries cannot be permanently suppressed. Other, less bureaucratized parts of the world—or at least, parts of the world with bureaucracies that are not quite so hostile to creative thinking—will, slowly, inevitably, attain the resources required to pick up where the United States and its allies have left off. The Internet does provide opportunities for collaboration and dissemination that may eventually help break us through the wall, as well. Where will the breakthrough come? We can't know. Over the last couple years, since the first version of this essay saw print, there has been a whole spate of new possibilities: 3-D printing, advances in materials technologies, self-driving cars, a new generation of robots, and as a result, a new spate of discussion of robot factories and the end of work. There are hints, too, of impending conceptual breakthroughs in physics, biology, and other sciences, made all the more difficult because of the absolute institutional lock of existing orthodoxies, but which might well have profound technological implications as well.

At this point, the one thing I think we can be fairly confident about it is that invention and true innovation will not happen within the framework of contemporary corporate capitalism—or, most likely, any form of capitalism at all. It's becoming increasingly clear that in order to really start setting up domes on Mars, let alone develop the means to figure out if there actually are alien civilizations out there to contact—or what would actually happen if we shot something through a wormhole—we're going to have to figure out a different economic system entirely. Does it really have to take the form of some massive new bureaucracy? Why do we assume it must? Perhaps it's only by breaking up existing bureaucratic structures that we'll ever be able to get there. And if we're going to actually come up with robots that will do our laundry or tidy up the kitchen, we're going to have to make sure that whatever replaces capitalism is based on a far more egalitarian distribution of wealth and power—one that no longer contains either the super-rich or desperately poor people willing to do their housework. Only then will technology begin to be marshaled toward human needs. And this is the best reason to break free of the dead hand of the hedge fund managers and the CEOs—to free our fantasies from the screens in which such men have imprisoned them, to let our imaginations once again become a material force in human history.

3

The Utopia of Rules, or Why We Really Love Bureaucracy After All

Everyone complains about bureaucracy. The essays in this book have themselves largely consisted of such complaints. Nobody seems to likes bureaucracy very much—yet somehow, we always seem to end up with more of it.

In this essay I'd like to ask why that is, and particularly, to consider the possibility that many of the blanket condemnations of bureaucracy we hear are in fact somewhat disingenuous. That the experience of operating within a system of formalized rules and regulations, under hierarchies of impersonal officials, actually does hold—for many of us much of the time, for all of us at least some of the time—a kind of covert appeal.

Now, I am aware this is not the only possible explanation. There is a whole school of thought that holds that bureaucracy tends to expand according to a kind of perverse but inescapable inner logic. The argument runs as follows: if you create a bureaucratic structure to deal with some problem, that structure will invariably end up creating other problems that seem as if they, too, can only be solved by bureaucratic means. In universities, this is sometimes informally referred to as the "creating committees to deal with the problem of too many committees" problem.

A slightly different version of the argument—this is really the core of Max Weber's reflections on the subject—is that a bureaucracy, once created, will immediately move to make itself indispensable to anyone trying to wield power, no matter what they wish to do with it. The chief way to do this is always by attempting to monopolize access to certain key types of information. Weber is worth quoting at length on this subject:

> Every bureaucracy seeks to increase the superiority of the professionally informed by keeping their knowledge and intentions secret. Bureaucratic administration always tends to be an administration of "secret sessions": in so far as it can, it hides its knowledge and action from criticism . . .
>
> The concept of the "official secret" is the specific invention of bureaucracy, and nothing is so fanatically defended by the bureaucracy as this attitude, which cannot be substantially justified beyond these specifically qualified areas. In facing a parliament, the bureaucracy, out of a sure power instinct, fights every attempt of the parliament to gain knowledge by means of its own experts or from interest groups . . .
>
> The absolute monarch is powerless opposite the superior knowledge of the bureaucratic expert—in a certain sense more powerless than any other political head. All the scornful decrees of Frederick the Great concerning the "abolition of serfdom" were derailed, as it were, in the course of their realization because the official mechanism simply ignored them as the

occasional ideas of a dilettante. When a constitutional king agrees with a socially important part of the governed, he very frequently exerts a greater influence upon the course of administration than does the "absolute monarch." The constitutional king can control these experts—better because of what is, at least relatively, the public character of criticism, whereas the absolute monarch is dependent for information solely upon the bureaucracy. The Russian czar of the old regime was seldom able to accomplish permanently anything that displeased his bureaucracy and hurt the power interests of the bureaucrats.[116]

One side effect, as Weber also observes, is that once you do create a bureaucracy, it's almost impossible to get rid of it. The very first bureaucracies we know of were in Mesopotamia and Egypt, and these continued to exist, largely unchanged, as one dynasty or ruling elite replaced another, for literally thousands of years. Similarly, waves of successful invaders were not enough to dislodge the Chinese civil service, with its bureaus, reports, and examination system, which remained firmly in place no matter who actually claimed the Mandate of Heaven. In fact, as Weber also noted, foreign invaders needed the skills and knowledge so jealously guarded by Chinese bureaucrats even more than indigenous rulers did, for obvious reasons. The only real way to rid oneself of an established bureaucracy, according to Weber, is to simply kill them all, as Alaric the Goth did in Imperial Rome, or Genghis Khan in certain parts of the Middle East. Leave any significant number of functionaries alive, and within a few years, they will inevitably end up managing one's kingdom.

The second possible explanation is that bureaucracy does not just make itself indispensable to rulers, but holds a genuine appeal to those it administers as well. One need not agree here with Weber's curious celebration of bureaucratic efficiency. The simplest explanation for the appeal of bureaucratic procedures lies in their impersonality. Cold, impersonal, bureaucratic relations are much like cash transactions, and both offer similar advantages and disadvantages. On the one hand they are soulless. On the other, they are simple, predictable, and—within certain parameters, at least—treat everyone more or less the same. And anyway, who really wants to live in a world where everything is soul? Bureaucracy holds out at least the possibility of dealing with other human beings in ways that do not demand either party has to engage in all those complex and exhausting forms of interpretive labor described in the first essay in this book, where just as you can simply place your money on the counter and not have to worry about what the cashier thinks of how you're dressed, you can also pull out your validated photo ID card without having to explain to the librarian why you are so keen to read about homoerotic themes in eighteenth century British verse. Surely this is part of the appeal. In fact, if one really ponders the matter, it's hard to imagine how, even if we do achieve some utopian communal society, some impersonal (dare I say, bureaucratic?) institutions would not still be necessary, and for just this reason. To take one obvious example: languishing on some impersonal lottery system or waiting list for a desperately needed organ transplant might be alienating and distressing, but it's difficult to envision any less impersonal way of allocating a limited pool of hearts or kidneys that would not be immeasurably worse.

This is, as I say, the simplest explanation. But in this essay I'd like to explore the possibility that all this goes much deeper. It's not just that the impersonal relations bureaucracies afford are convenient; to some degree, at least, our very ideas of rationality, justice, and above all, freedom, are founded on them. To explain why I believe this to be the case, let me begin, first of all, by examining two moments in human history when new bureaucratic forms actually did inspire not just widespread passive acquiescence but giddy enthusiasm, even infatuation, and try to understand precisely what it was about them that seemed, to so many people, so exciting.

I. The Enchantment of Disenchantment, or The Magical Powers of the Post Office

One reason it was possible for Weber to describe bureaucracy as the very embodiment of rational efficiency is that in the Germany of his day, bureaucratic institutions really did work well. Perhaps the flagship institution, the pride and joy of the German civil service was the Post Office. In the late nineteenth century, the German postal service was considered one of the great wonders of the modern world. Its efficiency was so legendary, in fact, that it casts a kind of terrible shadow across the twentieth century. Many of the greatest achievements of what we now call "high modernism" were inspired by—or in many cases, built in direct imitation of—the German Post Office. And one could indeed make a case that many of the most terrible woes of that century can also be laid at its feet.

To understand how this could be, we need to understand a little of the real origins of the modern social welfare state, which we now largely think of—when we think of them at all—as having been created by benevolent democratic elites. Nothing could be further from the truth. In Europe, most of the key institutions of what later became the welfare state—everything from social insurance and pensions to public libraries and public health clinics—were not originally created by governments at all, but by trade unions, neighborhood associations, cooperatives, and working-class parties and organizations of one sort or another. Many of these were engaged in a self-conscious revolutionary project of "building a new society in the shell of the old," of gradually creating Socialist institutions from below.

For some it was combined with the aim of eventually seizing control of the government through parliamentary means, for others, it was a project in itself. One must remember that during the late nineteenth century, even the direct heirs of Marx's Communist Party had largely abandoned the idea of seizing control of the government by force, since this no longer seemed necessary; in a Europe at peace and witnessing rapid technological progress, they felt that it should be possible to create a social revolution through peaceful, electoral means.

Germany was one of the places where such parties were most successful. Even though Chancellor Otto von Bismarck, the great mastermind behind the creation of the German state, allowed his parliament only limited powers, he was confounded by the rapid rise of workers' parties, and continually worried by the prospect of a Socialist majority, or a possible Paris Commune-style uprising in his new united Germany. His reaction to Socialist electoral success from 1878 was twofold: on the one hand, to ban the Socialist party, trade unions, and leftist newspapers; on the other, when this proved ineffective (Socialist candidates continued to run, and win, as independents), to create a top-down alternative to the free schools, workers' associations, friendly societies, libraries, theaters, and the larger process of building socialism from below. This took the form of a program of social insurance (for unemployment, health and disability, etc.), free education, pensions, and so forth—much of it watered-down versions of policies that had been part of the Socialist platform, but in every case, carefully purged of any democratic, participatory elements. In private, at least, he was utterly candid about describing these efforts as a "bribe," an effort to buy out working-class loyalties to his conservative nationalist project.[116] When left-wing regimes did later take power, the template had already been established, and almost invariably, they took the same top-down approach, incorporating locally organized clinics, libraries, mutual banking initiatives, workers' education centers, and the like into the administrative structure of the state.

In Germany, the real model for this new administrative structure was, curiously, the post office—though when one understands the history of the postal service, it makes a great deal of sense. The post office was, essentially, one of the first attempts to apply top-down, military forms of organization to the public good. Historically, postal services first emerged from the organization of armies and empires. They were originally ways of conveying field reports and orders over long distances; later, by extension, a key means of keeping the resulting empires together. Hence Herodotus' famous quote about Persian imperial messengers, with their evenly spaced posts with fresh horses, which he claimed allowed the swiftest travel on earth: "Neither snow, nor rain, nor heat, nor gloom of night stays these couriers from the swift completion of their appointed rounds" still appears carved over the entrance to the Central Post Office building in New York, opposite Penn Station.[118] The Roman Empire had a similar system, and pretty much all armies operated with postal courier systems until Napoleon adopted semaphore in 1805.

One of the great innovations of eighteenth- and especially nineteenth-century governance was to expand what had once been military courier systems into the basis for an emerging civil service whose primary purpose was providing services for the public. It happened first in commerce, and then expanded as the commercial classes also began to use the post for personal or political correspondence—until finally it was being used by just about everyone.[119] Before long, in many of the emerging nation-states in Europe and the Americas, half the government budget was spent on—and more than half the civil service employed in—the postal service.[120]

In Germany, one could even make the argument that the nation was created, more than anything else, *by* the post office.

Under the Holy Roman Empire, the right to run a postal courier system within imperial territories had been granted, in good feudal fashion, to a noble family originally from Milan, later to be known as the Barons von Thurn and Taxis (one later scion of this family, according to legend, was the inventor of the taximeter, which is why taxicabs ultimately came to bear his name). The Prussian Empire originally bought out the Thurn and Taxis monopoly in 1867, and used it as the basis for a new German national post—and over the next two decades, the sure sign that a new statelet or principality had been absorbed into the emerging nation-state was its incorporation into the German postal system. Partly for this reason, the sparkling efficiency of the system became a point of national pride. And indeed, the German post of the late nineteenth century was nothing if not impressive, boasting up to five or even nine delivery times a day in major cities, and, in the capital, a vast network of miles of pneumatic tubes designed to shoot letters and small parcels almost instantly across long distances using a system of pressurized air:

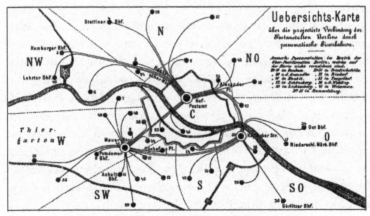

Map of Berlin pneumatic tube postal system, 1873

Fig. 613. Rohrpostamt.

Mark Twain, who lived briefly in Berlin between 1891 and 1892, was so taken with it that he composed one of his only known non-satirical essays, entitled "Postal Service," just to celebrate its wondrous efficiency.[121] Nor was he the only foreigner to be so impressed. Just a few months before the outbreak of Russian revolution, Vladimir Ilych Lenin wrote:

> A witty German Social-Democrat of the seventies of the last century called the *postal service* an example of the socialist economic system. This is very true. At present the postal service is a business organized on the lines of a state-*capitalist* monopoly. Imperialism is gradually transforming all trusts into organizations of a similar type . . .
>
> To organize the *whole* national economy on the lines of the postal service, so that the technicians, foremen, bookkeepers, as well as *all* officials, shall receive salaries no higher than "a workman's wage," all under the control and leadership of the armed proletariat—this is our immediate aim.[122]

So there you have it. The organization of the Soviet Union was directly modeled on that of the German postal service.

Neither were state socialists the only ones to be impressed. Even anarchists joined the chorus; though they were less interested in the national system than in relations between them— the fact that it was possible to send a letter from Venezuela to China despite the absence of any single overarching state. In fact, Peter Kropotkin often cited the international "universal postal union" of 1878 (along with accords between railroad companies) as a model for anarchism—again, emphasizing that this was something that was *already* taking shape at the top of imperial systems:

> The Postal Union did not elect an international postal parliament in order to make laws for all postal organizations adherent to the Union . . . They proceeded by means of agreement. To agree together they resorted to congresses; but, while sending delegates to their congresses they did not say to them, "Vote about everything you like—we shall obey." They put forward questions and discussed them first themselves; then they sent delegates acquainted with the special question to be discussed at the congress, and they sent *delegates*—not rulers.[123]

This vision of a potential future paradise emerging from within the Post Office was not confined to Europe. Indeed, the country that was soon to emerge as Germany's chief rival for global influence, the United States, was also held out as a model for a new type of civilization, and the efficiency of its own Post Service was considered *prima facie* evidence. Already in the 1830s, Tocqueville had been startled by the size of the postal system and the sheer volume of letters being moved about even on the frontier. During one journey through Kentucky to Michigan he noted: "There is an astonishing circulation of letters and newspapers among these savage woods," far more, he calculated, than in even the most populous and commercial provinces of France. In the words of one later historian of the American Republic:

> Americans would soon make their postal system larger than the postal systems of either Britain or France. By 1816 the postal system had over thirty-three hundred offices, employing nearly 70 percent of the entire federal civilian workforce. The amount of mail increased just as quickly. In the year 1790 the postal system had carried only three hundred thousand letters, one for about every fifteen persons in the country. By 1815 it transmitted nearly seven and a half million letters during the year, which was about one for every person . . . And, unlike the situation in Great Britain and other European nations, the mail was transmitted without government surveillance or control.[124]

In fact, for much of the century, from the perspective of a majority of Americans, the postal service effectively *was* the Federal government. By 1831, its staff already far outnumbered that of all other branches of government combined, it was substantially larger than the army, and for most small-town dwellers, postal employees were the only Federal officials they were ever likely to meet.

In Europe, the United States was at that time itself seen as a kind of utopian experiment, with its rejection of laissez-faire economics, and widespread reliance on cooperatives and government-sponsored projects and tariff protections. It was only with the rise of corporate capitalism after the Civil War that the United States also adopted something closer to the German model of bureaucratic capitalism. When it did, the post office model came to be seen, by Populists and especially Progressives, as the major viable alternative. Again, the forms of a new, freer, more rational society seemed to be emerging within the very structures of oppression itself. In the United States, the term used was "postalization"—a unique American coinage for nationalization (and one which has, significantly, since completely disappeared from the language). Yet at the same time as Weber and Lenin were invoking the German post office as a model for the future, American Progressives were arguing that even private business would be more efficient were it run like the post office, and scoring major victories for postalization, such as the nationalization of the once-private subway, commuter, and interstate train systems, which in major American cities have remained in public hands ever since.

In retrospect, all these fantasies of postal utopia seem rather quaint, at best. We now associate national postal systems mainly with the arrival of things we never wanted in the first place: utility bills, overdraft alerts, mail-order catalogs, solicitations, sweepstakes, calls to jury duty, tax audits, one-time-only credit-card offers, and charity appeals. Insofar as Americans have a popular image of postal workers, it has become increasingly squalid. But this didn't just happen. It is the result of intentional policy choices. Since the 1980s, legislators have led the way in systematically defunding the post office and encouraging private alternatives as part of an ongoing campaign to convince Americans that government doesn't really work.[125] As a result, the Postal Service quickly became the very definition of everything we were supposed to think was wrong with state bureaucracies: there were endless newspaper stories about strikes, drug-addled workers, houses full of years' worth of undelivered mail, and of course, most famously, employees periodically "going postal" and opening fire on managers, fellow workers, and members of the police or general public. In fact the only reference I could find to the term "postalization" in contemporary literature is an essay on workplace violence called "the postalization of corporate America," decrying how an epidemic of violent attacks on bosses and co-workers was spreading from the public sector into private corporations, too.

In a fascinating book called *Going Postal: Rage, Murder, and Rebellion from Reagan's Workplaces to Clinton's Columbine and Beyond*, Mark Ames carefully picked through journalistic accounts of such events (which did, indeed, quickly spread from the Post Office to private offices and factories, and even to private postal services like UPS, but in the process, became so commonplace that many barely made the national news) and noted that the language they employ, which always described these events as acts of inexplicable individual rage and madness—severed from any consideration of the systematic humiliations that always seem to set them off—bears an uncanny resemblance to the way the nineteenth-century press treated slave revolts.[126] Ames notes that there were remarkably few organized slave rebellions in American history. But there were a fair number of incidents in which individual slaves, or small groups, struck out in a similar fashion against overseers, masters, and their families with axes, knives, poison, or whatever means of immediate violence were at hand. In both cases, journalists treated such outbreaks as the result of either individual insanity, or inexplicable malice. In fact, to even suggest possible structural explanations—to speak of the evils of slavery, or to point out that before the eighties reforms in corporate culture that destroyed earlier assurances of secure lifetime employment and protections for workers against arbitrary and humiliating treatment by superiors, there had not been a single workplace massacre in all American history (*other* than by slaves)—seemed somehow immoral, since it would imply such violence was in some way justified.

It can't be denied, too, there was a major racial component

in the rhetoric. Just as for much of the twentieth century the post office stood, in the eyes of working-class African-American communities, as the very paradigm of stable, secure, but also respectable and community service-oriented employment,[127] so after Reagan it came to be pictured as embodying all the supposed degradation, violence, drug abuse, and inefficiency of a welfare state that was viewed in deeply racist terms. (This identification of African-Americans both with the stuffy bureaucrat, and with scary random violence, appears again and again in U.S. popular culture—though rarely, it's true, both at the same time. It is a strange, repetitive feature of action movies that the infuriating go-by-the-rules boss of the maverick hero is almost invariably Black.)[128]

Yet at the very same time that symbolic war was being waged on the Postal Service—as it was descending in the popular imagination into a place of madness, degradation, and violence—something remarkably similar to the turn-of-the-century infatuation with the Postal Service was happening again. Let us summarize the story so far:

1. A new communications technology develops out of the military.
2. It spreads rapidly, radically reshaping everyday life.
3. It develops a reputation for dazzling efficiency.
4. Since it operates on non-market principles, it is quickly seized on by radicals as the first stirrings of a future, non-capitalist economic system already developing within the shell of the old.
5. Despite this, it quickly becomes the medium, too, for government surveillance and the dissemination of endless new forms of advertising and unwanted paperwork.

Put it in these terms, it should be obvious enough what I'm referring to. This is pretty much exactly the story of the Internet. What is email, after all, but a giant, globe-spanning, electronic, super-efficient Post Office? Has it not, too, created a sense of a new, remarkably effective form of cooperative economy emerging from within the shell of capitalism itself—even as it has deluged us with scams, spam, and commercial offers, and allowed the government to spy on us in new and creative ways?

Obviously, there are differences. Most obviously, the Internet involves a much more participatory, bottom-up form of cooperation. This is important. But for the moment, I am less interested in the larger historical significance of the phenomenon than I am in asking: what does this tell us about the appeal of bureaucracy itself?

Well, first of all, it seems significant that while both postal services and the Internet emerge from the military, they could be seen as adopting military technologies to quintessential anti-military purposes. Organized violence, as I've argued, insofar as it is a form of communication, is one that radically strips down, simplifies, and ultimately prevents communication; insofar as it as a form of action, it is really a form of anti-action, because its ultimate purpose is to prevent others from being able to act (either to act in certain ways, or, if one kills them, to ever act in any way ever again.) Yet here we have a way of taking those very stripped-down, minimalistic forms of action and communication typical of military systems—whether chains of command or binary codes—and turning them into the invisible base on which everything they are not can be constructed: dreams, projects, declarations of love and passion, artistic effusions, subversive manifestos, or pretty much anything else. They allow for the creation and maintenance of social relations that could never have existed otherwise. But all this also implies that bureaucracy appeals to us—that it seems at its most liberating—precisely when it disappears: when it becomes so rational and reliable that we are able to just take it for granted that we can go to sleep on a bed of numbers and wake up with all those numbers still snugly in place.

In this sense, bureaucracy enchants when it can be seen as a species of what I've called poetic technology, that is, one where mechanical forms of organization, usually military in their ultimate inspiration, can be marshaled to the realization of impossible visions: to create cities out of nothing, scale the heavens, make the desert bloom. For most of human history this kind of power was only available to the rulers of empires or commanders of conquering armies, so we might even speak here of a democratization of despotism. Once, the privileged of waving one's hand and having a vast invisible army of cogs and wheels organize themselves in such a way as to bring your whims into being was available only to the very most privileged few; in the modern world, it can be subdivided into millions of tiny portions and made available to everyone able to write a letter, or to flick a switch.[129]

All this implies a certain very peculiar notion of freedom. Even more, I think, it marks a reversal of earlier ways of thinking about rationality whose significance could hardly be more profound.

Let me explain what I mean by this.

Western intellectual traditions have always tended to assume that humans' powers of reason exist, first and foremost, as ways of restraining our baser instincts. The assumption can already be found in Plato and Aristotle, and it was strongly reinforced when classical theories of the soul were adopted into Christianity and Islam. Yes, the argument went, we all have animalistic drives and passions, just as we have our powers of creativity and imagination, but these impulses are ultimately chaotic and antisocial. Reason—whether in the individual or the political community—exists to keep our lower nature in check, to repress, channel, and contain potentially violent energies in such a way that they do not lead to chaos and mutual destruction. It is a moral force. This is why, for instance, the word *polis*, the political community and place of rational order, is the same root that gives us both "politeness" and "police." As a result, too, there is always a lurking sense in this tradition that there must be something at least vaguely demonic about our powers of creativity.

The emergence of bureaucratic populism, as I've been describing it, corresponds to a complete reversal of this conception of rationality—to a new ideal, one most famously summed up by David Hume: that "reason is and ought only to be the slave of the passions."[130] Rationality, in this view, has nothing to do with morality. It is a purely technical affair—an instrument, a machine, a means of calculating how to most efficiently achieve goals that could not themselves be in any way assessed in rational terms. Reason cannot tell us what we should want. It can only tell us how best to get it.

In both versions, reason was somehow outside of creativity, desire, or the passions; however, in one, it acted to restrain such passions; in the other, to facilitate them.

The emerging field of economics might have developed this logic the furthest, but it is a logic that traces back at least as much to bureaucracy as to the market. (And one must remember, most economists are, and always have been, employed by large bureaucratic organizations of one sort or another.) The whole idea that one can make a strict division between means and ends, between facts and values, is a product of the bureaucratic mind-set, because bureaucracy is the first and only social institution that treats the means of doing things as entirely separate from what it is that's being done.[131] In this way, bureaucracy really has become embedded in the common sense of at least a very substantial part of the world's population for quite a long period of time.

But at the same time, it's not as if the older idea of rationality has ever entirely gone away. To the contrary: the two coexist, despite being almost completely contradictory—in constant friction. As a result, our very conception of rationality is strangely incoherent. It's entirely unclear what the word is supposed to mean. Sometimes it's a means, sometimes it's an end. Sometimes it has nothing to do with morality, sometimes it's the very essence of what's right and good. Sometimes it's a method for solving problems; other times, it is itself the solution to all possible problems.

II. Rationalism as a Form of Spirituality

This bizarre state of affairs is worth reflecting on, because it is at the very core of our conception of bureaucracy. On the one hand, we have the notion that bureaucratic systems are simply neutral social technologies. They are just ways of getting from A to B, and have no implications whatsoever for the rights and wrongs of the matter. I well remember a friend who attended the Woodrow Wilson School of Public and International Affairs at Princeton, a world-renowned training ground for top-level administrators, reporting to me with an almost shocked delight that he had just been obliged to sign up for a course in "value free ethics." On the face of it, this sounds absurd. But really the concept follows necessarily from this notion of the role of bureaucrats: that they are public servants, and it is the responsibility of servants to do their masters' bidding, no matter what that bidding is. Insofar as their master is something called "the public," however, this creates certain problems: how to figure out what, exactly, the public really wants them to do. This was what they taught budding functionaries in the "value free ethics" course: how, for example, in the case of planners designing a highway system, one might apply quantitative methods to determine the relative importance to the public of (a) getting to work on time, and (b) not being killed or maimed in a car accident (in economic jargon, their "revealed preferences" on the matter), and then set the speed limit accordingly.

On the other hand, in complete contradiction with this, there remains a modern incarnation of the earlier idea of rationality as moral order and therefore as an end in itself. Pretty much anyone with a utopian vision, whether Socialist, free market, or for that matter religious fundamentalist, dreams of creating a social order that will, unlike current arrangements, make some sort of coherent sense—and which will, therefore, represent the triumph of reason over chaos.[132] Needless to say, creating an effective bureaucracy always turns out to be the cornerstone of any such project.

Arguments about the role of "rationality" in politics almost invariably play fast and loose with these two contradictory ideas.

If one tries to go back to basic definitions, things don't get much better. In many ways they become considerably worse. There is no consensus amongst philosophers about what the word "rationality" even means. According to one tradition, for instance, rationality is the application of logic, of pure thought untempered by emotions; this pure, objective thought is then seen as the basis of scientific inquiry. This has attained a great deal of popular purchase, but there's a fundamental problem: scientific inquiry itself has proved it cannot possibly be true. Cognitive psychologists have demonstrated again and again that there is no such thing as pure thought divorced from emotions; a human being without emotions would not be able to think at all.[133]

Others prefer a more pragmatic approach, claiming merely that a rational argument can be defined as one that is both grounded in empirical reality, and logically coherent in form. The problem here is that these two criteria don't really have much to do with one another. One is about observation; the other is about reasoning.[134] What *do* they have in common? Mainly, it seems, that when someone makes an argument that is either delusional or incoherent, we are equally likely to write that person off as not right in the head. On one level, that's fair enough: we do call crazy people "irrational." But if so, calling someone, or an argument, "rational" is saying almost nothing. It's a very weak statement. You're just saying they are not obviously insane.

But the moment you turn it around, you realize that claiming one's own political positions are based on "rationality" is an extremely strong statement. In fact, it's extraordinarily arrogant, since it means that those who disagree with those positions are not just wrong, but crazy. Similarly, to say one wishes to create a "rational" social order implies that current social arrangements might as well have been designed by the inhabitants of a lunatic asylum. Now, surely, all of us have felt this way at one time or another. But if nothing else, it is an extraordinarily intolerant position, since it implies that one's opponents are not just wrong, but in a certain sense, wouldn't even know what it would mean to be right, unless, by some miracle, they could come around and accept the light of reason and decide to accept your own conceptual framework and point of view.

This tendency to enshrine rationality as a political virtue has had the perverse effect of encouraging those repelled by such pretentions, or by the people who profess them, to claim to reject rationality entirely, and embrace "irrationalism." Of course, if we simply take rationality in its minimal definition, any such position is absurd. You can't really make an argument against rationality, because for that argument to be convincing, it would itself have to be framed in rational terms. If one is willing to argue with another person at all, one must accept, at least on a tacit level, that arguments based in an accurate assessment of reality are better than ones that are not (that is, that any argument that proceeds from the assumption that all buildings are made of green cheese is not worth taking seriously), and that arguments that follow the laws of logic are better than those that violate then (i.e., that an argument that since the Mayor of Cincinnati is human, all humans are the Mayor of Cincinnati, can be similarly dismissed).

This is not the place to enter into all the logical traps and contradictions that result from this situation. I simply wish to ask how we ever got to this point at all. Here I think we have no choice but to go back to the very beginning, and look at the historical origins of the Western concept of "rationality" in the Greek cities of Southern Italy in the middle of the first millennium BC.

The first philosophical school to represent themselves as rationalists, and to treat rationality as a value in itself, were the Pythagoreans, who were simultaneously a philosophical and scientific school, and a kind of political cult or confraternity that managed, at one point or another, to take control of several Italian cities.[135] Their great intellectual discovery was that there was a formal similarity between the kind of mathematical ratios that could be observed in geometry, musical intervals, and the movements of the planets. The conclusion they reached was that the universe was, on some ultimate level at least, composed of numbers—a notion now largely remembered for the rather charming concept of the inaudible "music of the spheres." The cosmos, according to the Pythagoreans, was rational because it was ultimately an expression of the principles of number, pitch, and vibration, and when the human mind (or soul) exercised its powers of reason, it was simply participating in that larger rational order, the cosmic "world soul" that animated all.[136]

This was the picture of the universe Plato largely adopted in *Timaeus*, and it had enormous influence. By the first and second century of the Roman Empire, in fact, variations on the basic Pythagorean set of ideas had been adopted by pretty much all major philosophical schools—not just the Neoplatonists but the

Stoics and even, to some extent, the Epicureans. What's more, it formed the philosophical basis of what Hans Joas originally dubbed the emerging "cosmic religion" of late Antiquity, a fusion of elements of Greek cosmological speculation, Babylonian astrology, and Egyptian theology, often combined with strains of Jewish thought and various traditions of popular magic.[137] As Joas noted, this cosmic religion—which assumed that God, Reason, and the Cosmos were the same, and the higher faculties in humans were themselves a form of participation in this rational cosmic order—for all its grandeur, represented a kind of political retreat. The Pythagoreans, like most Greek philosophers, had been avid participants in the political life of the city, which they often sought to reconstitute on rational grounds. Under the Roman Empire, this was impossible. All political questions were now settled. A single—and apparently eternal—legal and bureaucratic order regulated public affairs; instead of aspiring to change this structure, intellectuals increasingly embraced outright mysticism, aspiring to find new ways to transcend earthly systems entirely, rising through the various planetary spheres, purging themselves of materiality, to the rarified sphere of pure reason, a divine realm of transcendent mathematical laws that governed time and motion and ultimately rendered them illusory. God did not impose these laws, He *was* those laws. Human reason, then, was simply the action of that divine principle within us. In this sense, rationality was not just a spiritual notion, it was mystical: a technique for achieving union with the divine.

This set of assumptions about the nature of rationality, absorbed into Christianity through Augustine, informs pretty much all Medieval philosophy as well, however difficult it was to reconcile with the notion of a transcendent willful Creator (and indeed, much Medieval philosophy was precisely concerned with arguing about different ways of reconciling them).

In many ways, all these assumptions are very much still with us. Take the notion, which we all learn as children and most of us accept as self-evident truth, that what sets humans apart from other animals is rationality (that we, as a species, "possess the faculty of reason.") This is very much a Medieval notion.[138] If you think about it, it also doesn't make a lot of sense. If "rationality" is just the ability to assess reality more or less as it is and to draw logical conclusions, then most animals are extremely rational. They solve problems all the time. Most might not be nearly as good at it as humans but there is no fundamental difference in kind. There are plenty of other faculties that would make much better candidates—ones that actually do seem to be unique to humans. One obvious choice would be imagination. Animals act in what seem like rational, calculating, goal-directed ways all the time, but it's harder to make a case that most of them engage in creating self-conscious fantasy worlds.[139] Hence the anthropologist Edmund Leach once remarked that what sets humans apart from animals is not that they possess an immortal soul, but rather, that they are capable of imagining that they have one.[140] But of course, if the soul is the seat of Reason, the divine element in Man, to say that humans are in possession of an immortal soul, and to say that they are rational creatures, is to say precisely the same thing.[141]

This conclusion inevitably followed from the logic of the Great Chain of Being, where all living creatures were ranked in a single hierarchy of increasing rationality according to their proximity to God, with humans placed at the top of the natural order, between animals and angels.

It's easy to see the grand cosmic hierarchies of late Antiquity, with their archons, planets, and gods, all operating under the unfolding of abstract rational laws, as simply images of the Roman legal bureaucratic order writ very, very large. The curious thing is how this ultimately bureaucratic picture of the cosmos was maintained for a thousand years after the Roman Empire had collapsed. Medieval and Renaissance theologians produced endless speculative tracts about angelic hierarchies that if anything represented the universe as more systematically bureaucratic than anything ancient philosophers had imagined:[142]

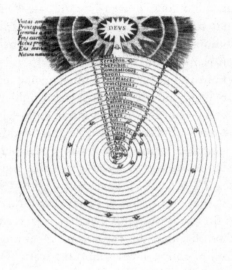

So, for instance, in the sixteenth century, Marsilio Ficino provided the following summary of the angelic hierarchy, drawing from the work of a fourth century Christian Neoplatonist whose real name has long since been forgotten, via the elaborations of Saint Thomas Aquinas and Dante:

Seraphim speculate on the order and providence of God.

Cherubim speculate on the essence and form of God.

Thrones also speculate, though some descend to works.

Dominions, like architects, design what the rest execute.

Virtues execute, and move the heavens, and concur for the working of miracles as God's instruments.

Powers watch that the order of divine governance is not interrupted and some of them descend to human things.

Principalities care for public affairs, nations, princes, magistrates.
Archangels direct the divine cult and look after sacred things.
Angels look after smaller affairs and take charge of individuals as their guardian angels.[143]

Angels are "celestial intelligences" ranked in order from those who engage in pure thought to those who concern themselves with the actual governance of worldly affairs. At a time when actual governance in Europe was as broken and fragmented as it could possibly be, its intellectuals were busying themselves arguing about the exact division of powers within a single, grand, unified, imaginary system of cosmic administration.

Nowadays, the grand synthesis of late Antiquity, revived by Renaissance alchemists and mages like Ficino, Agrippa, and Giordano Bruno (and in the process infused with Cabala, and other spiritual traditions), survives largely as the basis of Western ceremonial magic. The Enlightenment is supposed to have marked a fundamental break with it. But the fundamental structure of assumptions did not really change. The appeal to rationality in Descartes and his successors remains a fundamentally spiritual, even mystical, commitment, that the mathematical or math-like abstractions that are assumed to be the essence of thought, are also the ordering principles that regulate nature—and this remained true whether they were identified with God, or seen as the ultimate proof of God's nonexistence.

It is hard to think this way because of course we have by now come to identify the soul not with reason, but with everything that makes us unique, idiosyncratic, or imaginative. But this view is a product of the Romantic era, and one that, at the time, marked a near total break from earlier conceptions. Again, this is hardly the place to go into detail concerning the arguments about the relation between reason, imagination, and desire that came out of it, but it does help us understand why it is that the notion of "rationality," and particularly, of bureaucratic rationality, never seems to be able to contain itself to simple questions of deductive reasoning, or even technical efficiency, but almost invariably ends up trying to turn itself into some grandiose cosmological scheme.

III. On the Bureaucratization of the Antibureaucratic Fantasy

> "The point when I decided I just didn't care about that [academic] job any more was when I stopped turning off the sound on my computer games during office hours. There'd be some student waiting outside for feedback on his assignment and I was like, 'Wait, just let me finish killing this dwarf and I'll get back to you.' "
> —academic friend (name withheld for obvious reasons)

The fact that modern science is to some degree founded on spiritual commitments, of course, in no way implies that its findings are not true. But I think it does suggest that we might do well to step back and think very carefully the moment whenever someone claims to be trying to create a more rational social order (especially, when they could have just as easily described that social order as reasonable, more decent, less violent, or more just.)

We have seen how the European Middle Ages produced the vision of a virtual celestial bureaucracy, based distantly on that of ancient Rome,[144] which was seen as the embodiment of cosmic rationality, in a time when real bureaucracy was particularly thin on the ground. Over time, of course, it grew considerably less so. But as new bureaucratic states did emerge, and particularly as bureaucratic rationality became the predominant principle of governance in eighteenth and nineteenth century Europe and America, we witness a kind of countermovement: the rise of an equally fantastic vision of the Middle Ages, full of princes, knights, faeries, dragons, sorcerers, and unicorns; and eventually, hobbits, dwarves, and orcs. In most important ways, this world is explicitly antibureaucratic: that is, it evinces an explicit rejection of virtually all the core values of bureaucracy.

In the last essay, I observed that science fiction has come to assemble a fairly standardized list of future inventions—from teleportation to warp drive—and to deploy them so regularly—not just in literature but in games, TV shows, comics, and similar material—such that pretty much any teenager in Canada, Norway, or Japan can be expected to know what they are. The same could be said of the basic constituents of this fantasy literature, which, though obviously varying from text to text, movie to movie, nonetheless center on a remarkably consistent basic set of character types, systems of government (mostly magical), technologies, beasts, and cultural traditions. Needless to say it bears almost no resemblance, on any level, to what the Middle Ages were really like. But to understand the real historical origins of this world requires going much further back in time.

We are used to speaking of "the state" as a single entity but actually, I think, modern states are better seen as the confluence of three different elements, whose historical origins are quite distinct, have no intrinsic relation with one another, and may already be in the process of finally drifting apart.

I will call these sovereignty, administration, and politics.

Sovereignty is usually taken to be the defining feature of the state: a sovereign state is one whose ruler claims a monopoly over the legitimate use of violence within a given territory. Most governments in the ancient world, or for that matter the Middle Ages, never claimed sovereignty in this sense. Nor would it have occurred to them to do so: this was the logic of conquering empires, not of any sort of civilized community.

The second principle is administration, which can and often does exist without any single center of power to enforce its decisions. It could also, of course, simply be referred to as bureaucracy. In fact, the most recent archeological evidence from Mesopotamia indicates that bureaucratic techniques emerged not just before sovereign states, but even before the existence of the first cities. They were not invented to manage scale, as ways of organizing societies that became too big for face-to-face interaction. Rather, they seem to have been what encouraged people to assemble in such large communities to begin with. At least, this is what the record seems to show. The standardization of products, storage, certification, record-keeping, redistribution, and accounting all seem to have emerged in small towns along the Tigris and Euphrates and its tributaries in the fifth millennium BCE, a thousand years before the "urban revolution."[145] We don't really know how or why; we don't even know whether there were actual bureaucrats (in the sense of a distinct class of trained officeholders) or whether we are simply talking about the emergence of bureaucratic techniques. But by the time historical records do kick in there certainly are: we find vast temple and palace complexes with a hierarchy of trained scribes carefully registering and allocating resources of every sort.

We can refer to the third principle as "politics" if one takes that word in what might be termed its maximal sense. Obviously, there is a minimal sense in which anything people do can be said to have a political aspect, insofar it involves jockeying for power. But there are only some social systems in which politics in this sense becomes a spectator sport in its own right: where powerful figures engage in constant public contests with one another as a way of rallying followers and gathering support. We now think of this as an aspect of democratic systems of government, but for most of human history, it was seen as more of an aristocratic phenomenon. One need only think of the heroes of Homeric, or for that matter Germanic or Celtic or Hindu epics, who are constantly engaged in boasting, dueling, vying to organize the most splendid feasts or most magnificent sacrifices, or to outdo one another with the giving of extravagant gifts.[146] Such "heroic" social orders, as they've been called, represent the quintessence of the political. They recognize no principle of sovereignty, but create no system of administration either; sometimes there is a high king but usually he has very limited power, or is a pure figurehead; real power fluctuates continually as charismatic aristocrats assemble bands of followers, the most successful poaching off their rivals' retinues, while others crash magnificently, or decline into brooding obscurity.

Politics in this sense has always been an essentially aristocratic phenomenon. (There is a reason why the U.S. Senate, for example, is inhabited entirely by millionaires.) This is why for most of European history, elections were assumed to be not a democratic, but an aristocratic mode of selecting public officials. "Aristocracy" after all literally means "rule by the best," and elections were seen as meaning that the only role of ordinary citizens was to decide which, among the "best" citizens, was to be considered best of all, in much the same way as a Homeric retainer, or for that matter, a Mongol horseman might switch allegiance to some new charismatic war-leader. (The democratic way of selecting officials, at least from Greek times onwards, was in contrast assumed to be sortition, whereby ordinary citizens were chosen for posts by random lottery.)

What does all this have to do with dragons and wizards? Quite a lot, actually. Because all evidence we have suggests that such heroic orders did not just emerge spontaneously, alongside bureaucratic societies; they emerged in a kind of symbiotic rivalry with them; and they were remembered long after because they embodied a rejection of everything bureaucracy was supposed to be about.

Here again I must return to archeology, and particularly to the work of my friend David Wengrow on the ancient Middle East.[147] The actual origins of what I'm calling "heroic societies" seem to lie on the hills, mountains, deserts, or steppes on the fringes of the great commercial-bureaucratic societies of Mesopotamia, Egypt, and the Indus Valley, and then, later, empires like Rome, Persia, or China. Economically, these societies were in many ways linked to the urban centers. They tended to supply the cities with raw materials, and to import all sorts of fabulous wealth and treasures from urban workshops. However, from quite early on, both sides also came to define themselves as everything the other one was not. Urbanites came to define civilization as not acting like a barbarian; the barbarians, in turn, ended up creating social orders that took the key values of commercial-bureaucratic civilization and turned them precisely on their heads. Where one created and treasured literary masterworks, the other rejected the use of writing, but celebrated bards who could extemporize works of epic verse afresh each time. Where one carefully stored and registered items of material value, the other sponsored vast potlatch-like festivals in which priceless treasures were either distributed to followers or rivals as a gesture of contempt towards the pretentions of material wealth, or even abandoned, set on fire, or thrown into the sea. Where one developed a self-effacing bureaucracy that offered predictable stability, the other organized public life around charismatic egomaniacs in a never-ending struggle for supremacy.

The original heroic societies emerged in the Bronze Age, and by the time of Plato, or Confucius, they must have been only very distant memories. Yet nonetheless, those memories remained vivid. Almost all the great literary traditions begin with heroic epics that are, essentially, later fanciful reconstructions of what those Bronze Age heroic societies must have been like. We might well ask why this happened. Why did the very sorts of people ridiculed as ignorant barbarians by one civilization of urbanites so often become reimagined as distant heroic ancestors of a later one? Why were stories of their exploits told and retold, in many cases, for thousands of years?

I think part of the answer is that heroic societies are, effectively, social orders designed to generate stories. This takes us back to questions about the very nature of politics. One might well argue that political action—and this is true even on the micro-level—is a matter of acting in a way that will influence other people at least partially by their hearing or finding out about it.[148] Everyday politics—whether in a rural village or corporate office—has everything to do with the manufacture of official narratives, rumors, and accounts. It stands to reason that heroic societies, which turned political self-aggrandizement into an art form, would also have been organized in such a way as to become vast engines for the generation of stories. Everything was turned into a platform for some sort of contest, some narrative of perseverance, treachery, revenge, impossible challenges, epic quests, or magnificent acts of self-sacrifice. This is why poets were so important. The whole point of life was to do things that other people might wish to sing about. Even from the beginning, the inhabitants of bureaucratic societies like Egypt or Babylonia could not help develop a certain fascination with the barbarian hinterlands, which quickly became murky lands full of monsters and strange magical powers. And of course, dramatic stories about violent barbarians became even more compelling in ages when actual violent barbarians were no longer much around.

Barbarians always exist in a symbiotic relation to bureaucratic civilization. Over the course of Eurasian history, the pattern recurred again and again. Heroic societies formed at the fringes of empire; often (like the Germanic societies that formed on the fringes of the Roman Imperium, or the Northern Barbarians across the Great Wall from China, or the Huns that spent time on the borders of both) they would even sweep in and overwhelm those empires; in such cases, though, they would usually quickly dissolve away into legend.[149]

Modern fantasy literature might be said to have its origins in late chivalric romances like Amadis of Gaul or Orlando Furioso, but the genre really takes recognizable form in the Victorian Age, around the same time as the height of popular enthusiasm for the postal service. It is set in a very peculiar sort of time. In a way, this time is just a modern version of the "once upon a time" of fairy tales, which was both a kind of floating, unspecified past, and another dimension existing simultaneously with our own (as many stories confirm, there are, still, portals between our world and fairyland, a land where time and space work entirely differently). But the temper of such fantasy literature is not at all the same. Fairy tales reflect a women's and children's perspective on Medieval and Early Modern society; their heroes are more likely to be milkmaids and crafty cobblers' sons than courtiers and princes; in what has to be come to known as fantasy literature, in contrast, this "once upon a time" has been transformed entirely by a massive infusion of heroic epic. By "fantasy literature," here, I am referring above all to what's sometimes called the "sword and sorcery" genre, whose origins lie in late Victorian figures like George MacDonald and Lord Dunsany, and whose most shining avatars remain J.R.R. Tolkien, C. S. Lewis, and Ursula K. Le Guin.[150] It's within this tradition that the standard set of characters (warrior, cleric, mage), types of spells, types of monstrous creature, etc., formed: a standard repertoire that recurs, in endless idiosyncratic variations, in hundreds if not thousands of works of contemporary fiction.

These books are not just appealing because they create endless daydream material for the inhabitants of bureaucratic societies. Above all, they appeal because they continue to provide a systematic negation of everything bureaucracy stands for. Just as Medieval clerics and magicians liked to fantasize about a radiant celestial administrative system, so do we, now, fantasize about the adventures of Medieval clerics and mages, existing in a world in which every aspect of bureaucratic existence has been carefully stripped away.

Why do we do so? Well, the simplest explanation is that we are dealing with a form of ideological inoculation. Historically, one of the most effective ways for a system of authority to tout its virtues is not to speak of them directly, but to create a particularly vivid image of their absolute negation—of what it claims life would be like in the total absence of, say, patriarchal authority, or capitalism, or the state. As an ideological ploy, the trick works best when the image is on some level, profoundly appealing.[151] One is first drawn in to the vision of the alternative world, experiences a kind of vicarious thrill imagining it—only to ultimately recoil in horror at the implications of one's own desires.

Roman games provide an excellent example. Until the coming of the empire, most Mediterranean cities had had some form of self-governance, with public assemblies debating matters of public concern. In democracies, even legal cases were tried by public juries consisting of hundreds of citizens. Under the Empire, of course, these were stripped of all authority, and eventually disappeared. Instead, the main occasion when large numbers of citizens assembled in public was at the Coliseum or the Circus, for chariot races or gladiatorial games, or to watch criminals be torn to pieces by wild animals. Insofar as those citizens had any experience of voting for anything, it was to put their thumbs up or down over the question of whether some defeated gladiator would be put to death.

In other words, the Empire not only justified itself largely by imposing a uniform system of law over its subjects, it also made a point of encouraging those subjects to form organized lynch mobs (the games were often sponsored by the very magistrates who presided over the courts), as if to say, "Democracy? Now you know where that will lead." This was so effective that for the next two thousand years, warnings about the perils of democracy—and almost all educated Europeans for most of this period were staunchly opposed to democracy—insisted that "the people" in such a system would inevitably end up behaving like the mob at the Roman circus: riven by violent factionalism, careening irrationally between extremes of mercy and cruelty, between blindly following charismatic idols and destroying them again. And to this day, almost all educated people still feel that, even if they are willing to grudgingly accept a few democratic elements in some aspects of society, they need to be kept entirely separate from the administration of justice and the law.

I don't want to leave the reader with the impression that all such institutions are simply tricks set up by the ruling classes to manipulate the masses. Or that even insofar as they are, they can't backfire. The Roman circuses might have been unusually effective—they were truly one of the most brilliant antidemocratic institutions ever created—but Medieval carnivals, to take one famous example, with their drunken celebration of gluttony, revolt, and sexuality, were clearly contested ground. Its wealthier patrons no doubt saw carnival as a way of warning the masses of the horrors that might ensue were the hierarchical orders of society to dissolve, but it's obvious many of the common folk who were responsible for actually organizing and putting on the bulk of the celebrations did not see this prospect as nearly so horrible (indeed, carnivals often became the occasion for actual revolts).[152]

No doubt fantasy literature, too, is contested ground.

Its authors themselves were often unsure about the political implications of their work. J.R.R. Tolkien for example once remarked that politically, he was either an anarchist, or an "unconstitutional" monarchist—it seems he could never make up his mind quite which.[153] The one thing both positions have in common of course is that they are both profoundly anti-bureaucratic. This is true of almost all fantasy literature: only evil people maintain systems of administration. In fact, one could survey the key features of fantasy literature point by point and see each as a precise negation of some aspect of bureaucracy:

- Fantasy worlds tend to be marked by an absolute division of good and evil (or at best, ambiguous good and absolute evil), implying the existence of forces between which war is the only possible relationship. In fact, when it comes to conflict with such absolute villains, even war tends to be absolute, unmediated by custom, etiquette, or chivalry. This is in striking contrast either with heroic or Medieval societies, where organized violence—an aristocratic pastime—tended more often to resemble a ritualized game in which honor was everything. The principle of absolute evil seems to exist to negate **the bureaucratic principle of value-free rule-bound neutrality**, the fact that principles such as good and evil are utterly alien to administrative orders of any kind. Fantasy worlds create values so absolute it is simply impossible to be value-free.

- The existence in fantasy universes of demi-human species—gnomes, drow, trolls, and so on—which are fundamentally human, but absolutely impossible to integrate under the same larger social, legal, or political order, creates a world where racism is actually true. Often the language of race is directly invoked: "the race of elves," "the race of dwarves," and so on. Even when it is not, these are worlds where there actually *are* different stocks of humanoid creatures who can speak, build houses, cultivate food, create art and rituals, that is, who look and act basically like humans, but who nonetheless have profoundly different moral and intellectual qualities. This is among other things the absolute negation of the **bureaucratic principle of indifference,** that the rules are the same for everyone, that it shouldn't matter who your parents are, that everyone must be treated equally before the law. If some people are orcs and others are pixies, equal treatment is ipso facto inconceivable.

- Legitimate power in fantasy worlds tends to be based on pure charisma, or the memory of past charisma. Aragorn never coerces anyone to follow him. Neither does Aslan. Or Ged. Only bad guys ever create a state-like apparatus, and when they do, that apparatus is one of pure coercion. What's more, charismatic authority that is not constantly renewed tends to wither and become corrupt (e.g., Denethor, Gormenghast), or develop into creepy, Gothic, undead forms. Since the very possibility of real, vital, charismatic authority is always founded on war, this means legitimate authority is itself impossible without constant physical insecurity. In other words, the political ideal of modern "democratic" Republics, in which politicians constantly vie for followers, is maintained—hardly surprisingly, since as I emphasized this was always the heroic/aristocratic element in such Republics anyway—but it is entirely divorced both from principles of sovereignty, and above all, from the **regularity and predictability of bureaucratic procedures, and the routinization of force, which in a bureaucratic order is**

seen as legitimate only insofar as it is used to uphold that principle of regularity. In short, in fantasy worlds, truly legitimate figures of authority are usually violent, but they don't employ violence to enforce the rules.

- As a corollary: in fantasy, as in heroic societies, political life is largely about the creation of stories. Narratives are embedded inside narratives; the storyline of a typical fantasy is often itself about the process of telling stories, interpreting stories, and creating material for new ones. This is in dramatic contrast with the **mechanical nature of bureaucratic operations**. Administrative procedures are very much *not* about the creation of stories; in a bureaucratic setting, stories appear when something goes wrong. When things run smoothly, there's no narrative arc of any sort at all.

- What's more, protagonists are endlessly engaging with riddles in ancient languages, obscure myths and prophecies, maps with runic puzzles and the like. Bureaucratic procedures in contrast are based on a **principle of transparency**. The rules are supposed to be clear, uniformly expressed, and accessible to all. As we all know, this is rarely actually the case. But it is supposed to be true in principle. For most of us, administrative forms are at least as obscure as elvish riddles that only become visible at certain phases of the moon. But they are not supposed to be. In fact, one of the most infuriating bureaucratic tactics is to disguise information through a false pretense of transparency: for instance, to bury a key piece of information in a flurry of departmental emails—so many that no one could possibly read all of them. When we complain that we were not informed of a new policy or responsibility, the bureaucrats triumphantly produce the date (usually months in the past) and details of the documents where the new rules were listed.[154] Compared to this, there is certainly a kind of pleasure in the fantasy materials: puzzles actually are puzzles, they are supposed to be puzzles, and there is no officious person who will show up to lecture you on how this is all perfectly transparent and simple and there's obviously something wrong with you for not having immediately figured it out.

As the last example makes clear, when we discuss these constants, we are speaking of a certain abstract ideal of how bureaucratic systems should work, not the way they actually do. In reality, bureaucracies are rarely neutral; they are almost always dominated by or favor certain privileged groups (often racial groups) over others; and they invariably end up giving administrators enormous individual personal power by producing rules so complex and contradictory that they cannot possibly be followed as they stand. Yet in the real world, all these departures from bureaucratic principle are experienced as abuses. In fantasy worlds, they are experienced as virtues.

Still, those virtues are clearly intended to be fleeting. Fantasyland is a thrilling place to visit. Few of us would really want to live there. But if I am right that—whatever the authors' intentions—such literature largely ends up operating in such a way as to cause readers to question the ultimate implications of their own suspicions of bureaucratic existence, this is precisely the point.

Fantasy literature then, is largely an attempt to imagine a world utterly purged of bureaucracy, which readers enjoy both as a form of vicarious escapism and as reassurance that ultimately, a boring, administered world is probably preferable to any imaginable alternative.

Still, bureaucracy and bureaucratic principles are not entirely absent from such worlds. They creep in from several directions.

For one thing, the old imaginary cosmic administration of the Middle Ages is not entirely negated in most fantasy worlds. This is because these are almost invariably worlds where, though technology is limited to the wind and water mill level, magic actually works. And the type of magic that appears in the stories tends most often to be drawn from the Western ceremonial magic tradition that runs from ancient theurgists like Iamblichus to Victorian mages like MacGregor Mathers, full of demons invoked in magic circles, chants, spells, robes, talismans, scrolls, and wands. So the cosmic hierarchies, the complex logical orders of spells, orders, powers, influences, celestial spheres with their different powers and denominations and areas of administrative responsibility: all these tend to be preserved, in one form or another, as at least one hidden potential form of power within the fabric of the antibureaucratic universe itself. True, in the earliest, and most resolutely antibureaucratic universes, sorcerers are either evil (Zukala in *Conan the Barbarian* or a million similar pulp fiction villains, or even Michael Moorcock's amoral Elric),[155] or, if they are good, the technical aspect of their art is minimized (Gandalf's power seems to be an extension of his personal charisma rather than deriving from arcane knowledge of spells). But as time moved on from there to *The Wizard of Earthsea* to *Harry Potter*, magic—and magical knowledge—took more and more a central place. And of course by the time we get to Harry Potter, we have also traveled all the way from expressly heroic realms like Cimmeria or Elfland or Hyperborea, to an antibureaucratic narrative that's set *within* a classic bureaucratic institution: a British boarding school, in a magical world that is nonetheless replete with banks, Wizard Boards, Commissions of Enquiry, and even prisons. In the Harry Potter books, that's exactly the joke: let's take the most drab, stuffy, institutions responsible for the disenchantment of the world, and try to concoct the most wildly enchanted versions of them we can possibly imagine.

How could this have happened? Well, one reason is that genres of popular fiction are increasingly not confined to books. (This is especially true if children or adolescents are in any way involved.) Nor do they just extend into movies and television series: there are also everything from board games to models, puzzles, and action figures, multiple forms of fan literature, zines, fan art, video and computer games. In the case of the fantasy genre, it's impossible to understand the later direction of the literature without first of all understanding the rise, in the late seventies, of the role-playing game Dungeons & Dragons, which allowed hundreds of thousands of teenagers across the world to effectively improvise their own fantasy worlds and fantasy adventures, as if they were collectively writing the story or script of their own adventures in real time.

D&D, as its aficionados call it, is on one level the most free-form game imaginable, since the characters are allowed to do absolutely anything, within the confines of the world created by the Dungeon Master, with his books, maps, and tables and preset towns, castles, dungeons, wilderness. In many ways it's actually quite anarchistic, since unlike classic war games where one commands armies, we have what anarchists would call an "affinity group," a band of individuals cooperating with a common purpose (a quest, or simply the desire to accumulate treasure and experience), with complementary abilities (fighter, cleric, magic-user, thief . . .), but no explicit chain of command. So the social relations are the very opposite of impersonal bureaucratic hierarchies. However, in another sense, D&D represents the ultimate bureaucratization of antibureaucratic fantasy. There are catalogs for everything: types of monsters (stone giants, ice giants, fire giants . . .), each with carefully tabulated powers and average number of hit points (how hard it is to kill them); human abilities (strength, intelligence, wisdom, dexterity, constitution . . .); lists of spells available at different levels of capacity (magic missile, fireball, passwall . . .); types of gods or demons; effectiveness of different sorts of armor and weapons; even moral character (one can be lawful, neutral, or chaotic; good, neutral, or evil; combining these produces nine possible basic moral types . . .). The books are distantly evocative of Medieval bestiaries and grimoires. But they are largely composed of statistics. All important qualities can be reduced to number. It's also true that in actual play, there are no rules; the books are just guidelines; the Dungeon Master can (indeed really ought to) play around with them, inventing new spells, monsters, and a thousand variations on existing ones. Every Dungeon Master's universe is different. The numbers are in a sense a platform for crazy feats of the imagination, themselves a kind of poetic technology.

Still, the introduction of numbers, the standardization of types of character, ability, monster, treasure, spell, the concept of ability scores and hit-points, had profound effects when one moved from the world of 6-, 8-, 12- and 20-sided dice to one of digital interfaces. Computer games could turn fantasy into an almost entirely bureaucratic procedure: accumulation of points, the raising of levels, and so on. There was a return to the command of armies. This in turn set off a move in the other direction, by introducing role-playing back into the computer games (Elfquest, World of Warcraft . . .), in a constant weaving back and forth of the imperatives of poetic and bureaucratic technology. But in doing so, these games ultimately reinforce the sense that we live in a universe where accounting procedures define the very fabric of reality, where even the most absolute negation of the administered world we're currently trapped in can only end up being yet another version of the exact same thing.

IV. The Utopia of Rules

One reason I have seen fit to spend so much time on fantasy worlds is because the topic opens up some fundamental questions about the nature of play, games, and freedom—all of which, I believe, lie at the core of bureaucracy's covert appeal. One the one hand, a bureaucracy is anything but playful. Mechanistic and impersonal, it would appear to represent the negation of any possibility of playfulness. On the other hand, being trapped in a bureaucratic runaround feels very much like being caught inside some kind of horrific game.

Bureaucracies create games—they're just games that are in no sense fun. But it might be useful here to think more carefully about what games really are, and what it is that makes them fun in the first place. First of all, what is the relationship between play and games? We play games. So does that mean play and games are really the same thing? It's certainly true that the English language is somewhat unusual for even making the distinction between the two—in most languages, the same word covers both. (This is true even of most European languages, as with the French *jeu* or German *spiele*.) But on another level they seem to be opposites, as one suggests free-form creativity; the other, rules.

The great Dutch sociologist Johann Huizinga wrote a book called *Homo Ludens* that is ostensibly a theory of play. In fact, the book makes for a very bad theory of play, but it's not at all a bad theory of games.[156] According to Huizinga, games have certain common features. First, they are clearly bounded in time and space, and thereby framed off from ordinary life. There is a field, a board, a starting pistol, a finish line. Within that time/space, certain people are designated as players. There are also rules, which define precisely what those players can and cannot do. Finally, there is always some clear idea of the stakes, of what the players have to do to win the game. And, critically:

that's all there is. Any place, person, action, that falls outside that framework is extraneous; it doesn't matter; it's not part of the game. Another way to put this would be to say that games are pure rule-governed action.

It seems to me this is important, because this precisely why games are fun. In almost any other aspect of human existence, all these things are ambiguous. Think of a family quarrel, or a workplace rivalry. Who is or is not a party to it, what's fair, when it began and when it's over, what it even means to say you won—it's all extremely difficult to say. The hardest thing of all is to understand the rules. In almost any situation we find ourselves in, there *are* rules—even in casual conversation, there are tacit rules of who can speak in what order, pacing, tone, deference, appropriate and inappropriate topics, when you can smile, what sort of humor is allowable, what you should be doing with your eyes, and a million other things besides. These rules are rarely explicit, and usually there are many conflicting ones that could, possibly, be brought to bear at any given moment. So we are always doing the difficult work of negotiating between them, and trying to predict how others will do the same. Games allow us our only real experience of a situation where all this ambiguity is swept away. Everyone knows exactly what the rules are. And not only that, people actually *do* follow them. And by following them, it is even possible to win! This— along with the fact that unlike in real life, one has submitted oneself to the rules completely voluntarily—is the source of the pleasure.

Games, then, are a kind of utopia of rules.

This is also how we can understand the real difference between games and play. True, one can play a game; but to speak of "play" does not necessarily imply the existence of rules at all.[157] Play can be purely improvisational. One could simply be playing around. In this sense, play in its pure form, as distinct from games, implies a pure expression of creative energy. In fact, if it were possible to come up with a workable definition of "play" (this is notoriously difficult) it would have to be something along these lines: play can be said to be present when the free expression of creative energies becomes an end in itself. It is freedom for its own sake. But this also makes play in a certain sense a higher-level concept than games: play can create games, it can generate rules—in fact, it inevitably does produce at least tacit ones, since sheer random playing around soon becomes boring—but therefore by definition play cannot itself be intrinsically rule-bound. This is all the more true when play becomes social. Studies of children's play, for example, inevitably discover that children playing imaginary games spend at least as much time arguing about the rules than they do actually playing them. Such arguments become a form of play in themselves.[158]

On one level, all this is obvious: we are just talking about the emergence of form. Freedom has to be in tension with something, or it's just randomness. This suggests that the absolute pure form of play, one that really is absolutely untrammeled by rules of any sort (other than those it itself generates and can set aside at any instance) itself can exist only in our imagination, as an aspect of those divine powers that generate the cosmos.

Here's a quote from Indian philosopher of science Shiv Visvanathan:

> A game is a bounded, specific way of problem solving.
> Play is more cosmic and open-ended. Gods play, but
> man unfortunately is a gaming individual. A game has
> a predictable resolution, play may not. Play allows for
> emergence, novelty, surprise.[159]

All true. But there is also something potentially terrifying about play for just this reason. Because this open-ended creativity is also what allows it to be randomly destructive. Cats play with mice. Pulling the wings off flies is also a form of play.

Playful gods are rarely ones any sane person would desire to encounter.

Let me put forth a suggestion, then.

What ultimately lies behind the appeal of bureaucracy is fear of play.

For the social theorist, there is one obvious analogy to play as a principle that generates rules, but is not itself bound by them. This is the principle of sovereignty. The reader will remember sovereignty was one of the three principles—along with administration and politics—that ultimately came together in our current notion of "the state." The term "sovereignty" is mostly used in political theory nowadays as a synonym for "independence" or "autonomy"—the right of a government to do what it likes within its own borders—but it originally emerged from very specific European debates about the power of kings. Basically, the question was: is it possible to say that the supreme ruler of a kingdom is in any sense bound by its laws?

Those who argued that sovereigns were not bound by those laws drew an analogy with divine power. God is the creator, and ultimate enforcer, of any system of cosmic morality. But in order to create a system, one must be prior to it; for this reason God himself cannot be bound by moral laws. This is not at all an unusual conclusion. In Madagascar, proverbial wisdom was quite explicit about this: God was represented as both the ultimate judge—watching from on high and punishing transgressions—and simultaneously, as a completely arbitrary figure tossing lightning bolts and blasting mortals for no reason whatsoever. Occasional African kings tried to make themselves human embodiments of this absolute principle: the most famous example was the Kabaka of the Ganda kingdom. When he met with English visitors who tried to impress him by presenting him with some new efficient English rifle, he would, in turn, impress *them* by testing the rifle out on random subjects on the street. (He was also known to execute his wives for sneezing.) Yet at the same time, the Kabaka's legitimacy, as monarch, lay above all in his reputation for imposing impartial justice in his capacity as the kingdom's highest court judge. Again, the two were seen as connected: since the King could do (or take) absolutely anything he wanted, he also could not be bribed, so he really had no reason *not* to be impartial. The Ganda kingdom was unusual in taking the principle to such extremes (and it should be noted that in Africa, kings who did take things this far almost invariably came to a bad end eventually), but still, there is a direct line of continuity between this absolute conception of transcendent sovereignty and, say, Carl Schmitt's "Political Theology," which argues that in modern states, sovereign power is ultimately the power to set aside the laws.[160]

Sovereignty in this sense is ultimately identical to play as the generative principle that produces games; but if so, it is also play in its most terrifying, cosmic form. Some have called this the notion of "top-down" play, a concept that seems to be most explicitly developed in Indian theology, where the cosmos itself is essentially the play of the divine forces.[161] But as Brian Sutton-Smith notes in his book *The Ambiguity of Play*, this was the dominant view throughout the ancient world, where human beings were the playthings of destiny and fate; the exemplary *human* game, in such a universe, is gambling, where we willingly submit ourselves to the random whims of the gods.[162]

In such a universe, freedom really is a zero-sum game. The freedom of gods or kings is the measure of human slavery.

It shouldn't be hard to see where all this is going. Modern states are based on a principle of popular sovereignty. Ultimately, the divine power of kings is in the hands of an entity called "the people." In practice, though, it's increasingly unclear what popular sovereignty in that sense is even supposed to mean. Max Weber famously pointed out that a sovereign state's institutional representatives maintain a monopoly on the right of violence within the state's territory.[163] Normally, this violence can only be exercised by certain duly authorized officials (soldiers, police, jailers), or those authorized by such officials (airport security, private guards . . .), and only in a manner explicitly designated by law. But ultimately, sovereign power really is, still, the right to brush such legalities aside, or to make them up as one goes along.[164] The United States might call itself "a country of laws, not men," but as we have learned in recent years, American presidents can order torture, assassinations, domestic surveillance programs, even set up extra-legal zones like Guantanamo where they can treat prisoners pretty much any way they choose to. Even on the lowest levels, those who enforce the law are not really subject to it. It's extraordinary difficult, for instance, for a police officer to do *anything* to an American citizen that would lead to that officer being convicted of a crime.[165]

Brian Sutton-Smith argues that in the contemporary world the older, "top-down" view of play, what some have called "dark play," no longer really holds sway. Since the Romantic era, it has been largely replaced by a whole host of more cheerful bottom-up rhetorics that see play variously as subversive, or educational, or imaginative. No doubt all this is true. But it seems to me that the older conception has not vanished entirely.[166] If nothing else, it is preserved on a political level, where every arbitrary act of power tends to reinforce a feeling that it's not power, but arbitrariness—that is, freedom itself—that is the problem.[167]

This is, indeed, almost precisely what has happened wherever the republican form of government (now largely mislabeled "democracy") has become the norm. The legal order, and hence the zones where state violence is the ultimate enforcer of the rules, has expanded to define and regulate almost every possible aspect of human activity. Thus, as I've said earlier, we end up with regulations prescribing everything from where one can serve or consume different sorts of beverages, how one can work, when one can and can't walk off from work, to the size of advertisements visible from the street. The threat of force invades practically every aspect of our existence, in ways that would have simply been inconceivable under the rule of Elagabalus, Genghis Khan or Suleiman the Magnificent.

I've already written about this invasion of regulation, and violence, into every aspect of our lives. What I want to argue here is that this imperative ultimately derives from a tacit cosmology in which the play principle (and by extension, creativity) is itself seen as frightening, while game-like behavior is celebrated as transparent and predictable, and where as a result, the advance of all these rules and regulations is itself experienced as a kind of freedom.

This occurs even in contexts where the threat of state violence is maximally far away. A good example is the management of academic departments. As I've discussed, anthropologists are notoriously reluctant to turn their tools of analysis on their own institutional environments, but there are exceptions, and one excellent one is Marilyn Strathern's analysis of what in the UK has come to be known as "audit culture." The basic idea behind audit culture is that in the absence of clear, "transparent" criteria to understand how people are going about their jobs, academia simply becomes a feudal system based on arbitrary personal authority. On the surface, it's hard to argue with this. Who could be against transparency? Strathern was head of the anthropology department at Cambridge when these reforms were imposed, and in her book *Audit Cultures*, she documented the actual consequences of this kind of bureaucratization.[168] Cambridge was in its own way the quintessential feudal institution, with an endless accretion of customs and traditions, and anthropology, though a relatively new department, had its own traditional ways of going about everything that no one could entirely articulate; indeed, that no one completely understood. But in order to become "transparent" to the administration, they had to start articulating them; in practice, what this meant was that they had to take what had always been a subtle, nuanced form of procedures and turn them into an explicit set of rules. In effect, they had to turn custom into a kind of board game. Faced with such demands, everyone's first impulse was just to say, "Well, sure, we'll just write that for the authorities and proceed as we always have." But in practice this quickly becomes impossible, because the moment any conflicts crop up, both parties will automatically appeal to the rule-book.

Such reforms may aim to eliminate arbitrary personal authority, but of course they never actually do. Personal authority just jumps up a level, and becomes the ability to set the rules aside in specific cases (a sort of miniature version of sovereign power again). However, in practice, the fact that the reforms do not in any sense achieve their stated goals doesn't have the effect of undermining their legitimacy. Instead, the effect is quite the opposite, since anyone who objects to such personalized power can only do so by demanding even more rules and even more "transparency." Suddenly, freedom and justice really do become a matter of reducing everything to a game.

If we think about it, this sort of thing happens all the time— and even in contexts that have nothing to do with arbitrary personal authority. The most obvious example is language. Call it the grammar-book effect. People do not invent languages by writing grammars, they write grammars—at least, the first grammars to be written for any given language—by observing the tacit, largely unconscious, rules that people seem to be applying when they speak. Yet once a book exists, and especially once it is employed in schoolrooms, people feel that the rules are not just descriptions of how people do talk, but prescriptions for how they *should* talk.

It's easy to observe this phenomenon in places where

grammars were only written recently. In many places in the world, the first grammars and dictionaries were created by Christian missionaries in the nineteenth or even twentieth century, intent on translating the Bible and other sacred texts into what had been unwritten languages. For instance, the first grammar for Malagasy, the language spoken in Madagascar, was written in the 1810s and '20s. Of course, language is changing all the time, so the Malagasy spoken language—even its grammar—is in many ways quite different than it was two hundred years ago. However, since everyone learns the grammar in school, if you point this out, people will automatically say that speakers nowadays are simply making mistakes, not following the rules correctly. It never seems to occur to anyone—until you point it out—that had the missionaries came and written their books two hundred years later, current usages would be considered the only correct ones, and anyone speaking as they had two hundred years ago would themselves be assumed to be in error.

In fact, I found this attitude made it extremely difficult to learn how to speak colloquial Malagasy. Even when I hired native speakers, say, students at the university, to give me lessons, they would teach me how to speak nineteenth-century Malagasy as it was taught in school. As my proficiency improved, I began noticing that the way they talked to each other was nothing like the way they were teaching me to speak. But when I asked them about grammatical forms they used that weren't in the books, they'd just shrug them off, and say, "Oh, that's just slang, don't say that." In the end I found the only way I could really learn contemporary spoken Malagasy was to tape-record conversations, try to transcribe them myself, and then ask friends to clarify every time I came across an unfamiliar usage or expression. Nothing else would work: once they had decided these grammatical forms were errors, they simply could not describe them to me in grammatical terms.

In the case of the Cambridge anthropology department, the rules were made explicit, and were then frozen in place, ostensibly as a way of eliminating arbitrary, personal authority. The Malagasy attitudes towards rules of grammar clearly have nothing to do with a distaste for arbitrary authority, and everything to do with a distaste for arbitrariness itself—a distaste which leads to an unthinking acceptance of authority in its most formal, institutional form. After all, what is our first experience of formal, rule-governed authority if not our grade-school teachers? This is as much true in Madagascar as anywhere else. In fact, when I asked my friends why people didn't really speak the language described in the textbooks, the inevitable reply was always to the effect of "well, you know, people are lazy." Clearly, the problem was that the entire population had failed to memorize their lessons properly. But what they were actually denying was the legitimacy of collective creativity, the free play of the system.

It's worth thinking about language for a moment, because one thing it reveals, probably better than any other example, is that there is a basic paradox in our very idea of freedom. On the one hand, rules are by their nature constraining. Speech codes, rules of etiquette, and grammatical rules, all have the effect of limiting what we can and cannot say. It is not for nothing that we all have the picture of the schoolmarm rapping a child across the knuckles for some grammatical error as one of our primordial images of oppression. But at the same time, if there were no shared conventions of any kind—no semantics, syntax, phonemics—we'd all just be babbling incoherently and wouldn't be able to communicate with each other at all. Obviously in such circumstances none of us would be free to do much of anything. So at some point along the way, rules-as-constraining pass over into rules-as-enabling, even if it's impossible to say exactly where. Freedom, then, really is the tension of the free play of human creativity against the rules it is constantly generating. And this is what linguists always observe. There is no language without grammar. But there is also no language in which everything, including grammar, is not constantly changing all the time.

We rarely ask ourselves why that should be. Why is it that languages always change? It's easy enough to see why we need to have common agreements on grammar and vocabulary in order to be able to talk to one other. But if that's all that we need language for, one would think that, once a given set of speakers found a grammar and vocabulary that suited their purposes, they'd simply stick with it, perhaps changing the vocabulary around if there was some new thing to talk about—a new trend or invention, an imported vegetable—but otherwise, leaving well enough alone. In fact, this never happens. We don't know of a single recorded example of a language that, over the course of, say, a century, did not change both in sound and structure.[169] This is true even of the languages of the most "traditional" societies; it happens even where elaborate institutional structures have been created—like grammar schools, or the Académie Française—to ensure that it does not. No doubt some of this is the result of sheer rebelliousness (young people trying to set themselves off from elders, for example) but it's hard to escape the conclusion that ultimately, what we are really confronting here is the play principle in its purest form. Human beings, whether they speak Arapesh, Hopi, or Norwegian, just find it boring to say things the same way all the time. They're always going to play around at least a little. And this playing around will always have cumulative effects.

What this suggests is that people, everywhere, are prone to two completely contradictory tendencies: on the one hand, a tendency to be playfully creative just for the sake of it; on the other, a tendency to agree with anyone who tells them that they really shouldn't act that way. This latter is what makes the game-ification of institutional life possible. Because if you take the latter tendency to its logical conclusion, all freedom becomes arbitrariness, and all arbitrariness, a form of dangerous, subversive power. It is just one further step to argue that true freedom is to live in an utterly predictable world that is free from freedom of this sort.

Let me finish with another example from my own political experience.

Over the last thirty or forty years, anti-authoritarians around the world have been working on creating new, and more effective, modes of direct democracy—ones that might operate without any need for a bureaucracy of violence to enforce them. I've written about these efforts extensively elsewhere. A lot of progress has been made. But those working on such projects often find themselves having to deal with exactly this sort of horror of "arbitrary" power. Part of the work of developing new forms of consensus process, for example, is to create institutional forms that encourage, rather than inhibit, improvisation and creativity. As activists sometimes put it: in most circumstances, if you bring together a crowd of people, that crowd will, as a group, behave less intelligently, and less creatively, than any single member of the crowd is likely to do if on their own. Activist decision-making process is, instead, designed to make that crowd smarter and more imaginative than any individual participant.

It is indeed possible to do this, but it takes a lot of work. And the larger the group, the more formal mechanisms have to be put in place. The single most important essay in this whole activist tradition is called "The Tyranny of Structurelessness,"[170] written in the 1970s by Jo Freeman, about organizational crises that occurred in early feminist consciousness-raising circles when those groups began to attain a certain size. Freeman observed that such groups always started out with a kind of rough-and-ready anarchism, an assumption that there was no need for any formal, parliamentary rules-of-order type mechanisms at all. People would just sit down in a sisterly manner and work things out. And this was, indeed, what happened at first. However, as soon as the groups grew to over, say, twenty people, informal cliques invariably began to emerge, and small groups of friends or allies began controlling information, setting agendas, and wielding power in all sorts of subtle ways. Freeman proposed a number of different formal mechanisms that might be employed to counteract this effect, but for present purposes, the specifics don't really matter. Suffice it to say that what is now referred to as "formal consensus process" largely emerges from the crisis Freeman described, and the debate her intervention set off.

What I do want to bring attention to is that almost everyone who is not emerging from an explicitly anti-authoritarian position—and no insignificant number even of those who are—completely misread Freeman's essay, and interpret it not as a plea for formal mechanisms to ensure equality, but as a plea for more transparent hierarchy. Leninists are notorious for this sort of thing, but Liberals are just as bad. I can't tell you how many arguments I've had about this. They always go exactly the same way. First, Freeman's argument about the formation of cliques and invisible power structures is taken as an argument that any group of over twenty people will always have to have cliques, power structures, and people in authority. The next step is to insist that if you want to minimize the power of such cliques, or any deleterious effects those power structures might have, the only way to do so is to institutionalize them: to take the de facto cabal and turn them into a central committee (or, since that term now has a bad history, usually they say a coordinating committee, or a steering committee, or something of that sort.) One needs to get power out of the shadows—to formalize the process, make up rules, hold elections, specify exactly what the cabal is allowed to do and what it's not. In this way, at least, power will be made transparent and "accountable." (Notice that word again. It comes from accountancy procedures.) It won't in any sense be arbitrary.

From a practical, activist perspective, this prescription is obviously ridiculous. It is far easier to limit the degree to which informal cliques can wield effective power by granting them no formal status at all, and therefore no legitimacy; whatever "formal accountability structures" it is imagined will contain the cliques-now-turned-committees can only be far less effective in this regard, not least because they end up legitimating and hence massively increasing the differential access to information which allows some in otherwise egalitarian groups to have greater power to begin with. As I pointed out in the first essay, structures of transparency inevitably, as I've described, begin to become structures of stupidity as soon as that takes place.

So say one argues this point, and the critic concedes it (which usually they have to because it's pretty much common sense). If so, the next line of defense is generally aesthetic: the critic will insist it's simply distasteful to have structures of real power that are not recognized and that can, even if they entirely lack any degree of violent enforcement, be considered arbitrary. Usually, one's interlocutor won't go so far as actually admitting their objections are aesthetic. Usually they will frame their arguments in moral terms. But occasionally, you will find some honest enough to admit that's what's going on. I well remember having an Occupy Wall Street-sponsored debate in Central Park (I'm sure it's recorded somewhere) with Norman Finkelstein—a brilliant and altogether admirable activist, who had come of age with the Civil Rights Movement and still saw groups like the Southern Christian Leadership Conference as his inspiration. At this debate, Finkelstein stated the matter outright. Maybe it's true, he admitted, that the best way to keep such cliques from attaining too much power is to maintain a principle that they should not exist. But as long as such cliques are allowed to exist without being formally acknowledged and regulated, you're maintaining a system that says it's okay to be governed, even a tiny bit, from the shadows. It might not be that much of a practical problem. You might well be right that formally recognizing their existence might actually end up creating less overall freedom than leaving well enough alone. But in the final analysis, I just find the idea of being governed from the shadows, in any sense, distasteful.

In such arguments, we are witnessing a direct clash between two different forms of materialized utopianism: on the one hand, an anti-authoritarianism that, in its emphasis on creative synthesis and improvisation, sees freedom basically in terms of play, and on the other, a tacit republicanism that sees freedom ultimately as the ability to reduce all forms of power to a set of clear and transparent rules.

For the last two hundred years, in Europe and North America—and increasingly, elsewhere—that latter, bureaucratized notion of freedom has tended to hold sway. New institutional arrangements that operate by rules so strict and predictable they essentially disappear, so that one doesn't even know what they are (such as the physical or electronic post offices with which I began) tend to be put forward as platforms for human freedom that emerge from the very technical contingencies of running efficient structures of power. These arrangements seem to preserve the positive elements of play while somehow circumventing its more disturbing potentials.

But time and again, we have seen the same results. Whether motivated by a faith in "rationality" or a fear of arbitrary power, the end result of this bureaucratized notion of freedom is to move toward the dream of a world where play has been limited entirely—or, at best, boxed away in some remote location far from any serious, consequential human endeavor—while every aspect of life is reduced to some kind of elaborate, rule-bound game. It's not that such a vision lacks appeal. Who hasn't dreamed of a world where everyone knows the rules, everyone plays by the rules, and—even more—where people who play by the rules can actually still win? The problem is that this is just as much a utopian fantasy as a world of absolute free play would be. It will always remain a glimmering illusion that dissolves away as soon as we touch it.

Such illusions are not always bad things. One could make a case that most of the greatest human accomplishments were the result of such quixotic pursuits. But in this particular case, and in this larger political-economic context, where bureaucracy has been the primary means by which a tiny percentage of the population extracts wealth from the rest of us, they have created a situation where the pursuit of freedom from arbitrary power simply ends up producing more arbitrary power, and as a result, regulations choke existence, armed guards and surveillance cameras appear everywhere, science and creativity are smothered, and all of us end up finding increasing percentages of our day taken up in the filling out of forms.

Appendix

On Batman and the Problem of Constituent Power

I am appending this piece, ostensibly about the Christopher Nolan film The Dark Knight Rises—*the long version of a piece published under the title "Super Position" in* The New Inquiry *in 2012—as it expands on themes of sovereignty and popular culture broached in the third essay in this book. In that essay, I noted that there were three historically independent elements that I believed came together in our notion of "the state," which I described as sovereignty, bureaucracy, and (heroic) politics. My thoughts on sovereignty, however, were only minimally developed, so I thought it might interest the reader to see some further reflections on the subject, written in the same broad, discursive vein.*

On Saturday, October 1, 2011, the NYPD arrested seven hundred Occupy Wall Street activists as they were attempting to march across the Brooklyn Bridge. Mayor Bloomberg justified it on the grounds that protestors were blocking traffic. Five weeks later, that same Mayor Bloomberg closed down the nearby Queensboro Bridge to traffic for two solid days to allow for shooting of Christopher Nolan's last installment of his Batman Trilogy, *The Dark Knight Rises*.

Many remarked upon the irony.

A few weeks ago, I went to see the film with some friends from Occupy—most of whom had themselves been arrested on the bridge back in October. We all knew the movie was basically one long piece of anti-Occupy propaganda. That didn't bother us. We went to the theater hoping to have fun with that fact, in much the spirit of someone who was not a racist, or a Nazi, and would go to watch a screening of *Birth of a Nation* or *Triumph of the Will*. We expected the movie to be hostile, even offensive. But none of us expected it to be bad.

I'd like to reflect here, for a moment, on what made the film so awful. Because, oddly, it's important. I think the understanding of a lot of things—about movies, violence, police, the very nature of state power—can be furthered simply by trying to unravel what, exactly, made *The Dark Knight* so bad.

One issue I think we should get straight from the outset. The film really is a piece of anti-Occupy propaganda. Some still deny it. Christopher Nolan, the director, went on record to insist the script was written before the movement even started, and has claimed the famous scenes of the occupation of New York ("Gotham") were really inspired by Dickens's account of the French Revolution, not by OWS itself. This strikes me as disingenuous. Everyone knows Hollywood scripts are rewritten continually over the course of production, often to the point where they end up looking nothing like the original text; also, that when it comes to messaging, even details like where a scene is shot ("I know, let's have the cops face off with Bane's followers right in front of the New York Stock Exchange!") or a minor change of wording ("let's change 'take control of' to 'occupy'") can make all the difference.

Then there's the fact that the villains actually do occupy Wall Street, and attack the Stock Exchange.

What I'd like to argue is that it's precisely this desire for relevance, the fact that the filmmakers had the courage to take on the great issues of the day, which ruins the movie. It's especially sad, because the first two movies of the trilogy—*Batman Begins* and *The Dark Knight*—had moments of genuine eloquence. By making them, Nolan demonstrated that he does have interesting things to say about human psychology, and particularly, about the relation of creativity and violence (it's hard to imagine a successful action film director wouldn't). The *Dark Knight Rises* is even more ambitious. It dares to speak on a scale and grandeur appropriate to the times. But as a result, it stutters into incoherence.

Moments like this are potentially enlightening, for one thing, because they provide a kind of window, a way to think about what superhero movies, and superheroes in general, are really all about. That in turn helps us answer another question: What is the reason for the sudden explosion of such movies to begin with—one so dramatic that it sometimes seems comic book-based movies are replacing sci-fi as the main form of Hollywood special effects blockbuster almost as rapidly as the cop movie replaced the Western as the dominant action genre in the seventies?

Why, in the process, are familiar superheroes suddenly being given complex interiority: family backgrounds, emotional ambivalence, moral crises, anxiety, self-doubt? Or why (equally true but less remarked-on), does the very fact of their receiving a soul seem to force them to also choose some kind of explicit political orientation? One could argue that this happened first not with a comic-book character, but with James Bond, who in his traditional incarnation, as preternatural foil of evil masterminds, was always a kind of cinematic version of the same thing. *Casino Royale* gave Bond psychological depth. And by the very next movie, Bond was saving indigenous communities in Bolivia from evil transnational water privatizers.

Spiderman, too, broke left, just as Batman broke right. In a way this makes sense. Superheroes are a product of their historical origins. Superman is a Depression-era displaced Iowa farm boy; Batman, the billionaire playboy, is a scion of the military-industrial complex that was created, just as he was, at the beginning of World War II; Peter Parker, a product of the sixties, is a smartass working-class kid from Queens who got something weird shot into his veins. But again, in the latest movie, the subtext became surprisingly explicit ("you're not a vigilante," says the police commander, "you're an anarchist!"): particularly in the climax, where Spiderman, wounded by a police bullet, is rescued by an outbreak of working-class solidarity as dozens of crane operators across Manhattan defy city orders and mobilize to help him. Nolan's movie was the most politically ambitious, but it also falls the most obviously flat. Is this because the superhero genre does not lend itself to a right-wing message?

Certainly, this is not the conclusion cultural critics have tended to come to in the past.

What, then, can we say about the politics of the superhero genre? It seems reasonable to start by looking at the comic books, since this is where everything else (the TV shows, cartoon series, blockbuster movies) ultimately came from. Comic-book superheroes were originally a mid-century phenomenon and like all mid-century pop culture phenomena, they are essentially Freudian. That is to say, insofar as a work of popular fiction had anything to say about human nature, or human motivations, a certain pop Freudianism is what one would expect. Sometimes this even becomes explicit, as in *Forbidden Planet*, with its "monsters from the Id." Usually, it's just subtext.

Umberto Eco once remarked that comic book stories already operate a little bit like dreams; the same basic plot is repeated, obsessive-compulsively, over and over; nothing changes, even as the backdrop for the stories shifts from Great Depression to World War II to postwar prosperity, the heroes—whether Superman, Wonder Woman, the Green Hornet, or Dr. Strange—seem to remain in an eternal present, never aging, always fundamentally the same. The basic plot takes the following form: a bad guy—maybe a crime boss, more often a powerful supervillain—embarks on a project of world conquest, destruction, theft, extortion, or revenge. The hero is alerted to the danger and figures out what's happening. After trials and dilemmas, at the last possible minute, the hero foils the villain's plans. The world is returned to normal until the next episode when the exact same thing happens once again.

It doesn't take a genius to figure out what's going on here. The heroes are purely reactionary. By this I mean "reactionary" in the literal sense: they simply react to things; they have no projects of their own. (Or to be more precise, *as heroes* they have no projects of their own. As Clark Kent, Superman may be constantly trying, and failing, to get into Lois Lane's pants. As Superman, he is purely reactive.) In fact, superheroes seem almost utterly lacking in imagination. Bruce Wayne, with all the money in the world, can't seem to think of anything to do with it other than to design even more high-tech weaponry and indulge in the occasional act of charity. In the same way it never seems to occur to Superman that he could easily end world hunger or carve free magic cities out of mountains. Almost never do superheroes make, create, or build anything. The villains, in contrast, are relentlessly creative. They are full of plans and projects and ideas. Clearly, we are supposed to first, without consciously realizing it, identify with the villains. After all, they're having all the fun. Then of course we feel guilty for it, reidentify with the hero, and have even more fun watching the Superego pummel the errant Id back into submission.

Of course, the moment you start arguing that there's any message in a comic book, you are likely to hear the usual objections: "But these are just cheap forms of entertainment! They're no more trying to teach us anything about human nature, politics, or society than, say, a Ferris wheel." And of course, to a certain degree, this is true. Pop culture does not exist in order to convince anyone of anything. It exists for the sake of pleasure. Still, if you pay close attention, one will also observe that most pop culture projects do also tend to make that very pleasure into a kind of argument. Horror films provide a particularly unsubtle example of how this works. The plot of a horror movie is, typically, some kind of story of transgression and punishment—in the slasher film, perhaps the purest, most stripped-down, least subtle example of the genre, you always see the same movement in the plot. As Carol Clover long ago noted in her magisterial *Men, Women, and Chainsaws*, the audience is first tacitly encouraged to identify with the monster (the camera literally takes the monster's point of view) as he hacks away at the "bad girls," and only later, shifting to looking through the eyes of the androgynous heroine who will eventually destroy him. The plot is always a simple story of transgression and punishment: the bad girls sin, they have sex, they fail to report a hit-and-run accident, maybe they're just obnoxious, stupid teenagers; as a result, they are eviscerated. Then the virginal good girl eviscerates the culprit. It's all very Christian and moralistic. The sins may be minor and the punishment utterly disproportionate, but the ultimate message is: "Of course they really deserve it; we all do; whatever our civilized exterior, we are all fundamentally corrupt and evil. The proof? Well, look at yourself. You're not evil? If you're not evil, then why are you getting off on watching this sadistic crap?"

This is what I mean when I say the pleasure is a form of argument.

Next to this, a superhero comic book might seem pretty innocuous. And in many ways it is. If all a comic is doing is telling a bunch of adolescent boys that everyone has a certain desire for chaos and mayhem, but that ultimately such desires need to be controlled, the political implications would not seem to be particularly dire. Especially because the message still does carry a healthy dose of ambivalence, just as it does with all those contemporary action-movie heroes who seem to spend so much of their time smashing up suburban shopping malls and suchlike. Most of us would like to smash a bank or shopping mall at least once in our lives. And as Bakunin put it, "the urge for destruction is also a creative urge."

Still, I think there is reason to believe that at least in the case of most comic-book superheroes, the mayhem does have very conservative political implications. To understand why though I will have to enter into a brief digression on the question of constituent power.

Costumed superheroes ultimately battle criminals in the name of the law—even if they themselves often operate outside a strictly legal framework. But in the modern state, the very status of law is a problem. This is because of a basic logical paradox: no system can generate itself. Any power capable of creating a system of laws cannot itself be bound by them. So law has to come from someplace else. In the Middle Ages the solution was simple: the legal order was created by God, a being who, as the Old Testament makes abundantly clear, is not bound by laws or even any recognizable system of morality (again, this only stands to reason: if you created morality, you can't, by definition, be bound by it). Or if not by God directly, then by the divinely ordained power of kings. The English, American, and French revolutionaries changed all that when they created the notion of popular sovereignty—declaring that the power once held by kings is now held by an entity that they called "the people." This created an immediate logical problem, because "the people" are by definition a group of individuals united by the fact that they are, in fact, bound by a certain set of laws. So in what sense can they have created those laws? When this question was first posed in the wake of the British, American, and French revolutions, the answer seemed obvious: through those revolutions themselves. But this created a further problem. Revolutions are acts of law-breaking. It is completely illegal to rise up in arms, overthrow a government, and create a new political order. In fact, nothing could possibly be more illegal. Cromwell, Jefferson, or Danton were all clearly guilty of treason, according to the laws under which they grew up, just as much as they would have been had they tried to do the same thing again under the new regimes they created, say, twenty years later.

So laws emerge from illegal activity. This creates a fundamental incoherence in the very idea of modern government, which assumes that the state has a monopoly of the legitimate use of violence (only the police, or prison guards, or duly authorized private security, have the legal right to beat you up). It's legitimate for the police to use violence because they are enforcing the law; the law is legitimate because it's rooted in the constitution; the constitution is legitimate because it comes from the people; the people created the constitution by acts of illegal violence. The obvious question, then: How does one tell the difference between "the people" and a mere rampaging mob?

There is no obvious answer.

The response by mainstream, respectable opinion is to try to push the problem as far away as possible. The usual line is: the age of revolutions is over (except perhaps in benighted spots like Gabon, or maybe Syria); we can now change the constitution, or legal standards, by legal means. This of course means that the basic structures will never change. We can witness the results in the United States, which continues to maintain an architecture of state, with its electoral college and two party-system, that—while quite progressive in 1789—now makes us appear, in the eyes of the rest of the world, the political equivalent of the Amish, still driving around with horses and buggies. It also means we base the legitimacy of the whole system on the consent of the people despite the fact that the only people who were ever really consulted on the matter lived over two hundred years ago. In America, at least, "the people" are all long since dead.

We've gone then from a situation where the power to create a legal order derives from God, to one where it derives from armed revolution, to one where it is rooted in sheer tradition—"these are the customs of our ancestors, who are we to doubt their wisdom?" (And of course a not insignificant number of American politicians make clear they'd really like to give it back to God again.)

This, as I say, is how these matters are considered by the mainstream. For the radical Left, and the authoritarian Right, the problem of constituent power is very much alive, but each takes a diametrically opposite approach to the fundamental question of violence. The Left, chastened by the disasters of the twentieth century, has largely moved away from its older celebration of revolutionary violence, preferring nonviolent forms of resistance. Those who act in the name of something higher than the law can do so precisely because they *don't* act like a rampaging mob. For the Right, on the other hand—and this has been true since the rise of fascism in the twenties—the very idea that there is something special about revolutionary violence, anything that makes it different from mere criminal violence, is so much self-righteous twaddle. Violence is violence. But that doesn't mean a rampaging mob can't be "the people" because violence is the real source of law and political order anyway. Any successful deployment of violence is, in its own way, a form of constituent power. This is why, as Walter Benjamin noted, we cannot help but admire the "great criminal": because, as so many movie posters over the years have put it, "he makes his own law." After all, any criminal organization does, inevitably, begin developing its own—often quite elaborate—set of internal rules and regulations. They have to, as a way of controlling what would otherwise be completely random violence. But from the right-wing perspective, that's all that law ever is. It is a means of controlling the very violence that brings it into being, and through which it is ultimately enforced.

This makes it easier to understand the often otherwise surprising affinity between criminals, criminal gangs, right-wing political movements, and the armed representatives of the state. Ultimately, they all speak the same language. They create their own rules on the basis of force. As a result, such people typically share the same broad political sensibilities. Mussolini might have wiped out the mafia, but Italian Mafiosi still idolize Mussolini. In Athens, nowadays, there's active collaboration between the crime bosses in poor immigrant neighborhoods, fascist gangs, and the police. In fact, in this case it was clearly a political strategy: faced with the prospect of popular uprisings against a right-wing government, the police first withdrew protection from neighborhoods near the immigrant gangs, then started giving tacit support to the fascists (the result was the rapid rise of an overtly Nazi party. Roughly half of Greek police were reported to have voted for the Nazis in the last election). But this is just how far-right politics work. For them, it is in that space where different violent forces operating outside of the legal order (or in the case of the police, sometimes just barely inside it) inter-act where new forms of power, hence order, can emerge.

So what does all this have to do with costumed superheroes? Well, everything. Because this is exactly the space that superheroes, and super-villains, also inhabit. An inherently fascist space, inhabited only by gangsters, would-be dictators, police, and thugs, with endlessly blurring lines between them. Sometimes the cops are legalistic, sometimes corrupt. Sometimes the police themselves slip into vigilantism. Sometimes they persecute the superhero, at others they look the other way, or help. Villains and heroes occasionally team up. The lines of force are always shifting. If anything new were to emerge, it could only be through such shifting forces. There's nothing else, since in the DC and Marvel universes, God, or The People, simply doesn't exist.

Insofar as there is a potential for constituent power then, it can only come from purveyors of violence. And indeed, the supervillains and evil masterminds, when they are not merely dreaming of committing the perfect crime or indulging in random acts of terror, are always scheming of imposing a New World Order of some kind or another. Surely, if Red Skull, Kang the Conqueror, or Doctor Doom ever did succeed in taking over the planet, a host of new laws would be created very quickly. They wouldn't be very nice laws. Their creator would doubtless not himself feel bound by them. But one gets the feeling that otherwise, they would be quite strictly enforced.

Superheroes resist this logic. They do not wish to conquer the world—if only because they are not monomaniacal or insane. As a result, they remain parasitical off the villains in the same way that police remain parasitical off criminals: without them, they would have no reason to exist. They remain defenders of a legal and political order which itself seems to have come out of nowhere, and which, however faulty or degraded, *must* be defended, because the only alternative is so much worse.

They aren't fascists. They are just ordinary, decent, super-powerful people who inhabit a world in which fascism is the only political possibility.

Why, might we ask, would a form of entertainment premised on such a peculiar notion of politics emerge in early- to mid-twentieth-century America, at just around the time that actual fascism was on the rise in Europe? Was it some kind of fantasy American equivalent? Not exactly. It's more that both fascism and superheroes were products of a similar historical predicament: What is the foundation of social order when one has exorcised the very idea of revolution? And above all, what happens to the political imagination?

One might begin here by considering who are the core audience for superhero comics. Mainly, adolescent or preadolescent white boys. That is, individuals who are at a point in their lives where they are likely to be both maximally imaginative and at least a little bit rebellious; but who are also being groomed to eventually take on positions of authority and power in the world, to be fathers, sheriffs, small-business owners, middle managers, engineers. And what do they learn from these endless repeated dramas? Well, first off, that imagination and rebellion lead to violence; second, that, like imagination and rebellion, violence is a lot of fun; third, that, ultimately, violence must be directed back against any overflow of imagination and rebellion lest everything go askew. These things must be contained! This is why insofar as superheroes are allowed to be imaginative in any way, it could only be extended to the design of their clothes, their cars, maybe their homes, their various accessories.

It's in this sense that the logic of the superhero plot is profoundly, deeply conservative. Ultimately, the division between left- and right-wing sensibilities turns on one's attitude towards the imagination. For the Left, imagination, creativity, by extension production, the power to bring new things and new social arrangements into being, is always to be celebrated. It is the source of all real value in the world. For the Right, it is dangerous; ultimately, evil. The urge to create is also a destructive urge. This kind of sensibility was rife in the popular Freudianism of the day: where the Id was the motor of the psyche, but also amoral; if really unleashed, it would lead to an orgy of destruction. This is also what separates conservatives from fascists. Both agree that the imagination unleashed can only lead to violence and destruction. Conservatives wish to defend us against that possibility. Fascists wish to unleash it anyway. They aspire to be, as Hitler imagined himself, great artists painting with the minds, blood, and sinews of humanity.

This means that it's not just the mayhem that becomes the reader's guilty pleasure, but the very fact of having a fantasy life at all. And while it might seem odd to think any artistic genre is ultimately a warning about the dangers of the human imagination, it would certain explain why, in the staid forties and fifties, everyone did seem to feel there was something vaguely naughty about reading them. It also explains how in the sixties it could all suddenly seem so harmless, allowing the advent of silly, campy TV superheroes like the Adam West Batman series, or Saturday morning Spiderman cartoons. If the message was that rebellious imagination was okay as long as it was kept out of politics and simply confined to consumer choices (clothes, cars, accessories again), this had become a message that even executive producers could easily get behind.

•

We can conclude: the classic comic book is ostensibly political (about madmen trying to take over the world), really psychological and personal (about overcoming the dangers of rebellious adolescence), but ultimately, political after all.[171]

If this is so, then new superhero movies are precisely the reverse. They are ostensibly psychological and personal, really political, but ultimately, psychological and personal after all.

The humanization of superheroes didn't start in the movies. It actually began in the eighties and nineties, within the comic book genre itself, with Frank Miller's *The Dark Knight Returns* and Alan Moore's *Watchmen*—a subgenre of what might be called superhero noir. At that time, superhero movies were still working through the legacy of the sixties camp tradition, as in Christopher Reeve's *Superman* series, or Michael Keaton's *Batman*. Eventually, though, the noir subgenre, probably always somewhat cinematic in its inspiration, came to Hollywood as well. One might say it reached its cinematic peak in *Batman Begins*, the first of the Nolan trilogy. In that movie, Nolan essentially asks, "What if someone like Batman actually did exist? How would that happen? What would it actually take to make an otherwise respectable member of society decide to dress up as a bat and prowl the streets in search of criminals?"

Unsurprisingly, psychedelic drugs turn out to play an important role here. So do severe mental health issues and bizarre religious cults.

It is curious that commentators on the movie never seem to pick up on the fact that Bruce Wayne, in the Nolan films, is borderline psychotic. As himself he is almost completely dysfunctional, incapable of forming friendships or romantic attachments, uninterested in work unless it somehow reinforces his morbid obsessions. The hero is so obviously crazy, and the movie so obviously about his battle with his own craziness, that it's not a problem that the villains are just a series of ego-appendages: Ra's al Ghul (the bad father), the Crime boss (the successful businessman), the Scarecrow (who drives the businessman insane.) There's nothing particularly appealing about any of them. But it doesn't matter—they're all just shards and tessera of the hero's shattered mind. As a result, we don't have to identify with the villain and then recoil in self-loathing; we can just enjoy watching Bruce do that for us.

There's also no obvious a political message.

Or so it seems. But when you create a movie out of characters so dense with myth and history, no director is entirely in control of his material. The filmmaker's role is largely to assemble them. In the movie, the primary villain is Ra's al Ghul, who first initiates Batman into the League of Shadows in a monastery in Bhutan, and only then reveals his plan to destroy Gotham to rid the world of its corruption. In the original comics, we learn that Ra's al Ghul (a character introduced, tellingly, in 1971) is in fact a Primitivist and ecoterrorist, determined to restore the balance of nature by reducing the earth's human population by roughly 99 percent. The main way Nolan changed the story is to make Batman begin as Ra's al Ghul's disciple. But in contemporary terms that, too, makes a sort of sense. After all, what is the media stereotype that immediately comes to mind—at least since the direct actions against the World Trade Organization in Seattle—when one thinks of a trust-fund kid who, moved by some unfathomable sense of injustice, dons black clothing and a mask, and takes to the streets to create violence and mayhem, though always in a way calculated never to actually kill anyone? Let alone one who does so inspired by the teachings of a radical guru who believes we need to return to the Stone Age? Nolan made his hero a Black Bloc disciple of John Zerzan who breaks with his former mentor when he realizes what restoring Eden will actually entail.

In fact, none of the villains in any of the three movies wants to rule the world. They don't wish to have power over others, or to create new rules of any sort. Even their henchmen are temporary expedients—they always ultimately plan to kill them. Nolan's villains are always anarchists. But they're also always very peculiar anarchists, of a sort that seem to exist only in the filmmaker's imagination: anarchists who believe that human nature is fundamentally evil and corrupt. The Joker, the real hero of the second movie, makes all of this explicit: he's basically the Id become philosopher. The Joker is nameless, he has no origin other than whatever he, on any particular occasion, whimsically invents; it's not even clear what his powers are or where they came from. Yet he's inexorably powerful. The Joker is a pure force of self-creation, a poem written by himself; and his only purpose in life appears to be an obsessive need to prove to others first, that everything is and can only be poetry—and second, that poetry is evil.

So here we are back to the central theme of the early superhero universes: a prolonged reflection on the dangers of the human imagination; how the reader's own desire to immerse oneself in a world driven by artistic imperatives is living proof of why the imagination must always be carefully contained.

The result is a thrilling movie, with a villain both likeable—he's just so obviously having fun with it—and genuinely frightening. *Batman Begins* was merely full of people talking about fear. *The Dark Knight* actually produced some. But even that movie began to fall flat the moment it touches on popular politics. The People make one lame attempt to intervene in the beginning of when copycat Batmen appear all over the city, inspired by the Dark Knight's example. Of course they all die horribly and that's the end of that. From then on, they're put back in their place, as Audience, who like the mob in the Roman amphitheater exist only to judge the protagonists' performance: thumbs-up for Batman, thumbs-down for Batman, thumbs-up for the crusading DA . . . The end, when Bruce and

Commissioner Gordon settle on the plan to scapegoat Batman and create a false myth around the martyrdom of Harvey Dent, is nothing short of a confession that politics is identical to the art of fiction. The Joker was right. To a degree. As always, redemption lies only in the fact that the violence, the deception, can be turned back upon itself.

They would have done well leave it that.

The problem with this vision of politics is that it simply isn't true. Politics is not just the art of manipulating images, backed up by violence. It's not really a duel between impresarios before an audience that will believe most anything if presented artfully enough. No doubt it must seem that way to extraordinarily wealthy Hollywood film directors. But between the shooting of the first and second movies, history intervened quite decisively to point out just how wrong this vision is. The economy collapsed. Not because of the manipulations of some secret society of warrior monks, but because a bunch of financial managers who, living in Nolan's bubble world, shared his assumptions about the endlessness of popular manipulability, turned out to be wrong. There was a mass popular response. It did not take the form of a frenetic search for messianic saviors, mixed with outbreaks of nihilist violence;[172] increasingly, it took the form of a series of real popular movements, even revolutionary movements, toppling regimes in the Middle East and occupying squares everywhere from Cleveland to Karachi, trying to create new forms of democracy.

Constituent power had reappeared, and in an imaginative, radical, and remarkably nonviolent form. This is precisely the kind of situation a superhero universe cannot address. In Nolan's world, something like Occupy could only have been the product of some tiny group of ingenious manipulators (you know, people like me) who are really pursuing some secret agenda.

Nolan really should have left such topics alone, but apparently, he couldn't help himself. The result is almost completely incoherent. It is, basically, yet another psychological drama masquerading as a political one. The plot is convoluted and barely worth recounting. Bruce Wayne, dysfunctional again without his alter ego, has turned into a recluse. A rival business-man hires Catwoman to steal his fingerprints so he can use them to steal all his money; but really the businessman is being manipulated by a gas-mask-wearing supervillain mercenary named Bane. Bane is stronger than Batman but he's basically a miserable sort of person, pining with unrequited love for Ra's al Ghul's daughter Talia, crippled by mistreatment in his youth in a dungeon-like prison where he was cast unjustly, his face invisible behind a mask he must wear continually so as not to collapse in agonizing pain. Insofar as the audience identifies with a villain like that, it can only be out of sympathy. No one in her right mind would want to *be* Bane. But presumably that's the point: a warning against the dangers of undue sympathy for the unfortunate. Because Bane is also a charismatic revolution-ary, who, after disposing of Batman, reveals the myth of Harvey Dent to be a lie, frees the denizens of Gotham's prisons, and releases its ever-impressionable populace to sack and burn the mansions of the 1 percent, and to drag their denizens before revolutionary tribunals. (The Scarecrow, amusingly, reappears as Robespierre.) But really he's ultimately intending to kill them all with a nuclear bomb converted from some kind of green energy project. Why? Who knows? Maybe he too is some kind of Primitivist ecoterrorist like Ra's al Ghul. (He does seem to have inherited the headship of the same organization.) Maybe he's trying to impress Talia by finishing her father's work. Or maybe he's just evil and there's no need for further explanation.

Conversely, why does Bane wish to lead the people in a social revolution, if he's just going to nuke them all in a few weeks anyway? Again, it's anybody's guess. He says that before you destroy someone, first you must give them hope. So is the message that utopian dreams can only lead to nihilistic violence?

Presumably something like that, but it's singularly unconvincing, since the plan to kill everyone came first. The revolution was a decorative afterthought.

In fact, what happens to the city can only possibly make sense as a material echo of what's always been most important: what's happening in Bruce Wayne's tortured brain. After Batman is crippled by Bane halfway through the movie, he is placed in the same fetid dungeon where Bane himself was once imprisoned. The prison sits at the bottom of a well, so sunlight is always taunting its inhabitants—but the well is impossible to climb. Bane ensures Bruce is nursed back to health just so he can try and fail to scale it, and thus know that it's his failure that allowed his beloved Gotham to be destroyed. Only then will Bane be merciful enough to kill him. This is contrived, but psychologically, at least, you can say it makes some kind of sense. Translated onto the level of a city, it makes no sense at all: why would anyone want to give a population hope and then unexpectedly vaporize them? The first is cruel. The second is just random. And not only that, the filmmakers compound the metaphor by having Bane play the same trick on the Gotham police department, who—in a plot contrivance so idiotic it violates even the standards of plausibility expected from a comic book—are almost all lured beneath the city and then trapped there by well-placed bombs, except then for some reason allowed to receive food and water, presumably so they too can be tortured by hope.

Other things happen, but they're all similar projections. This time Catwoman gets to play the role usually assigned to the audience, first identifying with Bane's revolutionary project, then, for no clearly articulated reason, changing her mind and blowing him away. Batman and the Gotham police both rise from their respective dungeons and join forces to battle the evil Occupiers outside the Stock Exchange. In the end, Batman fakes his own death disposing of the bomb and Bruce ends up with Catwoman in Florence. A new phony martyr legend is born and the people of Gotham are pacified. In case of further trouble, we are assured there is also a potential heir to Batman, a disillusioned police officer named Robin. Everyone breathes a sigh of relief because the movie is finally over.

Is there supposed to be a message we can all take home from this? If there was, it would seem to be something along the lines of this: "True, the system is corrupt, but it's all we have, and anyway, figures of authority can be trusted if they have first been chastened and endured terrible suffering." (Normal police let children die on bridges. Police who've been buried alive for a few weeks can employ violence legitimately.) "True, there is injustice and its victims deserve our sympathy, but keep it within reasonable limits. Charity is much better than addressing structural problems. That way lies madness." Because in Nolan's universe, any attempt to address structural problems, even through nonviolent civil disobedience, really *is* a form of violence; because that's all it could possibly be. Imaginative politics are inherently violent, and therefore, there's nothing inappropriate if police respond by smashing apparently peaceful protestors' heads repeatedly against the concrete.

As a response to Occupy, this is nothing short of pathetic. When *The Dark Knight* came out in 2008, there was much discussion over whether the whole thing was really a vast metaphor for the war on terror: how far is it okay for the good guys (that's us) to go adapting the bad guy's methods? Probably the filmmakers were indeed thinking of such issues, and still managed to produce a good movie. But then, the war on terror actually was a battle of secret networks and manipulative spectacles. It began with a bomb and ended with an assassination. One can almost think of it as an attempt, on both sides, to actually enact a comic book version of the universe. Once real constituent power appeared on the scene, that universe shriveled into incoherence—even came to seem ridiculous. Revolutions were sweeping the Middle East, and the United States were still spending hundreds of billions of dollars fighting a ragtag bunch of seminary students in Afghanistan. Unfortunately for Nolan, for all his manipulative powers, the same thing happened to his world when even the hint of real popular power arrived in New York.

Notes

Introduction: The Iron Law of Liberalism and the Era of Total Bureaucratization

1. Elliot Jacques (Ann Arbor: University of Michigan Press, 1976).
2. Gordon Tullock (Washington, D.C.: Public Affairs Press, 1965).
3. Henry Jacoby (Berkeley: University of California Press, 1973).
4. C. Northcote Parkinson (Cambridge, MA: Riverside Press, 1957). "Work in an organization expands to fill the time allotted to do it."
5. Laurence J. Peter and Raymond Hill (London: Souvenir Press, 1969). The famous work on how those operating in an organization "rise to the level of their incompetence" also became a popular British TV show.
6. R. T. Fishall (London: Arrow Books, 1982). A now-classic text on how to flummox and discomfit bureaucrats, widely rumored to be by British astronomer and BBC host Sir Patrick Moore.
7. One could go further. The "acceptable" Left has, as I say, embraced bureaucracy and the market simultaneously. The libertarian Right at least has a critique of bureaucracy. The fascist Right has a critique of the market—generally, they are supporters of social welfare policies; they just want to restrict them to members of their own favored ethnic group.

8. Owing to a peculiar set of historical circumstances, the word "liberal" no longer has the same meaning in the United States as it does in the rest of the world. The term originally applied to free-market enthusiasts, and in much of the world, it still does. In the United States, it was adopted by social democrats, and as a result, became anathema to the right, and free-market enthusiasts were forced to take the term "libertarian," originally interchangeable with "anarchist," used in such terms as "libertarian socialist" or "libertarian communist" to mean the same thing.

9. In fact, Ludwig von Mises's position is inherently antidemocratic: at least insofar as it tends to reject state solutions of any kind, while, at the same time, opposing left-wing antistatist positions that propose the creation of forms of democratic self-organization outside it.

10. In the Durkheimian tradition this has come to be known as "the non-contractual element in contract," certainly one of the less catchy sociological phrases of all time. The discussion goes back to *The Division of Labor in Society* (New York: Free Press, 1984 [1893]), p. 162.

11. Michel Foucault's essays on neoliberalism insist that this is the difference between the old and new varieties: those promulgating markets now understand that they do not form spontaneously, but must be nurtured and maintained by government intervention. *Naissance de la biopolitique*, Michel Senellart, ed. (Paris: Gallimard, 2004).

12. "I don't know how many times I have used the term 'Government bureaucrat.' And you will never find a politician using that term that doesn't have some slightly pejorative connotation. That is, we know taxpayers resent the money they have to pay to the Government, and so we try to get credit by saying we're being hard on bureaucrats or reducing bureaucrats . . . But remember, most of those people are just like most of you: They love their children. They get up every day and go to work. They do the very best they can . . . After what we have been through in this last month, after what I have seen in the eyes of the children of those Government bureaucrats that were serving us on that fateful day in Oklahoma City, or in their parents' eyes who were serving us when their children were

in that daycare center, I will never use that phrase again." (www
.presidency.ucsb.edu/ws/?pid=51382)

13. From "Bureaucracy," Max Weber, in *From Max Weber: Essays in Sociology*, H. H. Gerth and C. Wright Mills, eds. (New York: Oxford University Press, 1946), pp. 197–98.

14. In many ways, the United States is a German country that, owing to that same early twentieth century rivalry, refuses to recognize itself as such. Despite the use of the English language there are far more Americans of German descent than English. (Or consider the two quintessentially American foods: the hamburger and the frankfurter). Germany in contrast is a country quite proud of its efficiency in matters bureaucratic, and Russia, to complete the set, might be considered a country where people generally feel they really ought to be better at bureaucracy, and are somewhat ashamed that they are not.

15. A British bank employee recently explained to me that ordinarily, even those working for the bank effect a kind of knowing doublethink about such matters. In internal communications, they will always speak of regulations as being imposed on them—"The Chancellor has decided to increase ISA allowances"; "The Chancellor has initiated a more liberal pension regime" and so on—even though everyone in fact knows bank executives have just had repeated dinners and meetings with the Chancellor in question lobbying them to bring these laws and regulations about. There is a kind of game where senior executives will feign surprise or even dismay when their own suggestions are enacted.

16. About the only policies that can't be referred to as "deregulation" are ones that aim to reverse some other policy that has already been labeled "deregulation," which means it's important, in playing the game, to have your policy labeled "deregulation" first.

17. The phenomenon I am describing is a planetary one, but it began in the United States, and it was U.S. elites who made the most aggressive efforts to export it, so it seems appropriate to begin with what happened in America.

18. In a way, the famous TV character of Archie Bunker, an uneducated

longshoreman who can afford a house in the suburbs and a non-working wife, and who is bigoted, sexist, and completely supportive of the status quo that allows him such secure prosperity, is the very quintessence of the corporatist age.

19. Though it is notable that it is precisely this sixties radical equation of communism, fascism, and the bureaucratic welfare state that has been taken up by right-wing populists in America today. The Internet is rife with such rhetoric. One need only consider the way that "Obamacare" is continually equated with socialism and Nazism, often, both at the same time.

20. William Lazonick has done the most work on documenting this shift, noting that it is a shift in business models—the effects of globalization and offshoring really only took off later, in the late nineties and early 2000s. (See, for example, his "Financial Commitment and Economic Performance: Ownership and Control in the American Industrial Corporation," *Business and Economic History*, 2nd series, 17 [1988]: 115–28; "The New Economy Business Model and the Crisis of U.S. Capitalism," *Capitalism and Society* [2009], 4, 2, Article 4; or "The Financialization of the U.S. Corporation: What Has Been Lost, and How It Can Be Regained," *INET Research Notes*, 2012.) A Marxian approach to the same class realignment can be found in Gérard Duménil and Dominique Lévy's *Capital Resurgent: The Roots of the Neoliberal Revolution* (Cambridge, MA: Harvard University Press, 2004), and *The Crisis of Neoliberalism* (Cambridge, MA: Harvard University Press, 2013). Effectively, the investor and executive classes became the same—they intermarried—and careers spanning the financial and corporate management worlds became commonplace. Economically, according to Lazonick, the most pernicious effect was the practice of stock buybacks. Back in the fifties and sixties, a corporation spending millions of dollars to purchase its own stock so as to raise that stock's market value would have likely been considered illegal market manipulation. Since the eighties, as executives' have increasingly been paid in stock, it has become standard practice, and literally trillions of dollars in corpo-

rate revenue that would in an earlier age have been sunk into expanding operations, hiring workers, or research, have instead been redirected to Wall Street.

21. A popular code word from the eighties onwards was "lifestyle liberal, fiscal conservative." This referred to those who had internalized the social values of the sixties counterculture, but had come to view the economy with the eyes of investors.

22. Just to be clear: this is by no means the case of major journalistic venues, newspapers like *The New York Times*, *The Washington Post*, or magazines like *The New Yorker*, *The Atlantic*, or *Harper's*. In such institutions, a degree in journalism would probably be counted as a negative. At this point, at least, it's only true of minor publications. But the general trend is always towards greater credentialism in all fields, never less.

23. www.aljazeera.com/indepth/opinion/2014/05/college-promise-economy-does-no-201451411124734124.html. The cited text is in *Saving Higher Education in the Age of Money* (Charlottesville: University of Virginia Press, 2005), p. 85. It continues, "Why do Americans think this is a good requirement, or at least a necessary one? Because they think so. We've left the realm of reason and entered that of faith and mass conformity."

24. This was certainly my own personal experience. As one of the few students of working-class origins in my own graduate program, I watched in dismay as professors first explained to me that they considered me the best student in my class—even, perhaps, in the department—and then threw up their hands claiming there was nothing that could be done as I languished with minimal support—or during many years none at all, working multiple jobs, as students whose parents were doctors, lawyers, and professors seemed to automatically mop up all the grants, fellowships, and student funding.

25. Loans directly from the government are not available for continuing education, so borrowers are forced to take private loans with much higher interest rates.

26. A friend gives me the example of master's degrees in library science,

which are now required for all public library jobs, despite the fact that the yearlong course of study generally provides no essential information that couldn't be obtained by a week or two of on-the-job training. The main result is to ensure that for the first decade or two of a new librarian's career, 20 to 30 percent of his or her income is redirected to repaying loans—in the case of my friend, $1,000 a month, about half of which goes to the university (principal) and half to the loan provider (interest).

27. This logic of complicity can extend to the most unlikely organizations. One of the premiere left journals in America has, as editor in chief, a billionaire who basically bought herself the position. The first criterion for advancement in the organization is of course willingness to pretend there is some reason, other than money, for her to have the job.

28. I outlined what happened in an essay called "The Shock of Victory." Obviously, the planetary bureaucracy remained in place, but policies like IMF-imposed structural adjustment ended, and Argentina's writing down of its loans in 2002, under intense pressure from social movements, set off a chain of events that effectively ended the Third World debt crisis.

29. The League of Nations and the UN up until the seventies were basically talking-shops.

30. In England, for instance, the anti–Corn Law legislation eliminating British tariff protections, which is seen as initiating the liberal age, was introduced by Conservative Prime Minister Sir Robert Peel, mainly famous for having created the first British police force.

31. I was reminded of this a few years ago by none other than Julian Assange, when a number of Occupy activists appeared on his TV show *The World Tomorrow*. Aware that many of us were anarchists, he asked us what he considered a challenging question: say you have a camp, and there are some people playing the drums all night and keeping everyone awake, and they won't stop, what do you propose to do about it? The implication is that police, or something like them—some impersonal force willing to threaten violence—

were simply necessary in such conditions. He was referring to a real incident—there had been some annoying drummers in Zuccotti Park. But in fact, the occupiers who didn't like the music simply negotiated a compromise with them where they would only drum during certain hours. No threats of violent force were necessary. This brings home the fact that, for the overwhelming majority of humans who have lived in human history, there has simply been nothing remotely like police to call under such circumstances. Yet they worked something out. One seeks in vain for Mesopotamian or Chinese or ancient Peruvian accounts of urban dwellers driven mad by neighbors' raucous parties.

32. It is possible that there could be market relations that might not work this way. While impersonal markets have been throughout most of history the creation of states, mostly organized to support military operations, there have been periods where states and markets have drifted apart. Many of the ideas of Adam Smith and other Enlightenment market proponents seem to derive from one such, in the Islamic world of the Middle Ages, where sharia courts allowed commercial contracts to be enforced without direct government intervention, but only through merchants' reputation (and hence creditworthiness). Any such market will in many key ways operate very differently from those we are used to: for instance, market activity was seen as much more about cooperation than competition (see *Debt: The First 5,00 Years* [Brooklyn: Melville House, 2011], pp. 271–82). Christendom had a very different tradition where commerce was always more entangled in war, and purely competitive behavior, especially in the absence of prior social ties, requires, pretty much of necessity, something like police to guarantee people keep to the rules.

33. There is some possibility this has begun to turn around somewhat in recent years. But it has been my own experience that pretty much any time I presented a paper that assumed that some form of social control is ultimately made possible by the state's monopoly of violence, I would be instantly faced with someone challenging

me on Foucauldian, Gramscian, or Althusserian grounds that such an analysis is foolishly outdated: either because "disciplinary systems" no longer work that way, or because we have now realized they never did.

34. *The Collected Works of Abraham Lincoln*, vol. 5. Roy P. Basler, ed. (New Brunswick, NJ: Rutgers University Press), p. 52. Anthropologist Dimitra Doukas provides a good historical overview of how this transformation worked itself out in small-town upstate New York in *Worked Over: The Corporate Sabotage of an American Community* (Ithaca, NY: Cornell University Press, 2003). See also E. Paul Durrenberger and Dimitra Doukas, "Gospel of Wealth, Gospel of Work: Counter-hegemony in the U.S. Working Class" *American Anthropologist*, Vol. 110, Issue 2 (2008), pp. 214–25, on the ongoing conflict between the two perspectives among contemporary American laborers.

35. It would be interesting to compare this campaign to the similarly well-funded effort to promulgate free-market ideologies starting in the sixties and seventies, which began with the establishment of think tanks like the American Enterprise Institute. The latter appears both to have come from a smaller sector of the capitalist classes and to have taken much longer to achieve broad effects on popular opinion—though in the end it was if anything even more successful.

36. Even the Soviet bureaucracy combined a celebration of labor with a long-term commitment to creating a consumer utopia. It should be noted that when the Reagan administration effectively abandoned antitrust enforcement in the eighties, they did it by shifting the criteria for approval of a merger from whether it operates as a restraint of trade to whether it "benefits the consumer." The result is that the U.S. economy is in most sectors, from agriculture to book sales, dominated by a few giant bureaucratic monopolies or oligopolies.

37. Similarly in the Classical world, or that of Medieval Christianity, rationality could hardly be seen as a tool because it was literally the

voice of God. I will be discussing these issues in more detail in the third essay.

38. Total number of civil servants employed in Russia in 1992: 1 million. Total number employed in 2004: 1.26 million. This is especially remarkable considering a lot of this time was marked by economic free-fall, so there was much less activity to administer.

39. The logic is analogous to Marxian notions of fetishism, where human creations seem to take life, and control their creators rather than the other way around. It is probably best considered a subspecies of the same phenomenon.

1. Dead Zones of the Imagination: An Essay on Structural Stupidity

40. This particular tactic is so common that I think there should be a name for it. I propose to call it the "one more word out of you and the kitten gets it!" move. If you complain about a bureaucratic problem, make it clear that the only result will to get some underling in trouble—whether or not that underling had anything to do with creating the initial problem. The complainer will then, unless unusually vindictive and cruel, almost immediately withdraw the complaint. In this case, someone did forget to tell me a key piece of information, but I have had the same move used when complaining about matters where the problem was clearly the fault of the very supervisor I was complaining to.

41. For example: "We expect everyone to work as hard as possible for the common good without expectation of reward! And if you are not capable of living up to such standards, clearly you are a counterrevolutionary bourgeois individualist parasite, and we'll have to send you to a gulag."

42. Insofar as anthropological studies of bureaucracy do exist—the classic here is Herzfeld's *The Social Production of Indifference: Exploring the Symbolic Roots of Western Bureaucracy* (New York: Berg, 1992)—they almost never describe such arrangements as foolish or idiotic. If it

does come up at all, the "bureaucracy as idiocy" perspective tends to be attributed to one's informants, represented as the naïve folk model, whose existence the anthropologist must explain. Why do Greek villagers, or Mozambiquan shopkeepers, they ask, make so many jokes about local officials in which those officials are represented as clueless idiots? The one answer never considered is that the villagers and shopkeepers are simply describing reality.

I suppose I should be careful here. I am not saying that anthropologists, and other social scientists, are entirely unaware that immersion in bureaucratic codes and regulations does, in fact, regularly cause people to act in ways that in any other context would be considered idiotic. Just about anyone is aware from personal experiences that they do. Yet for the purposes of cultural analysis, obvious truths are uninteresting. At best one can expect a "yes, but . . ."— with the assumption that the "but" introduces everything that's really important.

43. To some degree this is in open defiance of the way the institution constantly encourages them to see the world: I recently had to fill out an online "time allocation report" for my university. There were about thirty categories of admin, but no category for "writing books."

44. "Never" is no doubt an overstatement. There are a handful of exceptions. A very small handful. In anthropology Marilyn Strathern's excellent *Audit Cultures: Anthropological Studies in Accountability, Ethics and the Academy* (London, Routledge, 2000) is the most notable.

45. Talcott Parsons & Edward A. Shils, eds., *Toward a General Theory of Action* (Cambridge: Harvard University Press, 1951).

46. Eric Ross, "Cold Warriors Without Weapons." *Identities* 1998 vol. 4 (3–4): 475–506. Just to give a sense of the connections here, at Harvard, Geertz was a student of Clyde Kluckhohn, who was not only "an important conduit for CIA area studies funds" (Ross, 1998) but had contributed the section on anthropology to Parsons and Shils's famous Weberian manifesto for the social sciences, *Toward a General Theory of Action* (1951). Kluckhohn connected Geertz to MIT's

Center for International Studies, then directed by the former CIA Director of Economic Research, which in turn convinced him to work on development in Indonesia.

47. It is interesting to note here that Foucault was himself a relatively obscure figure in France, prior to '68, a one-time arch-structuralist who had spent many of his years in exile in Norway, Poland, and Tunisia. After the insurrection, he was, effectively, whisked out of Tunisia and offered the most prestigious position Paris has to offer, a professorship at the College de France.

48. In anthropology, see for instance Nancy Scheper-Hughes, *Death Without Weeping: The Violence of Everyday Life in Brazil* (Berkeley: University of California Press, 1992); Carolyn Nordstrom and Joann Martin, *The Paths to Domination, Resistance, and Terror* (Berkeley: University of California Press, 1992).

49. The term itself traces back to debates within Peace Studies in the 1960s; it was coined by Johann Galtung ("Violence, Peace, and Peace Research." *Journal of Peace Research* 1969 vol. 6:167–91; *Peace: Research, Education, Action, Essays in Peace Research* [Copenhagen: Christian Ejlers, Vol. 1, 1982]; Peter Lawler, *A Question of Values: Johann Galtung's Peace Research* [Boulder, CO, Lynne Rienner, 1995]), to meet the charge that to define "peace" as the mere absence of acts of physical assault is to overlook the prevalence of much more insidious structures of human exploitation. Galtung felt the term "exploitation" was too loaded owing to its identification with Marxism, and proposed as an alternative "structural violence": any institutional arrangement that, by its very operation, regularly causes physical or psychological harm to a certain portion of the population, or imposes limits on their freedom. Structural violence could thus be distinguished from both "personal violence" (violence by an identifiable human agent), or "cultural violence" (those beliefs and assumptions about the world that justify the infliction of harm). This is the how the term has mainly been taken up in the anthropological literature as well (e.g., Philippe Bourgois, "The Power of Violence in War and Peace: Post–Cold War

Lessons from El Salvador." *Ethnography* 2001 vol. 2 [1]: 5–34; Paul Farmer, "An Anthropology of Structural Violence." *Current Anthropology* 2004 vol. 45 [3]:305–25; *Pathologies of Power: Health, Human Rights, and the New War on the Poor* [Berkeley: University of California Press, 2005]; Arun Gupta, *Red Tape: Bureaucracy, Structural Violence, and Poverty in India* [Durham, NC: Duke University Press, 2012]).

50. Given the world as it actually exists, this clearly makes no sense. If, say, there are certain spaces women are excluded from for fear of physical or sexual assault, one cannot make a distinction between that fear, the assumptions that motivate men to carry out such assaults or police to feel the victim "had it coming," or the resultant feeling on the part of most women that these are not the kind of spaces women really ought to be in. Nor can one distinguish these factors, in turn, from the "economic" consequences of women who cannot be hired for certain jobs as a result. All of this constitutes a single structure of violence.

The ultimate problem with Johann Galtung's approach, as Catia Confortini notes ("Galtung, Violence, and Gender: The Case for a Peace Studies/Feminism Alliance." *Peace and Change* 2006 vol. 31 [3]:333–67), is that it views "structures" as abstract, free-floating entities, when what we are really referring to here are material *processes*, in which violence, and the threat of violence, play a crucial, constitutive, role. In fact one could argue it's this very tendency towards abstraction that makes it possible for everyone involved to imagine that the violence upholding the system is somehow not responsible for its violent effects.

51. It is true that slavery is often framed as a moral relation (the master takes a paternal interest in the slaves' spiritual welfare, that sort of thing), but as many have observed, such pretenses are never really believed by either masters or slaves; in fact, the ability to force the slaves to play along with such an obviously false ideology is itself a way of establishing the master's pure, arbitrary power.

52. Keith Breckenridge, "Power Without Knowledge: Three Colonial-

isms in South Africa." (www.history.und.ac.za/Sempapers/Breck-enridge2003.pdf)

53. Keith Breckenridge, "Verwoerd's Bureau of Proof: Total Information in the Making of Apartheid." *History Workshop Journal* 1985, vol. 59:84.

54. Andrew Mathews, "Power/Knowledge, Power/Ignorance: Forest Fires and the State in Mexico." *Human Ecology* 2005, vol. 33(6): 795–820; *Instituting Nature: Authority, Expertise, and Power in Mexican Forests, 1926–2011* (Cambridge: MIT Press, 2011).

55. David Apter, *The Politics of Modernization* (Chicago: University of Chicago Press, 1965); *Choice and the Politics of Allocation: A Developmental Theory* (New Haven: Yale University Press, 1971).

56. "Violent actions, no less than any other kind of behavioral expression, are deeply infused with cultural meaning and are the moment for individual agency within historically embedded patterns of behavior. Individual agency, utilizing extant cultural forms, symbols, and icons, may thus be considered 'poetic' for the rule-governed substrate that underlies it, and for how this substrate is deployed, through which new meanings and forms of cultural expression emerge" (Neil Whitehead, "On the Poetics of Violence," in *Violence*, James Currey, ed. [Santa Fe, NM: SAR Press, 2004], pp. 9–10).

57. In criminal matters, we tend to treat pointing a gun at someone's head and demanding their money as a violent crime, even though no actual physical contact takes place. However, most liberal definitions of violence avoid defining threats of physical harm as forms of violence in themselves, because of the subversive implications. As a result liberals tend to define violence as acts of nonconsensual harm, and conservatives, acts of nonconsensual harm that have not been approved by legitimate authorities—which of course makes it impossible for the state, or any state they approve of, anyway, to ever engage in "violence" (see C.A.J. Coady, "The Idea of Violence." *Journal of Applied Philosophy* 1986 vol. 3 [1]:3–19; also my own *Direct Action: An Ethnography* [Oakland: AK Press, 2009], pp. 448–49).

58. Hopefully at this point I do not have to point out that patriarchal

arrangements of this sort are prima facie examples of structural violence, their norms sanctioned by threat of physical harm in endless subtle and not-so-subtle ways.

59. Since first writing this passage I have tried in vain to locate the essay where I first read about these experiments (I first encountered them in a magazine I looked at in the American consulate in Antananarivo while doing my fieldwork around the year 1990, in an article about the movie *Tootsie*). Often when I tell the story, I am told that the real reason teenage boys object to imagining themselves as girls is simple homophobia, and this is surely true, as far as it goes. But then one has to ask why homophobia is so powerful in the first place, and why homophobia takes this particular form. After all, many teenage girls are equally homophobic, but it does not seem to stop them from taking pleasure in imagining themselves as boys.

60. bell hooks, "Representations of Whiteness," in *Black Looks: Race and Representation* (Boston: South End Press, 1992), pp. 165–78.

61. The key texts on Standpoint Theory, by Patricia Hill Collins, Donna Haraway, Sandra Harding, Nancy Hartsock and others, are collected in a volume edited by Harding (*The Feminist Standpoint Theory Reader: Intellectual and Political Controversies* [London: Routledge, 2004]). I might add that the history of this very essay provides a telling example of the sort of gendered obliviousness I'm describing. When I first framed the problem, I wasn't even aware of this body of literature, though my argument had clearly been indirectly influenced by it—it was only the intervention of a feminist friend that put me on to where many of these ideas were actually coming from.

62. Egon Bittner, *Aspects of Police Work* (Boston: Northeastern University Press, 1970); also, "The capacity to use force as the core of the police role." In *Moral Issues in Police Work*, Elliston and Feldberg, eds. (Savage, MD: Rowman and Littlefield, 1985), pp. 15–26; P. A. Waddington, *Policing Citizens: Authority and Rights* (London: University College London Press, 1999); Mark Neocleous, *The Fabrication of Social Order: A Critical Theory of Police Power* (London: Pluto Press, 2000).

63. This paragraph is addressed, of course, largely to those of a certain class status: I have often remarked that the real definition of being "middle class" is whether, when one sees a policeman on the street, one feels more, rather than less, safe. This is why only a very small percentage of the population of, say, Nigeria or India or Brazil feel that they are middle class, though most Danes or white Australians do. In most large cities in Europe or North America race is also a huge factor, though often those who face the most direct and consistent racist violence from police will nonetheless insist that fighting crime is what police are fundamentally about.

64. I am aware this is not really what Weber said. Even the phrase "iron cage" is apparently a mistranslation for a phrase that meant something more like "shiny metal casing"—not a drab prison but a high-tech wrapping superficially attractive in its own right. Nonetheless, this is how Weber was understood for most of the twentieth century and in a way the popular understanding was more important, and certainly more influential, than the author's actual meaning.

65. Ancient Egypt in contrast created whole genres of literature to warn young students against adventurous occupations. They would typically begin by asking whether the reader had ever dreamed of becoming the captain of a ship, or a royal charioteer, then go on to describe just how miserable such an apparently glamorous occupation would likely really turn out to be. The conclusion was always the same: don't do it! Become a bureaucrat. You'll have a prosperous job and all you'll be able to order around the soldiers and sailors who will treat you like a god.

66. The real joke in the Bond movies, it seems to me, is that Bond is a terrible spy. Spies are supposed to be discreet and unobtrusive. James Bond is anything but. It's just that he can get away with being a terrible spy because he's effortlessly, preternaturally flawless in the performance of any task *other* than spying. As for his inversions with Holmes, one could multiply these endlessly: Holmes has family history, Bond appears to be an orphan or anyway has no family ties, and further, seems to have constant sex without ever producing

offspring. Holmes works with one male partner who does well by their association; Bond with a series of female partners who usually die.

67. The full argument here would take much more time to make, and this is not really the place for it, but note that cop movies of the "rogue cop breaking all the rules" variety, that now seems the default mode for a Hollywood action movie, did not exist at all until the 1970s. In fact for the first half-century of American cinema there were hardly any movies at all that took a policeman's point of view. The rogue cop movie appeared at the moment the Western disappeared and is largely a transposition of Western plots into an urban bureaucratic setting. Clint Eastwood famously defined the transition: from Sergio Leone's *Man with No Name* (1964, 1965, 1966), to *Dirty Harry* (1971). As others have observed, the Western plot is typically an effort to contrive a situation where it is justifiable for a basically decent person to do things that in any other situation would be absolutely unjustifiable. Transposing that onto an urban bureaucratic environment has disturbing implications: indeed, one might well argue that Jack Bauer is the logical culmination of the genre.

68. Marc Cooper, "Dum Da Dum-Dum." *Village Voice* April 16, 1991, pp. 28–33.

69. This might seem to be similar to the fate of liberal or right libertarian free market ideas that oppose government interference but, according to what I've called the Iron Law of Liberalism, always produce more bureaucracy anyway. But I don't think that left-wing ideas always and necessarily create bureaucracy in the same way. Indeed, insurrectionary moments usually begin by eliminating existing bureaucratic structures entirely, and while these structures often creep back, they only do when the revolutionaries begin to operate through government: when they manage to maintain autonomous enclaves like, say, the Zapatistas, this does not take place.

70. I use the word "ontology" with some hesitation because as a philosophical term, it has recently undergone a great deal of abuse. Tech-

nically, ontology is theory about the nature of reality, as opposed to epistemology, which is theory about what we can know about reality. In the social sciences, "ontology" has come to be used merely as a pretentious way to say "philosophy," "ideology," or "set of cultural assumptions," often in ways that philosophers would find outrageous. Here I am using it in the specific sense of "political ontology," which admittedly is a sense I made up, but refers to a set of assumptions about underlying realities. When one says "let's be realistic here," what reality is it we're referring to? What is the hidden reality, the underlying forces, assumed to be moving below the surface of political events?

71. Even the rich and powerful will ordinarily concede that the world is a miserable place for most of those who live in it, but still, insist that this is inevitable, or that any attempt to change it will make it worse—not that we actually live in an ideal social order.

72. Unfortunately he never did. He called it *Crack Capitalism* (London: Pluto Press, 2010) instead, a far inferior title.

73. Key texts here are: James Engell, *The Creative Imagination: Enlightenment to Romanticism* (Cambridge MA: Harvard University Press, 1981), and Thomas McFarland, *Originality and Imagination* (Baltimore: Johns Hopkins University Press, 1985).

74. I might add that it is a profound reflection on the effects of structural violence on the imagination that feminist theory itself was so quickly sequestered away into its own subfield where it has had almost no impact on the work of most male theorists.

75. No doubt all this makes it easier to see the two as fundamentally different sorts of activity, making it hard for us to recognize interpretive labor—for example, or most of what we usually think of as women's work—as labor at all. To my mind it would probably be better to recognize it as the primary form of labor. Insofar as a clear distinction can be made here, it's the care, energy, and labor directed at human beings that should be considered fundamental. The things we care about most—our loves, passions, rivalries, obsessions—are always other people, and in most societies that are not capitalist, it's

taken for granted that the manufacture of material goods is a subordinate moment in a larger process of fashioning people. In fact, I
would argue that one of the most alienating aspects of capitalism is
the fact that it forces us to pretend that it is the other way around,
and that societies exist primarily to increase their output of things.

76. See my book *The Democracy Project* (New York: Spiegel & Grau,
2012). My own chosen title for it was, ironically, "As If We Were
Already Free," but in the end, I wasn't free to dictate my own title.

77. *A Paradise Built in Hell: The Extraordinary Communities That Arise in
Disaster* (New York, Penguin, 2010).

2. Of Flying Cars and the Declining Rate of Profit

78. Similarly, in 1949 Orwell had placed his futuristic dystopia, *1984*,
only thirty-five years in the future.

79. In fact, video telephones had first been debuted in the 1930s by the
German post office under the Nazis.

80. From Fredric Jameson's *Postmodernism; or, The Cultural Logic of Late
Capitalism* (Duke University Press, 1991), pp. 36–37. The original
essay was published in 1984.

81. The original book, in German, came out as *Der Spätkapitalismus* in
1972. The first English edition was *Late Capitalism* (London: Hu-
manities Press, 1975).

82. Probably the classic statement of this position is *Space and the American Imagination*, by Howard McCurdy (Washington, D.C.: Smith-
sonian, 1997), but other versions of this sort of rhetoric include:
Stephen J. Pyne, "A Third Great Age of discovery," in Carl Sagan
and Stephen J. Pyne, *The Scientific and Historical Rationales for Solar
System Exploration*, SPI 88-1 (Washington, D.C.: Space policy institute, George Washington University, 1988), or Linda Billings,
"Ideology, Advocacy, and Spaceflight: Evolution of a Cultural Narrative" in *The Societal Impact of Spaceflight*, Stephen J. Dick and Roger
D. Launius, eds. (Washington, D.C.: NASA, 2009).

83. Alvin Toffler, *Future Shock* (New York: Random House, 1970).

84. In this case, too, there's a Soviet equivalent: the Tupolev TU-144, which was actually the first supersonic passenger plane, and which first flew a few months before the Concorde in 1968, but was abandoned for commercial purposes in 1983.

85. Source: www.foundersfund.com/uploads/ff_manifesto.pdf.

86. Alvin Toffler, *The Third Wave* (New York: Bantam Books, 1980).

87. Toffler's own politics are slightly more ambiguous, but not much. Before the success of *Future Shock*, he had been known mainly as a business journalist, whose greatest claim to fame was probably that he had interviewed Ayn Rand for *Playboy*. Like most conservatives, he pays lip service to women's equality as an abstract principle, but never mentions actual feminists or feminist issues except to criticize them: for a typical example, see his *Revolutionary Wealth: How It Will Be Created and How It Will Change Our Lives*, Alvin Toffler and Heidi Toffler (New York: Doubleday, 2006), pp. 132–33. It is certainly curious that both Toffler and Gilder are so obsessed with the threat to motherhood: it's as if both are basing their politics on an opposition to the ideas of Shulamith Firestone, long before Firestone herself had actually appeared on the scene.

88. Eccentric though they were, it's hard to overestimate the influence of such figures on the Right, because they were considered its creative visionaries. Gilder's supply-side economic theories, for instance, are widely cited as one of the main inspiration for Reaganomics, and his "technology report" was so widely read that market observers spoke of a "Gilder effect," where the share values of any company he mentioned approvingly would almost invariably rise in value immediately thereafter.

89. Win McCormick, for instance, informs me that by the late sixties he was involved in a think tank founded by a former president of the University of Chicago, one of whose main concerns was trying to figure out how to head off the upheavals they assumed would ensue within a generation or so, when machines had completely replaced manual labor.

90. I have no time to describe in detail some of the actual political

conflicts of the early seventies described in the unpublished *Zero Work* volume that set the stage for the later emergence of the Midnight Notes Collective, but they reveal quite clearly that in many assembly-line industries, wildcat strikes during that period did focus on demands for replacing drudgery with mechanization, and for employers, abandoning factories in the unionized "Rust Belt" became a conscious strategy for sidestepping such demands (e.g., Peter Linebaugh and Bruno Ramirez, "Crisis in the Auto Sector," originally from *Zero Work*, published in *Midnight Notes*, 1992).

91. The United States sometimes likes to maintain the fantasy that it does not engage in industrial planning, but as critics have long since pointed out, it does. Much of the direct planning, and hence R&D, is carried out through the military.

92. The project was just called Energia, and it was the reason for the USSR's development of the gigantic booster rockets that are still the mainstay of the global space program, now that the Space Shuttle is out of commission. News of the project only really broke in the United States in 1987, two years before the Soviet collapse. www.nytimes.com/1987/06/14/world/soviet-studies-satellites-to-convert-solar-energy-for-relay-to-earth.html.

93. This raises an interesting question: how much of this particular mythological world was—at least partially—a Slavic import? Much research would have to be done to resolve this question, however.

94. Jeff Sharlet informs me these imaginary connections probably run much further than we think. In the fifties and sixties, many prominent Americans, including a significant number of Congressmen, appear to have strongly suspected that the Soviets actually *were* in contact with space aliens, and that UFOs were either Soviet allies, or actual Soviet craft built with borrowed alien technology (see e.g., Sharlet's *Sweet Heaven When I Die: Faith, Faithlessness, and the Country In Between* [New York: Norton, 2012], pp. 146–48).

95. As an example, in 368 pages, Judith Barad's *The Ethics of Star Trek* (New York: Perennial, 2000) does not mention democracy or issues of collective political decision-making even once.

96. Other sentences one would never hear are of this sort: "Did you hear that the Vulcan-Bejoran Traditionalist alliance is threatening to pull their support from the ruling coalition and force new elections if their candidate doesn't get the education portfolio this year?" Note too how in the absence of ideological differences, which have the potential to cross-cut ethnic ones, the only political divisions one can really imagine within the Federation are between species: the Andorians want this, the Betazoids want that. This too resembles what happened in the USSR and under similar regimes, where a combination of a centralized, redistributive system and an insistence on ideological conformity ensured that ethnic differences were the only ones that could find any open political expression—with ultimately disastrous political effects.

97. Though all ethnic groups seem to be represented in the Federation, I've always noticed one curious exception: Jews. It's all the more striking because both Kirk and Spock, in the original series, were played by Jewish actors—the Vulcan salute, famously, is actually an Orthodox Jewish blessing. But one never sees a Captain Goldberg or Lieutenant Rubinstein; as far as I'm aware not a single Jewish character has ever appeared.

98. The sequence of events is somewhat hypothetical here as, as I say, the history has not been written. I am certainly not suggesting Michael Moore himself sparked the debate, but rather that his comments gave a flavor for what was being talked about at the time. The Ferengi first appear quite early, in 1987, and the Borg even earlier, but they become much more prominent as contrasting alternatives to the Federation later on. All one has to do is Google (*Star Trek* creator) "Gene Roddenberry" and "communist" together to get a taste of the kind of ire the issue stirred up in conservative circles.

99. The term originally derives from "Franks," which was the generic Arabic term for Crusader. Thus the Ferengi have a curious Medieval heritage: their name is a hostile term Muslims applied to Christians, whom they considered barbarous, impious, and so greedy that they lacked all human decency, and their physical appearance and

behavior is an allusion to a hostile image those same Christians applied to Jews, for exactly the same reasons.

100. Thus for instance a recent study of work in the twenty-first century could begin: "Two broad developments reshaped work at the end of the twentieth century. The first was the implosion of the Soviet Union and the worldwide triumph of market capitalism. The second was the widespread use of computer-based production technologies and management command-and-control systems" (Rick Baldoz, Charles Koeber, Philip Kraft, *The Critical Study of Work: Labor, Technology, and Global Production* [Philadelphia: Temple University Press, 2001], p. 3).

101. Its designer, Mikhail Kalashinikov, who died in 2013, held a press conference where he pointed out that U.S. soldiers in Iraq regularly discard their own weapons in favor of captured AK-47s when they have the opportunity.

102. And of course just counting university staff is deceptive in itself, since it ignores the burgeoning numbers of administrators employed by foundations, and other grant-giving agencies.

103. Similarly Don Braben, a physicist at University College London, made headlines in the UK by pointing out that Albert Einstein would never have been able to get funding were he alive today. Others have suggested most of his major works would never even have passed peer review.

104. Jonathan L. Katz, "Don't Become a Scientist!" (wuphys.wustl.edu /~katz/scientist.html).

105. Even worse, as some friends in the industry point out, grant-givers regularly insist it's the scientists themselves who have to write the applications, progress reports, etc., rather than some subordinate, with the result that even the most successful scientists spend roughly 40 percent of their time doing paperwork.

106. It is true that certain capitalist firms of the Silicon Valley sort—the ones that consider themselves cutting-edge—will adopt some version of the old Bell Labs blue sky approach and make sure everyone knows that they are doing so. But these efforts always prove, on

investigation, to be largely publicity stunts. In Silicon Valley–style firms, innovation is largely outsourced to start-ups. At present, the most promising research is generally conducted neither in corporate nor in directly government-funded environments but in the nonprofit sector (which includes most universities), but here too, the corporatization of institutional culture ensures more and more time is taken up with grantsmanship.

107. David Harvie, "Commons and Communities in the University: Some Notes and Some Examples," *The Commoner* no. 8, Autumn/ Winter 2004. (www.commoner.org.uk/08harvie.pdf)

108. We cannot know, for instance, whether there really are alternative fuel formulae that have been bought up and placed in safes by oil companies, but it's widely speculated that there are. A Russian journalist I know told me about her friend, who invented a design for an Internet base station that could provide free wireless for an entire country. The patent was quickly purchased for several million, and suppressed by a major Internet provider. No such stories can by definition be verified, but it's significant in itself that they exist— that they have the complete aura of believability.

109. Neal Stephenson, "Innovation Starvation," *World Policy Journal*, Fall 2011, pp. 11–16.

110. It has often occurred to me that Steampunk really represents nostalgia for precisely this state of affairs. I once attended a museum panel on the topic, and it struck me as odd that all the commentators talked exclusively about the "steam" element, but none about the "punk." Punk rock in the seventies was about the lack of any redemptive future—"no future" was in fact one of its most famous mantras—and it strikes me that the taste for Victorian-era sci-fi futures is more than anything else a nostalgia for the last moment, before the carnage of World War I, when everyone could safely feel a redemptive future was possible.

111. Giovanni Arrighi, *The Long Twentieth Century: Money, Power, and the Origins of Our Times* (London: Verso, 1994).

112. Though possibly, this had at least as much to with his libertarian

communist political affinities than his devotion to the occult. His wife's sister, who seems to have been the ringleader in the magical society, eventually left him for L. Ron Hubbard; on leaving NASA, Parsons went on to apply his magic to creating pyrotechnic effects for Hollywood until he finally blew himself up in 1962.

113. Lewis Mumford, *The Myth of the Machine: Technics and Human Development* (New York: Harcourt Brace Jovanovich, 1966).

114. I note that Peter Thiel, who agreed with much of the original argument of this essay, has recently come out as an antimarket promonopoly capitalist for precisely the reason that he feels this is the best way to further rapid technological change.

115. For as long as I can remember, at least since I was in my twenties, I've heard at least one person every year or so tell me that a drug that will stop the aging process is approximately three years away.

3. The Utopia of Rules, or Why We Really Love Bureaucracy After All

116. "Bureaucracy" in *From Max Weber: Essays in Sociology*, H. H. Gerth & C. Wright Mills, eds. (New York: Oxford University Press, 1946), pp. 233–34.

117. As he put it to an American visitor at the time: "My idea was to bribe the working classes, or shall I say, to win them over, to regard the state as a social institution existing for their sake and interested in their welfare" (cited in William Thomas Stead, *On the Eve: A Handbook for the General Election* [London: Review of Reviews Publishing, 1892], p. 62). The quote is useful to bear in mind since I find that the general point—that the welfare state was largely created to pay off the working class for fear of their becoming revolutionaries—tends to be met with skepticism, and demands for proof that this was the self-conscious intention of the ruling class. But here we have the very first such effort described by its founder quite explicitly as such.

118. Herodotus, *Histories*, 8.98.

119. It's interesting that in *Imagined Communities*, Benedict Anderson barely mentions this phenomenon, focusing only on newspapers.

120. This is still true: in the United States right now, a third of government employees are in the military, and a quarter are in the postal service, far and away more than any other branch.

121. Unfortunately, the essay is lost. (See *The Mark Twain Encyclopedia*, J. R. LeMaster, James Darrell Wilson, and Christie Graves Hamric, eds. [New York: Routledge, 1993], p. 71; Everett Emerson, *Mark Twain, a Literary Life* [Philadelphia: University of Pennsylvania Press, 2000], p. 188.)

122. Lenin, *State and Revolution* (London: Penguin, 1992 [1917]), p. 52.

123. Peter Kropotkin, "Anarchist Communism," in *Anarchism: A Collection of Revolutionary Writings* (New York: Dover, 1974), p. 68.

124. Gordon Wood, *Empire of Liberty: A History of the Early Republic, 1789–1815 (Oxford History of the United States)* (Oxford: Oxford University Press, 2011), pp. 478–79.

125. Indeed, growing up in New York City, I was always struck by the fascinating disparity between the magnificence of public amenities created around the turn of the century, when that very grandeur was seen as reflecting the strength and power of the Republic, and the apparently intentional tawdriness of anything created by the city, for its citizens, since the 1970s. For me, at least, the two greatest exemplars of that earlier age were New York's monumental Central Post Office, with its sweeping, block-long marble steps and Corinthian columns, and the central branch of New York Public Library (which, incidentally, maintained its own system of pneumatic tubes for sending book requests into the stacks well into the 1980s). I remember once, as a tourist, visiting the summer palace of the Kings of Sweden—the first actual palace I'd ever been inside. My first reaction was: this looks exactly like the New York Public Library!

126. Brooklyn: Soft Skull Press, 2005.

127. This is beautifully conveyed in the great film *The Hollywood Shuffle*, featuring a hapless young African American hero willing to endure performing any humiliating racist stereotype in order to make it

in the movies—as his grandmother keeps gently reminding him, "There's always work at the Post Office."

128. This pattern actually extends to all sorts of movies: even if the maverick hero is a scientist, for example, the superior in a bureaucratic organization is almost invariably a person of color. The hero may occasionally be a person of color, but is usually white; the boss—at least, if the boss is an officious martinet and not a co-conspirator—pretty much never is.

129. Needless to say, as my comments on the fate of the Internet in the last essay made clear, such poetic technologies have an unfortunate tendency to themselves become bureaucratic ones.

130. Freud is a fascinating figure for trying to reconcile the two conceptions: rationality (the Ego) no longer represents morality, as it would have in a Medieval conception where reason and morality were the same, but, rather, is pushed and pulled in contradictory directions by the passions (the Id) on the one side, and morality (the Superego) on the other.

131. One might argue that this is developed most strongly in military bureaucracies, where officers often make it a point of pride to serve whatever civilian leaders political developments throw at them with equal dedication and efficiency, whatever their personal views. But this is just an extension of the bureaucratic mind-set. Armies dominated by, say, aristocratic officer corps behave quite differently.

132. There is a growing literature now on the social base of the more extreme form of Political Islam, for instance, that reveals that it has a particular appeal for students of engineering and the sciences.

133. There is a reason Mr. Spock was a fictional character. But of course Spock wasn't really supposed to be emotionless, he just pretended to be, so in a way he represented the ideal of rationality perfectly.

134. It is perfectly possible to come up with a logically coherent argument based on delusional premises, or to make a realistic assessment of a problem and then apply completely fallacious logic to its solution. People do both all the time.

135. I am referring here to the Pythagorean movement and not to its

founder, Pythagoras, because Pythagoras' own role in creating the doctrines that came to be known under his name is currently a matter of some contention. Walter Burkert has suggested that he was really only responsible for the doctrine of reincarnation, and not the mathematical cosmology, which has been variously attributed to later Pythagoreans such as Hippasus, Philolaus, and Archytas, or even, made up retrospectively and attributed to the Pythagoreans by Plato (this latter, however, strikes me as unlikely).

136. There is a story that such was the political importance of this doctrine that when one later Pythagorean, Hippasus, discovered the irrational number, his fellows drowned him in the sea. Actually, the legend in Antiquity was rather that Hippasus drowned by accident, as punishment from the Gods for his impiety in revealing such matters. Myself, I find more interesting the suggestion, in some sources, that Hippasus held that God was an irrational number: that God, in other words, represented a transcendent principle beyond the immanent rationality of the cosmos. If true, it would have been a major departure from the emerging logic of the "cosmic religion" of Antiquity and it might not be surprising if he thus aroused his comrades' antipathy. It is intriguing to consider how it relates to the reflections on sovereignty detailed below.

137. Hans Jonas (*The Gnostic Religion* [Boston: Beacon Press, 1958]) was, to my knowledge, the first to use the term "cosmic religion," in describing Gnosticism, which rejected the notion of an ideal cosmic order and saw human souls as fundamentally alien to creation, as its explicit negation. Augustinian Christianity actually contains elements of both, bringing together a Manichean dualism with a fundamentally Pagan insistence on the identity of mind and divinity.

138. It originates with the Stoics, but in Antiquity was not nearly so universal as it became in the European Middle Ages.

139. Insofar as they do, it's of course in play.

140. Edmund Leach, *Social Anthropology* (Oxford, Oxford University Press, 1982), p. 121.

141. It might have made better logical sense to see that what set hu-

mans apart from animals lay in imagination, but in Medieval terms this was quite inadmissible, because in the commonplace theology of the time, influenced by astrology and Neoplatonism, it corresponded to a lower order—imagination was a mediator between the divine intellect and the material world, just as the astral plane mediates heaven and earth; indeed, many at the time speculated our imaginative faculties were made of astral substance.

142. From Francis Yates, *Giordano Bruno and the Hermetic Tradition* (London: Routledge and Kegan Paul, 1964), p. 144; originally from Robert Fludd, *Meteorologica cosmtca* (Frankfort, 1626), p. 8.

143. Translation from Francis Yates, *op cit*, p. 119.

144. And also, of course, on the Church hierarchy that continued to be based in Rome, which did maintain the most elaborate and geographically far-reaching administrative system that existed in Europe at the time.

145. On proto-bureaucracy, see Hans Nissen et al., *Archaic Bookkeeping: Early Writing and Techniques of Economic Administration in the Ancient Near East* (Chicago/London: University of Chicago Press, 1993); see also David Wengrow, *What Makes a Civilization?* (Oxford: Oxford University Press, 2012), pp. 81–87.

146. Or in the anthropological record, one might think of the Maori, or the First Nations of the Northwest Coast of North America (often referred to as "potlatch societies," which were divided into aristocrats and commoners with no centralized system of government or administration), or, for that matter, more egalitarian heroic societies like the Iatmul of Papua New Guinea where all adult males were engaged in constant vainglorious behavior of this sort.

147. My key text here is David Wengrow's " 'Archival' and 'Sacrificial' Economies in Bronze Age Eurasia: An Interactionist Approach to the Hoarding of Metals," in *Interweaving Worlds: Systemic Interactions in Eurasia, 7th to the 1st Millennia BC*, T. C. Wilkinson, S. Sherratt, and J. Bennet, eds. (Oxford: Oxbow, 2011), pp. 135–44. I discuss heroic societies myself in "Culture as Creative Refusal," *Cambridge Anthropology* vol. 31 no. 2 (2013), pp. 1–19.

148. Indeed, I have, in an earlier book, *Lost People: Magic and the Legacy of Slavery in Madagascar* (Bloomington: Indiana University Press, 2007), pp. 129–31.

149. Attila the Hun, for example, appears as a character in both the Nibelungenlied and Volsunga Saga.

150. Obviously, "fantasy" can refer to a very wide range of literature, from *Alice in Wonderland* and *The Wonderful Wizard of Oz* to *The Call of Cthulhu*, and many critics include science fiction as a subgenre of fantasy as well. Still, Middle Earth style heroic fantasy remains the "unmarked term."

151. Elsewhere, I've referred to this as "the ugly mirror phenomenon." See David Graeber, "There Never Was a West: Democracy Emerges from the Spaces in Between," in *Possibilities: Notes on Hierarchy, Rebellion, and Desire* (Oakland: AK Press, 2007), p. 343.

152. The key difference here is no doubt that Medieval carnivals were, in fact, organized largely bottom-up, much unlike Roman circuses.

153. From a letter to his son written during World War II: "My political opinions lean more and more to Anarchy (philosophically understood, meaning abolition of control not whiskered men with bombs)—or to 'unconstitutional' Monarchy. I would arrest anybody who uses the word State (in any sense other than the inanimate realm of England and its inhabitants, a thing that has neither power, rights nor mind); and after a chance of recantation, execute them . . ." The letter adds that he feels relations of command are only appropriate within small face-to-face groups, and that the one bright spot in the world is "the growing habit of disgruntled men of dynamiting factories and power-stations." (Letter to Christopher Tolkien, November 29, 1943; in *The Letters of J.R.R. Tolkien*, Humphrey Carpenter, ed. [London: Allen & Unwin, 1981], #52.) Others have noted that this insistence that only personal authority is legitimate is a reflection of a lifelong hatred of bureaucracy in all its manifestations (Fascist, Communist, or Welfare State): i.e., John Garth, *Tolkien and the Great War: The Threshold of Middle-earth* [London: HarperCollins, 2011], p. 94, and Mark Home, *J.R.R. Tolk-*

ien [Nashville, TN: Thomas Nelson, 2011], pp. 124–27. The latter observes that "the fluctuation between kings and 'anarchy' is not odd for a student of northern European tribal history" (ibid., p. 125) but rather, is typical of what I've been referring to as heroic societies.

154. Douglas Adams fans will recall that *The Hitchhiker's Guide to the Galaxy*, another of the great midcentury bureaucratic satires, begins with precisely such a scenario, leading to the destruction of the planet.

155. The noble warrior chief versus evil magician scenario is basically a British colonial trope; colonial officials in Africa almost invariably tried to locate warrior elites, whom they admired, and if they did not find them, would assume they had been displaced by the wiles of "witch doctors" of one sort or another, whom they invariably saw as a maleficent influence. *King Solomon's Mines* is the ultimate fictional expression of this myth.

156. Huizinga actually assumes that play and games are the same thing. Johan Huizinga. *Homo Ludens: The Play Element in Culture* (Boston: Beacon Press, 1955).

157. And if one is playing a game, the "play" element is the unpredictable element, the degree to which one is not simply enacting rules, but applying skill, or rolling the dice, or otherwise embracing uncertainty.

158. To take just one typical example: J. Lowell Lewis, "Toward a Unified Theory of Cultural Performance" in *Victor Turner and Contemporary Cultural Performance*, Graham St. John, ed. (London: Berghahn, 2008), p. 47. But the point is made over and over in the literature. I might add that by this analysis, Dungeons & Dragons and similar role-playing games are so enjoyable because they have achieved the perfect mix of the play and the game principle.

159. "Alternative Futures," *Times of India*, February 10, 2007, in timesof india.indiatimes.com/edit-page/Alternative-Futures/article-show/1586903.cms.

160. Carl Schmitt, *Political Theology: Four Chapters on the Concept of Sover-*

eignty (Chicago: University of Chicago Press, 2004 [1922]). Schmitt's arguments were used by the Nazis to provide legal justification for concentration camps.

161. "In Indian cosmology, play is a top down idea. Passages to play and their premises are embedded at a high level of abstraction and generality. The qualities of play resonate and resound throughout the whole. But more than this, qualities of play are integral to the very operation of the cosmos," D. Handelman, 1992. "Passages to play: Paradox and process" *Play and Culture* vol 5 no. 1, p. 12. Cited in Brian Sutton-Smith, *The Ambiguity of Play* (Cambridge: Harvard University Press, 2001), p. 55.

162. Sutton-Smith op. cit., pp. 55–60. Bottom-up play, in contrast—the notion of play as intrinsically subversive—has always existed, but only really became our dominant way of thinking about such matters with Romanticism.

163. Or to be more precise, its representatives are the only people allowed to act violently in a given situation if they are both present and on the job.

164. During protests against the World Bank in 2002, police in Washington, D.C., decided to surround a public park and arrest everyone inside it. I well remember calling out to the commanding officer asking what we were being arrested for. He answered, "We'll think of something later."

165. It can happen, but it usually has to involve anal penetration with weapons. At least, the two cases that jump most readily to mind are officer Justin Volpe, who sodomized a man he mistakenly thought had earlier thrown a punch at him in a street fight with a broom handle in a precinct bathroom in New York in 1997, and Dennis Krauss, a Georgia police officer, who repeatedly responded to domestic violence calls by extorting sexual favors from the women who called him and in 1999, attempted to sodomize one with a gun. Both were sentenced to prison terms. But it usually takes an assault of that outrageousness for an officer to actually go to jail. For instance, during the Global Justice Movement and Occupy Wall

Street, there were repeated cases of police systematically breaking wrists and fingers of nonviolent protesters—often after announcing they would do so—but no police officer was ever so much as charged, let alone convicted of assault.

166. Notice the complex relation between this and the rationalist view described earlier, where creativity was seen as demonic because it was opposed to the divine or cosmic principle of reason. Here, creativity is seen as demonic because it *partakes* of the divine or cosmic principle of play!

167. Some contemporary political theorists are willing to more or less state this outright. I am thinking particularly here of that school of thought that is referred to as Civic Republicanism, as outlined by intellectual historians like Quentin Skinner and philosophers like Philip Pettit, who argue that "freedom" in the classic liberal tradition is not a matter of being able to act without the interference of power, or even threats of violence—since legal systems do threaten those who break the rules with violence—but rather, to act without the interference of *arbitrary* power. This is not the place to launch into a detailed analysis but the entire formulation thus comes to present a zero-sum view of freedom. "Arbitrary" after all just means "non-determined." In a system of arbitrary authority, decisions reflect the "will and pleasure" of the despot. But from the perspective of the despot, "arbitrariness" is freedom. So the people are free if the ruler is not. Powerful people have to follow the rules. But since all citizens have a certain degree of power, so does everyone else. Ultimately, since freedom means protection from the arbitrary (non-rule-bound) power of others, and since power is everywhere, the logic provides a charter for the reduction of all aspects of human life into sets of transparent rules. (For the key texts here: Philip Pettit, *Republicanism: A Theory of Freedom and Government* [Oxford: Clarendon Press, 1997]; Quentin Skinner, "Freedom as the Absence of Arbitrary Power," in *Republicanism and Political Theory*, Cécile Laborde and John Maynor, eds. [Malden, MA: Blackwell Publishing, 2008].)

168. Marilyn Strathern, *Audit Cultures: Anthropological Studies in Account-ability, Ethics and the Academy* (London: Routledge, 2000).

169. Not only do they change, they tend to change at a fairly constant rate, regardless of historical circumstances. There is, indeed, a whole science, glottochronology, premised on this fact.

170. Jo Freeman, "The Tyranny of Structurelessness." First officially published in *The Second Wave* (vol. 2, no 1). Reprinted in *Quiet Rumours: An Anarcha-Feminist Reader*, Dark Star Collective (Edinburgh: AK Press, 2002), pp. 54–61.

Appendix: On Batman and the Problem of Constituent Power

171. I note in passing that my analysis here is of mainstream comic book fiction, especially in the first several decades. When my piece first came out it was often critiqued for not taking consideration of the most sophisticated examples of the literature: Frank Knight's *Batman*, the *Watchmen* series, *V for Vendetta*, and other more explicitly political comic plots. And even mainstream comics have become more explicitly political over time (Lex Luthor, for example, became President!). Still, if one wants to understand the essence of a popular genre, one does not examine its most sophisticated, high-culture variants. If one wants to understand the essence of a popular genre, one looks at schlock.

172. Unless you want to count the case of one individual who had clearly seen far too many Batman movies.

<u>Also by David Graeber</u>

Debt
The First 5,000 Years

"Fresh . . . Fascinating . . . Graeber's book is not just thought-provoking, but also exceedingly timely. His sweeping narrative history essentially argues that many of our existing ideas about money and credit are limited, if not wrong."
—Gillian Tett, *Financial Times*

"Exhaustive . . . Engaging . . . An authoritative account of the background to the recent crisis. Both erudite and impertinent, his book helps illuminate the omissions of the current debate and the tacit political conflicts that lurk behind technical budget questions."
—Robert Kuttner, *The New York Review of Books*

"An alternate history of the rise of money and markets, a sprawling, erudite, provocative work." **—Drake Bennett, *Bloomberg Businessweek***

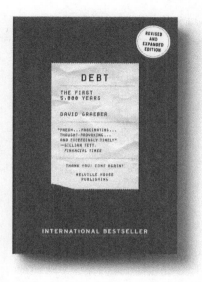

$22.00 U.S./Can.
Paperback: 978-1-61219-419-6
Ebook: 978-1-61219-420-2